DATE			

rary

8 rev. 1-94

© THE BAKER & TAYLOR CO.

Effective Reform
in
China

EFFECTIVE REFORM IN CHINA

An Agenda

HENRY K. H. WOO

 PRAEGER

New York
Westport, Connecticut
London

Library of Congress Cataloging-in-Publication Data

Woo, Henry K. H., 1946–
    Effective reform in China : an agenda / Henry K. H. Woo.
        p. cm.
    Includes bibliographical references (p.) and index.
    ISBN 0–275–93740–2
    1. China—Economic policy—1976– 2. China—Economic
conditions—1976– 3. Socialism—China. I. Title.
HC427.92.W655   1991
338.951—dc20   90–45197

British Library Cataloguing in Publication Data is available.

Library of Congress Catalog Card Number: 90–45197
ISBN: 0–275–93740–2

First published in 1991

Praeger Publishers, One Madison Avenue, New York, NY 10010
An imprint of Greenwood Publishing Group, Inc.

Printed in the United States of America

∞

The paper used in this book complies with the
Permanent Paper Standard issued by the National
Information Standards Organization (Z39.48–1984).

10 9 8 7 6 5 4 3 2 1

Contents

Preface

China is in a state of predicament. What it urgently needs is not more of its present policies or a continuation of the reform package executed under the days of Zhao Ziyang. Still less does it need the restoration of the command system from prior to Deng Xiaoping's reform. What it does need is an entirely new vision and a new direction. This requires a rethinking of the fundamental frameworks relevant to China's situation, namely, the feasibility of socialism, the basic principles governing development and the place of agriculture in development. It is hoped that from theoretical discussions of these first principles, sound and plausible development strategies can be prescribed. This work, in a nutshell, is an attempt in this direction. It is a work on the political economy of China's reform in the broadest sense. As such, this work is not concerned with the analysis of details, for its scope does not permit such treatment. Rather, it addresses questions of an abstract order and strategies of major import.

At various stages in the progress of this work, I received comments, suggestions and materials from many people. I would like to avail myself of this opportunity to thank all of them, especially my colleagues and associates at the Hong Kong Institute of Economic Science and at the China Foundation (Hong Kong) for their kind help and encouragement throughout the project. In particular, I wish to thank the following people for their help: Louis Lau, S. K. Ho, P. C. Lund, Richard Wong, Jonas Kan, and Patrick

Tai. Of course, I am entirely responsible for the ideas and opinions expressed in this work. Last, but not least, I should like to once again express my deepest gratitude to my secretary, Linda Lee, for her efficient typing of all the drafts of the work.

Effective Reform
in
China

1

China at the Crossroads

AUSTERITY AND MASSACRE

In spite of the official rhetoric for continuing reform that could still be heard well after the June 4, 1989, massacre, the reform momentum initiated by Deng Xiaping and Zhao Ziyang 10 years ago had come to a halt by the latter part of 1988. The last reform drive was headed by Deng Xiaoping, China's supreme leader, who decided in the middle of 1988 that it was imperative, at all costs, to implement a comprehensive price reform. Events in the following months quickly and completely smashed his bold declaration, and have silenced Deng henceforth on this subject. In response to a fast-developing double-digit inflation and rumors of impending shortages, panic prevailed among the public, causing bank runs and scrambles to stockpile consumer items in China's capital, Beijing, in July and August. To prevent the situation from deteriorating further, in September the Communist Party's Central Committee promised to dampen further price rises and to maintain price stability for the following year or so. In early October, the State Council issued a number of sweeping orders, including cutbacks on capital projects, reduction of investment in industries ranging from textile processing to electronics and plastics, tightening of bank credits, imposition of a 50-percent tariff on imported luxuries, purges of certain trading companies, and control of lending by the Construction Bank of China. Later in the month, the government announced that it would freeze or impose ceilings on the price of a wide range of goods. Public calm was subsequently restored, and what might have developed into a major crisis was temporarily averted.

The Swing toward Austerity

All these measures amounted, of course, to a major reversal of policy and, indeed, to the ushering in of a new phase of retrenchment and austerity. What was less clear was whether this new swing of the pendulum was a mere punctuation to the reform course, as were previous swings toward austerity in 1980–1981 and 1983–1984, or whether it signified the end of a 10-year economic liberalization. The events that subsequently ensued seemed to suggest that the swing was more than idle movement. By the end of November 1988, the number of projects that had been shelved or cancelled had risen to about 9,500.[1] Domestic credit agencies at all levels were further prohibited to make loans to nonstate enterprises or to projects that were not covered by state planning. By December, the government had moved to curb borrowing by its factories from abroad, to tighten its control over the use of foreign exchange by its state enterprises, and to restrict nonessential imports.[2] Even projects that came under the current five-year plan, which began in 1986, were stalled. In the same month, Finance Minister Wang Bingqian revealed his plan to tighten budget control and raise more tax revenues in order to contain the state's worsening budget deficit.[3] This series of measures retrenching economic liberalization was further endorsed by China's National People's Congress (which acts like a parliament) when it met in March 1989, and where Premier Li Peng, backed by the conservative faction of the party, further proposed to indefinitely postpone two critical reforms: price liberalization and selling shares of state enterprises to the public. To fortify his austerity program, Li also called for reducing state investment by 21 percent for the year 1989 and for a reduction of the state budget deficit.[4]

In the same congress, Li emphasized that China would not return to the command regime, which was characterized by overcentralized, excessive and rigid control, but neither would it embrace the other extreme of adopting private ownership, a budding idea hotly debated among the hard-line reformers themselves, and which in Li's view amounted to the negating of the socialist system. Since he took an essentially eclectic position, Li's proposals were not expected to contain anything new. As it turned out, all that he had to offer was a set of administrative measures and expedients that were alleged to be capable of correcting the blunders of the decade-old reform and of putting inflation under control. Also in the same congress, more severe measures were unveiled. The country's chief economic planner, Yao Yilin, revealed that the government would terminate some projects in key sectors such as energy, transport and raw materials. These were sectors that had formerly been exempted from such austerity measures. The government would also suspend operation of those enterprises producing inferior products or consuming excessive energy or raw materials.

Turmoil and Massacre

The abrupt swing toward austerity, though not completely unexpected, had colossal consequences for the economy. While it was unlikely that a milder course of action would have saved China's economy from plunging into the kind of predicament that it faced in the early part of 1989, the abruptness of the change intensified the looming economic crisis and precipitated the political crisis that subsequently unfolded. The economic problems that had surfaced by 1988 were the inevitable result of an ill-designed and ill-handled reform. By then, the economy had already moved to the point where one could characterize it as nonreformable by the measures available to the reformers. What the austerity measures did was to translate an economic problem into a political one, and to change a standing conflict between dissenting factions over economic issues into a political struggle.

The economic repercussions of these austerity measures were, of course, enormous, especially because many latent problems were brought to a boil. The imposition of credit freeze policies meant that a critical part of an enterprise's working capital was suddenly cut off, and immediately much of the intercompany flow of payments and short-term debts became locked in and thus translated into long-term debts. In response to this situation, enterprises would either cut back sales to existing debtors or would require cash payments for them. This entailed that the amount of working capital required by an enterprise to maintain its existing level of business activity had to be raised substantially. The results were as expected. A collective shortage of working capital, coupled with the already existing shortage of raw materials, forced drastic cutbacks on production, sales and employment, and threatened many enterprises with the possibility of bankruptcy. To maintain production or liquidity, many enterprises were forced to resort to less-than-legal courses of action and manipulative activities such as selling materials allocated by the state that are supposed to be used for meeting state-set production quota.

Moreover, the impact of the austerity measures went beyond the economic boundaries: The psychological effects they engendered were even more frightening. The reform had been looked on as a source of hope, not only by the government but also by the people at large. The economic crisis that had loomed since 1988 was a disillusionment to many, but there was still a lingering hope. The imposition of austerity measures confirmed the worry of many who feared that the government had changed its mind and had become more prepared to roll back the reform rather than try out new solutions to continue it. Even within the Chinese government, some delegates of the National People's Congress openly voiced their dissatisfaction with the severity of the austerity programs.

Given the state of the Chinese economy, the austerity measures were unlikely to yield positive results within a short period of time. By contrast, the negative impacts were quick to come about, and soon manifested themselves in various realms. The first few months of 1989 showed further signs of a deteriorating situation. Inflation was still running at a 30-percent high.[5] Corruption was rampant. Continuing public jitters caused new bursts of panic buying during March 1989 in several southern provinces. Many rural industries and enterprises, stripped of credit, were on the verge of bankruptcy and about to unleash massive unemployment. In response to the worsening situation, about a hundred managers from various enterprises gathered in mid-April and submitted a joint appeal to the government, expressing their fear of the continuing austerity measures and the possibility of the economy moving back toward recentralization, thereby negating the fruits of the 10-year reform.[6]

All these disillusionments, dissatisfactions and fears came to a head on April 15 at the death of Hu Yaobang, the former Communist Party chief, who was viewed by many Chinese students and intellectuals as the nation's most liberal reformer. His death triggered an outpouring of sympathy in memory of the ousted leader among students, who rallied together, putting up hundreds of posters supporting Hu and calling for more democracy and government actions to combat the existing economic ills. This soon developed into massive antigovernment protests and demands for political reform. In the following week or so, more than one hundred thousand students from two dozen universities defied stern government warnings and marched through Beijing's main thoroughfare to the cheers of hundreds of thousands of sympathetic onlookers. Not unexpectedly, the government response was negative. Criticizing the movement as "reactionary," it threatened to crack down. Undaunted, the students continued to defy government warnings and set up temporary shelters in the Tiananmen Square during that month in an attempt to strike a deal with the government. In May the student actions were subsequently reinforced by citywide demonstrations supporting reforms and more democracy. It was estimated that over a million people from almost all walks of life participated in these rallies, which also disrupted the schedule of the state visit of Soviet leader Mikhail Gorbachev. The overt confrontation came to an abrupt end on June 4 as the government brutally crushed the student demonstrators, dismissed the moderate Zhao Ziyang, the party's general secretary, and started to hunt and arrest thousands of dissenters and their supporters.

Post–June 4 Developments

The Tiananmen bloodshed and the dismissal of Zhao marked the beginning of a new era, as the military and the conservatives adopted the party line, and as Zhao's administrators and think tank were taken apart. The reform rhetoric stayed on, but how much of Zhao's reform remained in the post–June 4 era was very controversial. On the one hand, it was clear that Deng, whose power still remained relatively intact, wanted the reform to continue in one way or another. On the other hand, however, he also came to realize that the kind of liberal reform undertaken by Zhao was not politically tenable nor economically feasible after all. Whether or not Deng was entirely willing, it seemed that he felt compelled to adopt the conservatives' overall choice of recentralization and austerity, at least as a temporary solution to the staggering problems of the day.

On the part of the conservatives, it was clear that they would have preferred to make more drastic changes and reverse more of Zhao's reform measures, but they were also severely constrained in their power and resources, as well as being controlled by the force of circumstances. Apart from being constrained by Deng's explicit will to continue the reform, the conservatives who held the reins to the government faced a host of political, economic and financial problems that limited the options for implementing policies congenial to their ideology. In order not to stir great opposition from the provincial authorities, many of whom had already expressed dissent concerning the way the June 4 repression had been conducted, the conservatives were careful not to push their recentralization measures too quickly in spite of all their rhetoric. In order to pacify potential urban unrest, the conservatives had to increase food subsidies and allow private enterprises to continue their level of activities, notwithstanding the fact that it was the existence of massive private enterprises that had permitted the substantial support given to the student movement. In order not to overburden the worsening financial situation, the conservatives were forced to maintain the existing financial contracting system with the provinces, in spite of the fact that in so doing they had to make concessions concerning the financial and economic autonomy of these provinces. This is particularly true with respect to the southern provinces, where much free-wheeling reform had taken place and which were in command of substantial resources. In order to ensure a steady food supply from the countryside, the conservatives were forced to continue the policy of rural individualism. To alleviate continuing hostility from the international community, the government kept emphasizing its adherence to an open-door policy.

It would be a mistake to say that the conservatives were supportive, in even a halfhearted way, of Zhao's reform measures, or that they did little to reverse them. Reform-minded officials who served Zhao or were sympathetic toward his cause were mostly replaced. In spite of the constraints we have mentioned, recentralization was quietly but vigorously pursued wherever there was little resistance. The enterprise manager was no longer entirely responsible for all major matters in the enterprise. His power was to be shared, if not seriously challenged, by the party cadre, whose power was now reinstated. Bankruptcy laws that had been passed and were aimed to apply across the board to all enterprises were brushed aside when the government, out of political considerations, came to the rescue of the state enterprises, regardless of their persistent substandard performances.

However we label the measures adopted by the conservatives, the results of austerity and repression were a deepening economic crisis, the buildup of a staggering financial deficit, withdrawal of foreign investment, suspension of foreign loans and, most important, a demoralized work force. We will return to these developments in a later section. At this point, let us investigate in more detail the 10-year reform and explain the causes of its failure.

DENG'S REFORM IN RETROSPECT: A THEORETICAL ANALYSIS

Theoretical Framework

This section aims to give an explanatory account of Deng and Zhao's 10-year reform, and in particular, the causes of its failure. In line with an explanatory approach, it will be a rational reconstruction of historical events and a logical abstraction of detailed sequences. The explanatory sketch we offer will demonstrate how apparently rational policymakers and economic actors, operating under an initially less-than-rational system while adopting strategies that they individually perceive as rational, can unwittingly engender a "constraint-creating" process, whereby their options are gradually reduced over time, leading eventually to the kind of explosive disequilibrium that China's economy faced by the later part of 1988. The mode of analysis that was adopted might be called the methodology of the logic of the situation.[7] It consists in analyzing how rational actors can collectively, through a series of situations, one leading to the next, come to produce a highly unstable regime. In a sense, what happened to China is inevitable given the nature of the initially less-than-rational system and the logic of its economic actors.

In physics, chemical kinetics and theoretical biology, dynamic systems of the self-reinforcing or autocatalytic type (systems with local positive feedback) tend to possess symptotic states or "emergent" structures. This means that an initial starting state, combined with early random events or later fluctuations, can push the dynamics of the system into some emergent structures, which in turn bias the system toward the structures so selected. The result is that the system will gradually lock itself into some kind of steady state, and will eventually have little chance of exit unless a large dose of energy is applied to free it from the lock-in situation. In the course of selection, the system may undergo vigorous fluctuations or a phase of explosive disequilibrium before it settles down into the lock-in situation. When a huge amount of energy is applied to break up this situation, the dynamics leading to an explosive disequilibrium may also be set off, but it is not possible to tell beforehand whether the intended exit will be successful.

Not unexpectedly, some human systems, including economic systems of the dynamic kind, show properties similar to those described above. However, in the economic realm, mainstream neoclassical economics is ill-equipped to handle phenomena of this kind. This is because neoclassical economics, which is built on the assumption of diminishing returns on the margin (namely, local negative feedback), assumes equilibrium states to be the dominant mode of economic phenomena and the equilibrating principle to be the basic principle of economic fluctuation. By corollary, it underestimates the prevalence of disequilibrium phenomena in the economy, although the literature in economics is not without discussions of positive feedback mechanisms.

In the areas of international trade, regional economics, industrial organization and economic development, and under different conceptual tools such as increasing returns to scale, virtuous and vicious cycles, deviation-amplifying mutual causal processes, threshold effects and nonconvexities, there have been, albeit conducted in a nonsystematic manner, considerable discussions and analyses of self-reinforcing mechanisms not dissimilar to those discussed in other realms. W. Brian Arthur (1988), for example, observed that self-reinforcing mechanisms are variants of or usually derive from four generic sources: large set-up or fixed costs (which give the advantage of falling unit costs to increased output); learning effects (which act to improve products or lower their cost as their prevalence increases); coordination effects (which confer advantages to "going along" with other economic agents that are taking similar actions); and adaptive expectations (where increased prevalence on the market enhances beliefs of further prevalence).

Economists since the time of Alfred Marshall ([1890] 1961) have known that increasing returns can cause multiple equilibria and possible inefficiency, and there is no lack of approaches in modern economics dealing with these two subjects. A market may start out even and symmetrical, but it may end up asymmetrical, having experienced some kind of "symmetry-breaking" process in the course of development (for example, Arrow and Hahn 1971). In international trade theory, self-reinforcing mechanisms rooted in increasing returns or large set-up costs often lead to the existence of multiple equilibria with different welfare consequences (see Ohlin 1933). In industrial organization, network externalities and expectations are said to lead to multiple market-share equilibria (see Katz and Shapiro 1986). In spatial economics, historical incidents have clearly been shown to have selection and subsequent self-reinforcing effects even on regions with similar levels of endowment.

In spite of the usefulness of these studies, the level of abstraction at which they are formulated is not sufficiently high to enable us to grasp the underlying unity across these subfields or to develop a more generalized understanding. Arthur's (1988) taxonomy of the common causes of self-reinforcement, namely large set-up costs, learning effects, coordination effects and adaptive expectations, together with his analysis of the formal characteristics of lock-in and path-dependence, are useful steps toward a broader understanding of the nature of self-reinforcing mechanisms. However, they are far from constituting even first attempts to offer a comprehensive theory to unify these different theoretical pillars. It remains unclear, therefore, what ultimate ontological property is inherent in the initial state of an economic system or in the dynamics of that system, or both, that is responsible for that system's eventual performance.

One route by which to explore this basic ontological question would be to approach the subject via the study of autopoiesis and dissipative structures. These ideas were derived from the physical sciences where they were used to analyze the emergence of "far-from-equilibrium" physical states (see Prigogine 1984). An autopoietic system is conceived broadly to be

a unity realized through a closed organization of production processes such that (a) the same organization of processes is generated through the action of their own products (components) and (b) a topological boundary emerges as a result of the same constituent processes (Zeleny 1979, pp. 394–95).

Some researchers hold that autopoiesis is a central aspect of the dissipative system which is defined by its relations of stability to its environment or to that of other systems (see Jantsch 1979). In spite of their apparent fruitfulness, to date there has been much controversy over the specific meanings of these concepts, especially when they are applied beyond the original physical domain. In living systems, autopoiesis usually focuses on their capacity to develop and maintain their organization. In the social domain, the concept of autopoiesis generally focuses attention on the internal mechanisms or processes within a given system (see Coats 1988). Regardless of the theoretical immaturity in their applications to the social domain, the very ideas of an autopoietic system and dissipative structure, these above-mentioned researchers contend, should alert us to those aspects of reality that characterize today's accelerated social change; disorder, instability, diversity, disequilibrium, nonlinear relationships (in which small inputs can trigger massive consequences) and temporality (a heightened sensitivity to the flows of time).

Juxtaposing findings through the bottom-up approach (as found in Arthur's 1988 work) with the "promise" of the top-down approach (for example, Zeleny's 1979 conception of autopoiesis), one might notice that between these two poles there is a big gap for further theories to fill as far as our understanding of economic reality is concerned. It is doubtless important to continue to borrow concepts from the physical and biological disciplines in order to better our understanding of emergent systems, self-reinforcing mechanisms and disequilibrium states, as well as to continue to analyze different subfields in economics in order to yield more formal characteristics of the dynamics of these nonequilibrium movements, in the hope that the gap will be finally closed. However, in the absence of a general theory that can account at once for a diversity of equilibrium and disequilibrium paths and states in the economic domain, we need an intermediate, "indigenous" framework to help us, in the least, to throw light on the kind of development situation that China experienced during its 10-year reform. Specifically, we need a theoretical framework to adequately explain why and how the partial reform conducted by Deng and Zhao, instead of attaining its intended results, led to situations that practically went out of control and finally led to runaway situations in the Chinese economy in the later part of 1988. To this end, we must first posit ontological assumptions about the prereform socialist system of China. We will then analyze how these properties yield selection structures that bias a system toward certain unstable developmental pathways, which in turn eventually drive the economy onto a path of explosive disequilibrium.

Broadly speaking, we posit that the more a social or economic system is decentralized, namely, the more it consists of atomic units of a homogeneous kind that have, individually, minimal impacts on other units and thereby on the system as a whole, the more stable the overall system and the less it will tend toward a state of disequilibrium. Any effects caused by external disturbances on the system would then be temporary. As a corollary, the chance of exit from such a system is slim. Any lasting change in the system could only come internally by its atomic units gradually combining and forming into progressively less divisible "chunks" with a high degree of interdependence among themselves. Such "indivisible" chunks would then act as the spearhead or catalyst for change. A perfectly competitive market in the neoclassical framework, consisting of atomistic buyers and sellers of a homogeneous kind, is a divisible system in the perfect form. By contrast, a command economy capable of shuffling resources at will, controlling resources from a center and imposing its power on any part of its system is indivisible. Other familiar examples of indivisible systems are the family, the government, and political parties.

At the risk of oversimplification, one may posit that an indivisible system is more likely to be relatively less stable because the indivisible chunks, operating with either positive or negative local feedbacks, generally have a self-reinforcing character. On the other hand, a perfectly divisible order without, by definition, any "lead" sector is hardly capable of sustaining changes, for the system has an "innate" propensity to bounce back to its original state of equilibrium. The overall stability of an indivisible system, therefore, depends on the directions and the relative strengths of its indivisible chunks, as well as on external disturbances that act on the system or on parts of it. An indivisible system could be stable for a long period, even if there are local disturbances and disequilibria, but on the whole it is less stable than a highly divisible system.

In spite of its potential instability, a system characterized by large indivisible chunks may stand to gain in dynamism and vitality should they operate with positive local feedbacks. Under such conditions, they may yield benefits not only to themselves but may also spread them to the neighboring parts as well. However, the existence of indivisible chunks does not necessarily lead the overall system to higher levels of welfare. Certain types of indivisible chunks, especially those operating with negative local feedbacks, might deter their elements from their best performances and deprive the system of its ability to detect either internal or external threats. As an analogy, one might liken these chunks to groups of cancer cells that grow at the expense of the rest of the body. A system characterized by large indivisible chunks is therefore double-edged. It possesses formidable power to either initiate or block changes. Additionally, because it is an inherently unstable system, it may lock itself into a specific state for an indefinite period of time. An ideal system, it seems, is divisible and has sufficient power to restore the entire system to some kind of equilibrium, yet possesses lead indivisible chunks that operate in virtuous circles so that over time higher levels of performance and welfare for the entire system can be realized. The combination of divisibilities and indivisibilities in a system that is necessary to attain this desirable state is a subject for future research. For our purpose, we will confine ourselves to the discussion of the properties of the command system as an indivisible system.

From the above characterization, a command economy appears to be a thoroughgoing indivisible system. Being indivisible, its defects and problems are entirely transmittable to different parts of the system. As a result, its power to contain its own defects is very limited. Therein lies part of its instability. On the other hand, however, its indivisibility is of an artificial kind, cemented and sustained more by power than by internal coherence. Right from the start, the system embodies a decentralizing propensity suppressed by some lead chunks (for example, the party, or the military) and by its administrative instruments. This accounts again for part of its instability. Unlike a mixed system, where different indivisible chunks stand in competition among themselves and with the rest of the system, driving the system as a whole toward some higher planes of efficiency, the command system as an indivisible system faces little competition among different parts of itself, and hence has little internal drive to attain higher levels of performance. The prereform Chinese economy is a case in point.

Apart from being a divisible system, a decentralized economic system is essentially rational in that it tends to allocate its resources in the most efficient manner and that it unintentionally will maximize welfare or utility for the system as a whole most of the time. By this standard, the market economy, relying on the price mechanism for signaling scarcities and coordinating transactions, is conceivably the most efficient and thereby the most rational system, although it does admit of multiple equilibria under certain circumstances or by virtue of certain historical conditions. In principle, a competitive market system is, in the extreme, capable of attaining a Pareto-efficient state, an ideal state that is no longer capable of further improvement in efficiency or welfare. A social state is described as Pareto-optimal if and only if no one's utility can be raised without reducing the utility of someone else. Pareto-optimality thus is also Pareto-efficient for any economy that has maximized its overall level of utility. An economic system is a rational one if it is Pareto-efficient, and a price system is a rational one if the prices are entirely free to move in line with scarcities and thereby move toward a Pareto-efficient state.

By the above criteria, the Chinese economy in the prereform era can be described as at once an indivisible and an irrational system. We have pointed out that it was an indivisible system by virtue of being a command system. The indivisibility, however, goes beyond the economic aspects. It is manifested in every aspect of the social life of its economic actors. Apart from defining the role of economic actors in the system and their entitlement to its output, the command system predefines in a strict manner their social status and their relationships to others, as well as what constitutes acceptable or unacceptable behaviors. As we have pointed out, however, such indivisibility is artificial and is more apparent than real. In addition, the system is irrational in that the prereform economy was characterized by a regime of less-than-rational prices in the sense that many of its prices bore remote relations either to the cost structures or the demand structures. Not unexpectedly, such a price regime tacitly embodies income subsidies from government to enterprises and households, each of which regards such support as its rightful entitlement. Reflecting relative distributions of income rather than relative scarcities of resources, these prices are, out of political considerations and for historical reasons, usually kept at artificially low levels. This explains in part why price reform is such a delicate business. Part of the delicacy arises from the complexity of the price system, the price of one commodity being intricately related to the prices of many others. An economy in which a considerable number of its prices are kept artificially low will be liable to transmit such irrationalities across other parts of the system and thus infect a large range of commodities. In the case of China, as in most other socialist countries, the prices of consumer goods, and in particular food prices, are irrational prices. Heavily subsidized by the state, they bear little relation to the costs of production.

One less-than-rational characteristic of a socialist command system is that since it is an indivisible system, the rule of dessert is highly distorted. Whereas the market economy has a built-in reward and penalty system, whereby economic actions can in the least be consistently, if not always objectively, appraised; economic actions, especially those at the level of the individual in a command system, are, deliberately or nondeliberately, denied of objective appraisal. As a result, mistakes made at this level can hardly be identified, correctly labeled and treated accordingly, in addition to the fact that they can be easily concealed in an indivisible system and are covered up so that they are not shown at the level of collective results. In other words, a command system lacks the stick with which to discipline errors and wrong judgments. An alternative characterization would be what J. Kornai called the "soft budget constraint," namely, in a socialist economy there is an absence of effective sanctions against inefficiency at the enterprise level (1980). All this means that the effectiveness of any set of reform measures will be questionable unless it possesses both disciplinary components and a system of accountability for such disciplines to be effectively applied to the level of the individual economic actor.

The situation of China is further complicated by the fact that, unlike many other socialist economies, the provincial authorities play a crucial role in the reform process (see Shirk 1985). The prominence of localities in economic affairs in the Chinese socialist system was in part the result of Mao Tse-tung's long-time effort to promote and mobilize local power in both agriculture and industry. By the end of the Cultural Revolution, local governments had already gained control over vast amounts of resources. Chinese reformers seemed to wrongly believe that the delegation of power to the provinces or the counties represented a progressive step in reform. They did not seem to realize that because of the way provincial and local power is delegated in their system, instead of creating a rational regime for reform, more often than not it becomes an obstacle in the way of reform. With vast resources vested in their domains, these authorities could, for example, act out of self-interest to set up trade barriers to protect local industries. The mushrooming of high-cost firms operating with excess capacities and dominating small, fragmented markets in the different provinces of China during the reform period is a case in point.

Our contention is that the Chinese economy as an indivisible and irrational system is cemented and driven by political and administrative means. To reform the system for efficiency, it would be necessary to decentralize its decision-making base. Were the decentralization a complete and comprehensive one, the system would in principle be capable of being restored to a rational state over time. On the other hand, a less than full decentralization would not only fail to eliminate the irrationalities of the system, it would also render it highly unstable by creating indivisible chunks with unequal power and resources. Left to grow on their own, they would amplify rather than eliminate the original irrationalities in the system. The result would be a highly unstable regime capable of developing runaway situations. In the following section, we will demonstrate how the partial reform of Deng and Zhao, being a less than complete decentralization, in due course created a highly explosive situation.

We might also mention one constraint to effective reform in China: the Chinese reformers, ingrained in the socialist doctrine, invariably equated modernization with industrialization, the modernization of agriculture with the mechanization of agriculture, and the end of reform with rapid industrial growth. In 1982, Deng publicly proclaimed that the goal of his reform was to quadruple China's agricultural and industrial production by the end of the century. That worked out to be 7.2-percent annual growth rate in agricultural and industrial production between 1980 and 2000. Many provincial leaders and factory managers took this target seriously, believing that if they only would work hard enough, it would be within their reach.

As is typical of any reform, time is always a major constraint. A reform always runs out of time, and reformers are, as a rule, meanly treated. Unlike preservers of the status quo, reformers are usually given only limited time to prove their merit. Since reformers stick their neck out, they capture more attention and their shortcomings tend to be magnified. There is, in a sense, a deep-seated, fundamental asymmetry between the proponents of a reform and the preservers of the status quo. Unless the reformers are able to build on their strength and score repeated successes, the chance of an ultimate triumph always remains questionable.

Two Subphases of Deng's Reform

Broadly speaking, Deng's reform can be demarcated into two phases, 1979–1984 and 1984–1988. The first period was characterized by two features. First, it was a period of phenomenal success in rural reform. Second, as far as the reform of the urban industrial system was concerned, it was a period of experimentation, when reformers tried hard to kick the reform off the ground and gradually remove resistance from the conservatives. During the second period, 1984–1988, reform in the countryside took two divergent paths. Reform on the farms gradually lost its momentum, but the nonfarm sector, especially the rural and township industries, continued its boom until the imposition of austerity measures in late 1988. In the urban industrial system, reform began to gain momentum after the reformers came into full control in 1984. In a matter of three years, the adopted reform measures, instead of removing previously imposed less-than-rational constraints, had created new constraints and reduced the range of options available to the reformers. The narrowing of options compelled the reformers to adopt high-risk reform measures during the later stage, which ultimately led to the highly explosive disequilibrium situations of 1988–1989, and finally brought the reform to a halt. As the options available to the reformers were running out, neither the legitimatization of the reform by way of giving it an ideological backing (for example, Zhao's theory of the first phase of socialism, which was put forward in November 1987) nor the theoretical debates between the comprehensive reform camp and the property rights camp in 1987–1988 could be of any real help.[8] The dice had already been cast when the grand strategy of reform was formulated.

The Household Responsibility System: A Foretaste of Success

Few would deny that the starting point of the 10-year reform dates from the meeting of the Third Plenum of the Eleventh Central Committee in December 1978, which officially declared that the era of turbulent class struggle was over and the party should henceforth focus its attention on economic development. This change in direction was needed to correct the imbalances that existed in the economy and to improve the livelihood of both the urban and the rural populations. Specifically, it set out to attack the overconcentration of authority in economic management, to reform the agricultural system, and to upgrade living standards. With respect to agriculture, the plenum decided to raise farm prices substantially with a view to improving farm incentives, to forbid infringement by higher authorities on the rights of commune subunits, and to experiment with a partial decollectivization of agricultural organization.

Subsequent to these decisions, development in agriculture took a sharp upturn. The policy of enforced self-sufficiency in grain was subsequently relaxed. In its stead, encouragement was given to the diversification of production and the development of family sidelines. Rural free markets recovered and proliferated as the limit on the size of private plots was raised. The most important development was the permission, upon the issue of Document 75 by the Central Committee, to contract output to the individual households. Under this new policy, after meeting its quota and tax obligations and paying a contribution to the team to maintain some collective services, each household was free to dispose of its output as it wished. It might sell its surplus to the state at above-quota prices and beyond, at still higher, "negotiated" prices, or it might choose to sell it to the free market. Work points were eliminated altogether. Increased productivity thus entailed a more-than-proportional increase in income.

By the end of 1982, the household responsibility system (HRS) had become nearly universal in the countryside. After 1983, the extension of the reform consisted in lengthening the duration of land lease to 15 years and beyond, permitting lease-like arrangements between households, as well as permitting the free flow of peasant investment into various kinds of private and cooperative enterprises. As a result of these measures, a period of rural prosperity commenced, agricultural output rose sharply, and the rural markets flourished. A switch toward cash crop diversification and a phenomenal mushrooming of rural industries took place. We will discuss the details of these measures and changes in Chapter 4.

Piecemeal Reform in the Urban Industrial System: DPRR and Its Defects

The above-mentioned reform strategy was sometimes dubbed "streamlining administration and delegating power" or "delegating power and relinquishing revenues" (DPRR). It was applied not only to reform measures in the countryside but also to reform measures undertaken after 1979 in the urban industrial system. The essence of the formula consisted in "more decision-making power being granted to local authorities and production units and more benefits to the local authorities and the producers" (Wu 1988, p. 39). The formula was by no means an original one, for a similar formula had once been adopted in the 1958 reform. One major difference lay in the realm of application. The 1958 reform was confined largely to the state-owned industrial sector, whereas the 1979 reform was, in contrast, all-encompassing. Another difference was that the emphasis of the 1958 reform was on administrative decentralization, whereas the 1979 reform emphasized the autonomy of the enterprises. In its application to the urban industrial sector, the DPRR strategy consisted in the following measures: (a) expanding the private and collective sector, (b) vesting more managerial power in local authorities and enterprises, (c) sharing the revenue of enterprises between the central government, the local authority and the enterprise itself, (d) sharing the provincial revenue between the central government and the provinces, and (e) permitting foreign trade and cooperation schemes up to the level of localities and individual enterprises.

The guiding belief of the 1979 reform, in contrast to the previous ones, was that for reform measures to be effective, incentives must be vested in the proper unit or level of organization. Just as the household came to be recognized as the driving force of reform in the countryside, the enterprise was to be its counterpart in the urban industrial reform. This point was well established in September 1978 by Li Xiannian in a conference on Principles in Economic Work called by the State Council, who pointed out that the main defect of previous reforms was that authority was misplaced on administrative units, and that to be effective, the reform must vest an independent status in the enterprise.

Were the 1979 reform conducted in a way entirely compatible with Li's enlightened understanding; namely, had the reformers created truly autonomous enterprises as well as the necessary conditions for their smooth operation, the 1979 reform would at one stage or another have become a true success. This is the case because to guarantee the independent status of the enterprise and its autonomous operation would require nothing less than a full reinstatement of the price mechanism and the full-fledged operation of a market economy. A full restoration to the market economy, as numerous experiences tell us, is under normal circumstances the ultimate instrument of effective reform. Neither Li or Deng, nor any others saw at that moment the logical and inseparable link between the autonomy of enterprises and the free market. However, even had they had the knowledge, they did not have the ideological legitimacy to pursue the reform to such a radical point at that juncture. To opt for a reform of such encompassing scope and with such institutional ramifications would in a sense have been taking great political risks. Within the bounds of their resources and ideology, the reformers could only move in a cautious way, seeking step-by-step concessions from the hard-line conservatives as well as support from the neutral parties. Vesting more resources in enterprises and creating an environment for the enterprises to engage in some degree of competition among themselves, must even by the reformers' own standards, have been bold and daring steps at this point in time.

Reinforcing the belief that the reformers were going in the right direction, a foretaste of apparent success was achieved in the early days of the urban industrial reform. In 1978, a number of factories and plants in Sichuan were first given the autonomy to make production decisions, sell above-quota products, retain and make use of profits, adopt material incentive schemes, appoint lower-echelon personnel, promote personnel with higher levels of education and technical training, and impose stricter workplace discipline. The experiment was well received, and soon expanded to cover some 6,600 state enterprises, accounting for about 60 percent of total output (Riskin 1987). The results were encouraging. Enterprises vested with such autonomy soon displayed positive performances. The same liberal principle was immediately applied to the collective sector and beyond. For the first time since the mid-1950s, small private undertakings were permitted in commerce, services and handicrafts. The growth of these sectors was phenomenal. Between 1979 and 1984, there was an increase of 14.5 million people employed in the urban collective sector. In the private sector, employment grew from virtually zero to 3.4 million in the same period. To circumvent administrative barriers and tap new opportunities, new forms of enterprises and different systems of joint ventures between enterprises across different regions or under separate vertical chains of command sprang up. Joint stock companies with private participation were allowed, and a period of unprecedented competition ensued.

The puzzling question is, if decentralization is the proper strategy of reform, and if what the reformers did amounted to decentralizing the decision-making base of the economy, why did the reform fail to attain its intended results in the case of China? Why was it that the mushrooming of private enterprises, or of more flexible forms of enterprises as well as foreign participation and joint ventures, with their increased competition, could not lead China to the path of increasing productivity and real production? The overwhelming answer to this question, as we have already pointed out, is that the decentralization was not carried out far and deeply enough. The following sections show why this was the case.

Behavioral Strategies of Enterprise Managers under the Regime of Expanding Enterprise Autonomy: The Case of Profit Bargaining

In a centrally planned regime, the role of the state enterprise manager is, strictly speaking, an administrative one, devoid of entrepreneurial components. What is expected of him is that his production results must match the master plan. His job is to remove obstacles that inhibit the fulfillment of his plan in the respective processes of input acquisition, production and delivery of output. For the purpose of propaganda, he might be asked, once in a while, to overfulfill his preset quota. However, unlike his counterpart in the market economy, he is not required to act enterpreneurially on behalf of his firm, for instance, in spotting new opportunities, pooling and shuffling resources to meet the challenges of new market demands and consumer preferences and, as the bottom line, to earn a competitive rate of profit for his firm. The socialist enterprise manager, in other words, performs essentially a house-keeping function, comparable more to that of a controller in the Western firm, albeit a controller with less flexibility and less resources with which to manage changes. The result of confining the role of the enterprise manager to that of a controller operating under highly restrictive constraints is that he is always put on the defensive, and the achievements he scores are "negative" in char-acter.

To break it down, the behavioral strategies of the typical socialist enterprise manager consist in (a) fulfilling, as far as possible, the face value of the part of the plan for which he is responsible, (b) minimizing the risk of underfulfillment, and (c) minimizing his share of responsibility in the event of underfulfillment. With the aid of a few tricks, strategies (a) through (c) are readily attainable within a highly indivisible system. The fulfillment of the face value of a plan in many cases is not too difficult, because the manager can always trade off quality in order to achieve quantitative results. As far as (b) goes, the enterprise manager in the socialist system is generally smart enough either to stockpile sufficient resources, including labor, to buffer shortages caused by other enterprises, or to greatly understate his production capacities at any point of time. Moreover, in the unfortunate outcome of the underfulfillment of planned targets, the socialist enterprise manager can always point his finger at other parties. Not unexpectedly, his excuses are generally well justified because the fulfillment of preset production targets does critically depend on the timely availability of inputs from many other enterprises over which he has little control.

There are many other constraints in the system that entrench the housekeeping function of the enterprise manager. He is in no position to hire and fire his labor, although he has some leeway and can practice some favoritism in the allocation of some fringe benefits. He is always constrained by ideological considerations and by party cadres who are stationed in the enterprise. Under these constraints, the most valuable skill required of the enterprise manager to survive and maintain his status quo is that of political bargaining. A "capable" enterprise manager is one who is able to bargain for more resources without a corresponding increase in the level of production responsibilities. Clearly, a system of this kind has an innate propensity to generate increasing wastes and inefficiencies, particularly as the so-called skills of its enterprise managers become more sophisticated and as the more skillful managers replace the less skillful ones.

The urban industrial reform was supposed to correct the chronic decline in efficiency and productivity caused by the above-described management structure. It was reasoned by the reformers that if the enterprise manager could retain part of his profits, he would be more conscientious in the deployment of the resources under his control. Hidden resources would be unleashed if the enterprise manager were to be vested with more incentives and more autonomy. Quite naturally, the typical enterprise manager would be awakened from his inertia to improve the efficiency of his enterprise and to enter into competition with his rivals. This appeared to be sound logic and a straightforward step to take. Indeed, the first round of the reform between 1979 and 1980, which was endorsed by five reform documents on July 13, 1979, revolved around institutional experiments toward retaining a portion of the profits made by the enterprises. In return for retaining a certain portion of profits and certain depreciation charges, the enterprises concerned were required to pay fees for the fixed capital used and interest charges to the bank for all the circulating capital used. The essence of the design was that the enterprise retentions would increase only to the extent that realized profits increased, and that enterprises would, in theory, retain less funds than previously should their overall level of profit decline. That is, enterprises were required in theory to bear higher risks. To enhance their risk-bearing capacity, enterprises were allowed to enjoy expanded authority over labor and current production decisions, as well as the right to independently market output produced outside the state plan.

At the initial stage, this scheme was conservatively implemented. During the first nine months of 1979, the number of profit-retention enterprises stood at 1,366. However, the program was soon taken up by virtually all the large, profitable industrial enterprises. Uniform regulations for profit retention were issued at the beginning of 1980, and by June 1980, the total number of participating enterprises in the scheme had grown to 6,600. The rapid rate of conversion of enterprises to this scheme did not, however, radically alter the structure of responsibilities of the participating enterprises. The change, as it turned out, was more of an accounting nature. What actually changed was that the participating enterprises were put in control of the full sum of their depreciation retention, which had previously had to be remitted to the central government budget. Other items of the scheme, for example, payment for the use of fixed capital and payment of interest to the bank for all circulating capital, which were supposed to increase the accountability of the enterprises in resource deployment, were only very slowly pursued.

In other words, the scheme of profit retention turned out to be little more than an indirect way of transferring resources to enterprises, especially enterprises strongly endowed with fixed capital. Apart from the fact that the managers were now more inclined to put resources under their control toward industrial investment, especially those in the localities, the positive effects on managerial behavior were minimal, since the increase of resources came largely from depreciation funds, which was a kind of paper transfer. One might say that the scheme represented a paradigmatic case where the carrot is given but not the stick.

Owing to a financial crisis in the central government, the above-mentioned reform came to a halt in December 1980. A severe deflationary policy was then pursued as the central government drastically reduced spending and strengthened price controls on consumer goods. However, the deflation was short-lived, as the policymakers soon came to realize that these policies were too drastic and threatened to push the economy toward a sharp downturn. By the end of March 1981, the cutback had been held up and a second round of reform was in the making. The new scheme grew partly out of the chaos caused by the sharp deflationary policy and the subsequent revisions to it. In response to the chaos, the profit contract was offered as an expedient to resolve the financial conflicts between the central government and the enterprises. Under this scheme, the enterprise and its supervisory body were to negotiate a "base figure" of profits which the enterprise undertook to deliver to the state while retaining the rest under its control, the retention rate being tied to some kind of sliding scale. This "profit contract" scheme was taken up by most state enterprises at a rate more rapid than that at which the previous profit-retention scheme had been embraced. This was not surprising, if one considers the advantages that the new scheme conferred to the enterprises. Not only did the new scheme endow more autonomy on the enterprises, it also fitted well with the bargaining mentality of the enterprise managers. The results were to be expected. Total profits retained in enterprises increased substantially in 1981, with a part of the increases attributable to the low base figures negotiated in early 1981, when the economy had yet to recover from its low.

One can easily see that these schemes did not by themselves constitute any effective tools for reform. Instead of bargaining over production targets, the new schemes of profit retention and profit contracting merely switched the objects and contents of the bargaining. Interestingly, the enterprise managers stood to gain more in bargaining for profit than in bargaining over production targets. Production targets are highly specific, and it is therefore difficult to exaggerate the problems involved in their realization. Profits, on the other hand, are more controversial subjects. Bargaining for profit means that the managers could enlist more contingent factors and uncertainties in their arguments for more leeway and allowances. They could easily exaggerate some factors and make more stringent assumptions in their favor. There was a further complication. Many smaller enterprises were under the direct control of the local provinces. Since the revenue of the local authorities depended in part on contributions from the enterprises, the level of profit obtained by the enterprises was of great concern to this group. Under the profit-contract system, local authorities were given more leeway to manage the industrial systems under their jurisdiction. In other words, these authorities had a deep interest in seeing that their respective enterprises managed to bargain for the highest rates of profit retained.

The reformers were not utterly unaware of the kind of quasi-profits these enterprises then reaped. Subsequent developments consisted in attempts to work out a more rational formula, which eventually focused on the "tax-for-profit" scheme. In its fully developed form, this scheme amounted to demanding that enterprises pay a number of taxes directly to the state treasuries. The taxes included the following components: (a) charges on fixed and circulating capital (b) the existing sales tax (c) an income tax, and (d) an "adjustment" tax to equalize contingency factors. The intention of the scheme was to charge the enterprises realistically for all inputs used in the production process and to reduce opportunities for bargaining over profit targets and retention rates (Naughton 1985).

At the beginning of 1983, the government decreed that all enterprises would shift to the tax-for-profit system, which was to begin on July 1983. Stripped of its details, the upshot of the 1983 tax-for-profit system was that enterprises were required to pay a flat rate of 55 percent in income tax. Again, however, the change in formula did not materially affect the enterprises insofar as their current levels of profit were concerned. Profit-retention ratios or profit-contract base figures were to be recalculated on the basis of after-tax income in such a way that most enterprises were left with the same level of retained profits. Thus, the tax-for-profit scheme, while being a more rational plan, did not radically alter the behavior of the enterprise managers. Instead of inculcating a production-for-real-profit mentality, these changes in policy merely reinforced the

bargaining mentality and its accompanying rent-seeking ramfica-
tions, for through no effort of their own, the enterprises came to
enjoy a continued, uninterrupted increase in profit, although it was
really a quasi-profit. With every change in these reform schemes,
the enterprise managers became more confused over the ultimate
direction of the reform. Through a series of bargaining sessions
and changes, local authorities came to control vast amounts of
retained depreciation funds. Profits were, so to speak, thrust on
these enterprises, while losses, as a rule, were eventually to be
borne by the state (Naughton 1985).

The Strategy of Disposable Resources and Bonus Maximization in the Socialist Enterprise

Behind the facade of profit bargaining, there exists a level of
deeper motives that make the socialist enterprise manager behave
in ways fundamentally different from his counterpart in the market
economy and make bargaining the focal point of his management
strategy. We assume that the firm in the market economy aims to
maximize profit, growth or a combination of both, and that its
manager aims to maximize his income, with the level of income
being commensurate with the level of profit of his firm. The
interests of the firm and the manager are, therefore, largely convergent, if not fundamentally identical.[9] However, this is rarely the
case in the socialist system. Several reasons might explain the
difference. We have already pointed out that the socialist enterprise
manager performs essentially a housekeeping function. Since this
is an undemanding job, requiring more political skill than management expertise, it is always easy to replace one enterprise manager
with another. In fact, a competent manager intent on improving
real production and productivity is unlikely to stay in that position
for long because he would have to overcome the inertia of the
vested interests in his enterprise and might have to challenge the
political elements in that organization. Unable to reap a handsome
bonus through a short period of brilliant performance and then to
retire or change jobs like his counterpart in the market economy,

the socialist enterprise manager must strive to keep his job as long as he can. To maintain his position, he must develop healthy relations with the party cadres in his organization as well as with people with the correct political connections. The best way to develop these relations is to materially benefit these people and their close relatives, within the bounds of resources available officially for allocation by the manager himself and the bounds of official rules permitting such allocations. The more resources that are disposable by the manager, the better he will be able to serve this end, regardless of whether the resources allocated in this way will contribute to the overall well-being of his enterprise. In a similar vein, to keep his position as long as possible, the manager will avoid committing overt mistakes. As we have pointed out, understating production targets and stockpiling resources are common strategies to this end, in spite of the fact that they are inconsistent with the overall interest of the system as a whole. In other words, security considerations on the part of the enterprise manager, as well as his craving for power, drive a wedge between the interests of the manager and his enterprise.

The socialist enterprise manager also knows clearly that the government, whether for ideological or political reasons, will not let his enterprise fall, particularly if it is a large-scale one. This means that his security considerations, his pursuit of power and status, and so forth, while diverging from the interests of his enterprise, can be unscrupulously pursued without fear of the enterprise being destroyed by persistent substandard performances. Provided he can cover up his mistakes in one way or another, he can retain his position indefinitely. With such a fear taken away, it is natural that the manager will gather as many resources as possible under his control, regardless of their contribution to the real performance of his enterprise. Alternatively put, very much unlike the market economy, the socialist system possesses no impartial mechanism by which incompetent or unscrupulous managers can be easily identified and eliminated.

Since no private property rights of any significance are overtly permitted in the socialist system, the rewards to a brilliant enterprise manager or to anyone in the system cannot be translated into ownership of marketable properties or, for that matter, into any long-term investment instruments. His gains are thus biased in general toward consumption. In a political climate dominated by ideological purism, consumption is generally suppressed, but in a more liberal period, conspicuous consumption will suddenly erupt and become the rule rather than the exception. This is because conspicuous consumption is easily identified with the status of the consumer, especially consumption of commodities of a more exclusive kind. The occasional eruption of status-enhancing consumption in the socialist system should not surprise us if we consider that there are limited modes of expression of self-worth in a system where personal ability is not given proper recognition, and where overt competence is, more often than not, penalized. Conspicuously consumed goods of an exclusive kind thus serve as popular symbols to express the status and self-worth of their owners, no matter how unreal and superficial such symbols may be. Eager to please power brokers in order to stay in office, enterprise managers are rarely hesitant to exploit this particular means to their end. As a result, they will do anything within their power to gain access to such goods, even if they are of little economic value to their enterprise. Predictably, the more resources at the disposal of the enterprise managers, the more access they have to these goods.

Thus, given the constraints of his economic environment, the socialist enterprise manager invariably tends to maximize the amount of resources at his disposal. In a rigid command system where the wage bill is strictly set and where material resources are monitored in great detail, there is not much room for the enterprise manager to exercise his discretion, although he can still use certain fringe benefits such as housing to practice some degree of favoritism. A reform that emphasizes enterprise autonomy and thrusts resources on the enterprises changes these rules of the game in a practical way. Whereas previously the maximization of disposable resources was an implicit strategy, the reform made it legitimate. In the market economy, the manager has to depend on a subtle balance between business skill and luck in order to expand the amount of resources available to him, but the socialist enterprise manager in the reform regime need not expend similar efforts. With the policymakers giving more flexibility to the enterprise manager by permitting him to selectively reward his staff through bonus schemes, the resources of the enterprise increasingly were at the service of the personal interests of the enterprise manager, and the stage was set for a period of competition for personal gains. In the analytical language we have been using, we can say that the reform measures did not render the system truly divisible (namely: with quasi-profits and the absence of any possibility of bankruptcy). Instead, it made the system less rational (that is, through the increasing divergence between the interests of the enterprises and those of the enterprise managers). With more irrationalities, the system as a whole, in effect, degenerated with the implementation of these new measures.

Since 1979, the process of decentralization of both financial and material resources to provinces and enterprises was well underway. Local enterprises gained access to an increasing amount of funds for investment via different channels, including depreciation, retained profits, domestic loans, extra-budgetary funds of local government and nonprofit organizations, and foreign capital. At the same time, local provinces continued to register further control over a variety of key material resources such as cement, rolled steel, coal and timber. Conversely, the centrally controlled proportion of total capital construction and investments in state enterprises experienced a conspicuous decline over the period (Naughton 1985, Wong 1985). The stage was set for a phase of vigorous expansion at the provincial and enterprise levels.

The reform measures were not, of course, received with open arms by all parties. To have gone that far, the reformers had already overcome much covert resistance. This was well manifested in the temporary setbacks that occurred first in early 1982 and then between mid-1983 and mid-1984. By 1983, the mildly expansionist propensity of provinces and enterprises to siphon resources off key infrastructural projects conducted by the central government was keenly felt and caused great concern. Funds earmarked for investments to sectors that had been promised increases, such as agriculture, education, and scientific research, were not made available. To address the situation, in mid-1983 the Central Committee and the State Council reimposed administrative restraints on investment in the hope of regaining control of the priorities. A 10-percent levy on all nonbudgetary funds was imposed, and a rule was passed requiring local governments and enterprises to provide 30-percent down payments from their own funds for all projects they initiated. However, these controls were quickly shed as the reformers won the day and pushed the reform to its logical conclusion.

By 1984, the stage had been set for a full offensive on the part of the reformers. The overall spirit at that period was in favor of a full-scale reform. The private sector was flourishing, with the more enterprising practitioners now having many success stories to tell. A variety of organizations and joint ventures emerged to tap opportunities that were now emerging fast. Material incentive schemes adopted by enterprises seemed to meet with success, while hidden resources once held by enterprises were openly unleashed. The pent-up consumer demand and the rising income of different sectors provided a great potential for consumer sales. A fast-increasing amount of foreign capital and production contracts was crossing the border. It was against this background of optimism that in 1984 the reformers voiced their determination to carry out an urban economic "revolution" (Deng Xiaoping's term), to be equal in magnitude to the one enacted in the countryside. The reform gained new impetus.

In May 1984, the State Council promulgated the "provisional regulations concerning further extending the decision-making power of state-owned enterprises," empowering these enterprises, among other features, to (a) decide on the level of output beyond state-quota quantities to meet market demand, (b) market above-quota output and set prices on their own, (c) dispose of profits, retention funds and idle assets, (d) appoint middle-level administrative staff, and (3) distribute bonuses out of retained profits (Renmin Ribao

[People's Daily] 12 May 1984). To create a freer economic environment in line with such newly endorsed freedoms, in August 1984 the State Council further approved the "Provisional regulations concerning improving the planning system," prepared by the State Planning Commission, which expanded the scope of "guidance plans" and pure market regulations at the expense of mandatory plans (Wu 1988, p. 34). State mandatory plans would be reduced to key products, projects and key materials. State control over investment on fixed assets by enterprises and localities would be restricted to the overall level rather than to individual items. The document entitled "Decision of the Central Committee on Reform of the Economic Structure," and adopted in October of the same year, further divested government of its economic management role and undertook to proceed with price reforms. In addition, the banking system was finally given full control over the allocation of working capital to enterprises, a function it had been sharing with the Ministry of Finance.

Limited Price Reform: A Valuable Opportunity Forgone

The above-mentioned reform package, by all accounts, was a highly liberal one. However, it was lacking in one very crucial feature, namely, a comprehensive price decontrol. Indeed, at the risk of oversimplification, one could say that it was due to this missing feature that the reform eventually came to grief. With the benefit of hindsight, one might also say that were there a single most suitable moment at which to introduce a complete price decontrol in the course of the 10-year reform, it was the period 1984–1985. Moreover, had price reform been thoroughly pursued at that point, the history of China would have been very different.

The reformers came very close to embracing a radical price reform when, after a series of experiments conducted after 1979, the Central Committee announced on 20 October 1984 in a document entitled "Decision of the Central Committee on Reform of the Economic Structure" that price reform was "the key to reforming the entire economic structure" and that this reform would gradually be implemented. In the same month, the State Planning Commission issued a set of proposals to allow prices to fluctuate in response to market conditions. By late 1984, the pace and mode of price reforms on which the reformers finally decided to settle became clear. The reformers were to follow Hungary's use of a three-tiered price system—fixed prices for the most important goods, upper and lower limits to fluctuations for an intermediate range of goods and freely floating prices for a host of consumer and small-producers' goods. Industries with the greatest and most general forward linkages, such as steel, coal and petroleum, would remain under tight central control. At the other end of the spectrum, the production of most ordinary consumer goods and many small-producers' goods would respond freely to market conditions. An intermediate range of goods would be subject to state "guidance" rather than mandatory controls. By 1985, many food prices, including the prices of meat, poultry, fish, eggs and vegetables had been decontrolled.

With these events now behind us, one could say that the reformers at that stage did not fully grasp the importance and benefits of a complete price decontrol. Their change in attitude on this issue at the later stage of the reform was driven by the force of circumstances. Had the reformers implemented a comprehensive price reform at this point, the built-in logic of this measure would have corrected in a step-by-step fashion the irrational elements in the system, and would eventually have compelled the economic actors toward higher degrees of rationality. A complete price decontrol would have meant that the relatively indivisible system that characterized China's economy in the reform period would have undergone a complete and timely decentralization. With this change, all other features of the reform would have fallen neatly into place, eliminating over time what irrationalities that remained. For example, the impacts of local protectionism, which caused great difficulties in the reform, would have been effectively offset by a rational price regime. Similarly, under a rational price regime, the need for bankruptcy rules would have been compelling, and with bankruptcy permitted regardless of any excuse, a reform of labor would have soon ensued. In other words, once a comprehensive price reform had been instituted, the system would have inevitably moved toward greater degrees of rationality.

There were, of course, practical and ideological obstacles that inhibited the reformers from taking on this crucial strategy. A full decontrol of prices would mean the end of all mandatory planning, and one should not forget that there still existed strong opposition from the conservatives, who dominated the important sectors of heavy industries, as well as from bureaucrats and planners, who thrived on administrative control and state regulation. Formidable opposition also resided at the level of ideology. At this point, Zhao had yet to develop his "theory of the first stage of socialism," and comprehensive price reform was easily associated with a full surrender to the capitalist mode of economic operation. After all, the 1982 debate within the circle of policymakers over this issue had been settled in favor of a mixed system, which was perceived by them to be a safer one. The 1984 reform package, by all accounts, was already a daring move, and any further step would seem to be too risky politically. The reformers were hardly aware of the fact that without creating a truly divisible system (made possible only by a complete price decontrol), under reform, the irrationalities of the system would intensify instead of being removed by other reform measures. The runaway situation that developed after 1984 was the result of these irrational factors at work.

Scramble for Resources and Unreined Growth: 1985 to 1987

The subsequent period 1985–1987 was one of unreined expansion. It was a period during which the reformers were believed to have a free hand in their reform, but it was actually a period during which the reformers tried hard to alleviate troubles brought about by this phase of irrational expansion. As the reform forged ahead, problems of an unprecedented nature and magnitude gradually put the reformers on the defensive.

The 1984 reform package quickly brought about a new boom. Within a matter of months, industrial production had soared and began to grow at an annual rate of more than 20 percent. Capital construction investments surged ahead, pushing up inflation while quickly depleting foreign exchange reserves. This development was the result of the unchecked expanionist mentality of the enterprises and the local authorities, and was fueled by a banking system that was allowed to lend freely, as well as by the large number of organizations now permitted to have access to foreign exchange. The expansion was unchecked because it was in everyone's interest to participate in the game. Enterprises and localities were resource-rich, and it would have been stupid of them not to avail themselves of these opportuniites for profit. Enterprise managers wanted expansion because the amount of the depreciation fund they could retain was tied to the level of fixed capital. Both they and their workers wanted expansion because their bonuses were now pegged to the level of production, regardless of whether the output would find ultimate buyers. Local authorities wanted expansion because it fitted well with their revenue-maximizing objective, and out of self-interest, bankers too were more than willing to finance the expansion.

At the earlier phase of the expansion, there was no question of demand. First, there was much pent-up consumer demand in the system. Second, the sustained rural prosperity in the past five years had rapidly increased the purchasing power of many households. The private sector that gradually began to flourish in the urban areas also yielded much purchasing power. Moreover, worker bonus schemes in a variety of forms gave industrial workers an enhanced buying power. It was no wonder that in the post-1984 boom, and indeed throughout the entire reform period, the expansion concentrated largely on the supply of consumer goods. Apart from demand-side reasons, the orientation toward producing consumer goods was attributable to the fact that a lot of equipment and key materials that had previously been allocated only to large production units and higher levels became available to the smaller local plants, as the state enterprises were now permitted to sell their above-quota output in the market. The high profits that went to the production of consumer goods were first engendered by the pent-up demand. Later on, when the competition became vicious, they were sustained by protective barriers set up by the local authorities eager to protect their level of revenue. Consumer items that were formerly made by state enterprises now attracted small, local competitors. These projects yielded attractive profits partly because the new entrants were able to satisfy buyers who had no access to the old distribution channels, and partly because some of the prices were previously set at artificially high levels of virtue of the monopolistic positions enjoyed by the state enterprises. For example, even with production costs that were two to three times higher than those of the Shanghai plants, local watchmakers still made substantial profits at current prices (Wong 1985). For products whose demand far outstripped supply, small local industries enjoyed an unusually high rate of return in spite of their higher costs of production. This was because they were free to sell their output at negotiated or market prices, whereas for a considerable part of their output, the state enterprises still received the much lower state procurement prices. In other words, the original irrationalities of the system remained undissolved under this regime of constrained competition and, moreover, they gave rise to new irrationalities.

In a market economy, competition would eliminate the inefficient producers and eventually bring supply into balance with demand. Nothing of this sort, however, happened in China during the reform period. To protect its inefficient enterprises, the provincial governments set up barriers and segmented the national market in order to reduce "external" competition. For their part, the state enterprises, although facing shrinkages of market shares, were too inflexible to respond rationally. Since they operated with a rigid cost structure, and since there was no way they were allowed to go bankrupt, the losses they incurred were merely translated into a loss of state revenue.

The situation would have been easier to remedy if the bonuses, profits, funds, and so forth that were distributed by the enterprises and the local governments were all translated into demand for locally made products. In that case, the segmented markets could still come to some kind of local equilibrium, eventually compelling the provincial authorities and enterprises to reduce their capital investment in line with demand. Unfortunatley, there existed another factor that inhibited the system from reaching such suboptimal equilibria. Typical of other developing countries and other socialist economies, imported luxury goods, in particular consumer durables, cast a magical spell on consumers via a chain of demonstration effects. Not only did enterprise managers and party cadres wish to possess such luxuries, workers and farmers alike also came to see their possession as an improvement in their status. Not only did they crave these goods, they came to crave the latest models and the best-known brands. Gradually, a scramble for these status-enhancing goods intensified, with the more affluent going after the most desired models and brands, and the less affluent purchasing whatever they could afford. In a system where private property rights of any lasting value or significant scope are denied, and where there is a lack of reliable, longer-term media in which to store value, imported luxuries serve unwittingly as the media of both value and status.[10]

The result of this craving for imported luxuries was an upsurge of imports and, other things being equal, a deterioration of the balance of trade. It meant that foreign exchange now commanded an additional premium, and that access to foreign exchange became an enviable channel to develop. As a result, exporting meant more than the earning of profits, it also meant access to foreign exchange. In the same vein, joint ventures with foreign interests became the royal road to special privileges. In competition for foreign exchange contracts, many exports were sold below cost, and some joint ventures were hastily concluded. The situation quickly deteriorated as more and more regional enterprises were permitted to export their outputs directly, which in turn provided both the motive and the justification for expanding their capacities.

Shortage, Corruption and the Rescue of the Reform

It did not take long for the scramble among enterprises to expand capacity and muster resources to produce an acute economy-wide shortage. A huge amount of resources became locked into half-finished plants or uncompleted projects, and were intent on producing more of the same. Even the state enterprises began to feel the pinch, as they had to acquire some of their inputs from the market under the new three-tiered price system. In fact, the state enterprises were facing a double predicament. They had to sell a part of their output at fixed, low government procurement prices, while local enterprises protected by provincial trade barriers took away part of their market shares. With more regionally based enterprises now permitted to conduct foreign trade, they stood to lose an important part of their foreign trade business and foreign exchange earnings, especially as the small, locally based enterprises were often in a position to sell at below their cost. On the side of inputs, the state enterprises had to face keen competition from local enterprises in their scramble for increasingly scarce resources. With good reason, they could ask the central government for additional assistance. However, with more resources now under the control of the local authorities, the central government itself became too impoverished to meet the demands of these state enterprises. As a result, they had to acquire inputs from the market at fluctuating and rising prices. To meet the increasing bill for materials, they had to resort to the banks for more finances, leading in part to the rapid expansion of the money supply in the later days of the reform.

By 1986, it had become clear that more and more of China's state-owned factories were operating at a loss. Quite naturally, operating under such confusing and deteriorating conditions, these enterprises were hardly inclined to improve their productivity, which in any case would have been too slow a process to show any effect. As could be expected, they were more inclined to employ easier ways to rescue their position. One way was that, instead of using all the inputs allocated to them for meeting the mandatory targets of production by the state, these enterprises saved some of these resources for the production of more profitable items. Such a diversion of resources did affect the fulfillment of preset production targets, but, as we have explained, accounting for underfulfillment was not a difficult task for these enterprises. A still more effective way was to save some of these resources and sell them in the market for a profit. As prices of raw materials were on the rise, the latter turned out to be a more attractive route.

This practice, needless to say, had serious repercussions. Its widespread adoption meant that fewer and fewer of the resources allocated from the center were used for production. Instead, they were merely converted, through the multitiered irrational price system, into rents to make up for the losses incurred by the state enterprises. However, part of such rents continued to be distributed among workers in the form of bonuses, much of which was spent on purchasing imported consumer goods. In other words, an increasing portion of resources allocated from the central government was converted after several rounds into "transfer payments" for consumption. This state of affairs was not confined to the state enterprises. It was in part generated by the universal inability of the primitive accounting systems of Chinese enterprises to take inflation into account. Since bonuses were tied to profits, and since such profits were inflated by capital asset buildup and price increases, the level of profit on which the bonuses were calculated became disproportionately exaggerated. This meant that in reality a considerable part of the bonuses distributed to workers was actually the working capital of the enterprises.

Another serious repercussion was that such practice gave golden opportunities to the enterprise managers and their middlemen to reap handsome profits. This was an unfortunate development. Although enterprise managers were inclined toward maximizing disposable resources, during the reform period they were generally keen to show positive performances for their enterprises. In fact, the reform leaders, intent on making the reform a success, had during the reform period promoted many of their younger, more enthusiastic followers to these "key" positions as enterprise managers. The new enterprise managers were mostly in their fifties or early sixties, and were better educated and technically equipped than their predecessors. As early as 1984, four-fifths of state enterprises were reported to have younger and more competent directors. Under normal circumstances, where opportunities for reaping personal windfall gains were scant, these officials would hardly have been subject to the temptation of corruption (however, see Fung 1983). Nonetheless, under a regime of shortage and fluctuating prices, both opportunities for personal gain and the instruments to cover up such gains were amply available. In addition, from game-theoretic perspectives, the unethical behaviors of a small group could easily trigger others to follow suit. As a result, the situation changed drastically. Soon, different kinds of abuses emerged, syphoning state resources into private channels and eventually into the creation of an "underground private economy." The same processes operated at the local level. As resources under the command of the local authorities dwindled, they were compelled to trade them in the market for a profit. Local enterprises, facing the same shortage situations and the pressing demand for bonuses by workers, also resorted to selling part of their resources to finance their activities. The result was nothing less than an inflationary spiral.

The reformers did not, of course, expect such developments. In spite of their deep worries, they remained undaunted. Since 1985, the reformers had hoped that their indirect, nonadministrative measures would have some positive effects on the economy. Part of these measures included economic levers such as interest rates and taxation. They were meant to regulate rather than force the economy into some kind of equilibrium. However, by late 1987 it had become clear to them that these indirect measures were futile. In full awareness of the need to strengthen the "stick" side of the reform, the State Council turned to sterner measures to deal with the situation and to penalize those who were found engaging in corruption and profiteering. Propaganda, coupled with efforts to close tax loopholes as well as crackdowns on tax evasions and similar activities became part of the government's routine.[11] Aimed toward disciplining the inefficient, bankruptcy laws were vigorously legislated.[12] In spite of the laws being rejected by the National People's Congress in March 1987, the reformers continued to push such legislation. The reformers finally had their way, but only shortly before their loss of power. Meanwhile, in the absence of bankruptcy rules, the reformers encouraged corporate takeover as a second-best solution. Moreover, in September 1987 when Beijing Gears Work bought up a metal factory (another state-owned enterprise), reformers hailed the event as signifying the "third wave" on the reform.[13]

True to their own aims, the reformers continued to draft laws to protect private and individual businesses from bureaucratic interference, illegitimate tax extortions, and so forth. To enable enterprise managers to be free of local bureaucratic influences, reformers continued to put forth rules that permitted them more say in resources and staff management. To vest managers in all state enterprises with more power with which to deal with their labor, a contract system was introduced after October 1986, granting the former the power to dismiss any workers hired under such contracts who violated rules.[14] Additionally, changes were introduced permitting stock issues in state-owned and non-state-owned enterprises and in-company issues of stock to workers.[15] They also permitted some collective enterprises to have their shareholders elect managers, as well as permitting the floating of bonds and bond trading after August 1986.[16]

Meanwhile, the reformers engaged among themselves in a grand debate over the direction of reform. Two schools of thought emerged (Wu 1988). One favored comprehensive reform transforming the present economy into a "planned commodity economy," namely, a market economy with macroeconomic management. It was envisaged that under macro-regulation, the market mechanism would play a leading role in the Chinese economy. In effect, this approach recommended a full decontrol of prices. Accompanying price decontrol would be a tax reform and a fiscal reform. The second school of thought contended that a comprehensive price reform would be too risky, since it would involve a fundamental readjustment of vested interests. A two-track system, it was contended, would enable reform to take place in a constrained way and would, therefore, be a safer route. The root of the problem in the Chinese economy, in this view, lay in the vague boundaries among property rights, especially in the state-owned sector. Priority should, therefore, be given to ownership reform in order to create a new foundation for the microeconomy. Also according to this school, aggregate demand in the developing socialist economy would always exceed aggregate supply, and a balance would be reached only upon nearing the end of the reform. If one were to suppress such demand and limit money supply through artificial macro-control, growth would be retarded. Retardation of growth would then affect the interest of different social groups and would thereby reduce the social base supporting the reform. By the last quarter of 1986, the latter view had emerged as the more prominent one among the reformers themselves.

Besides arguing among themselves and their various think tanks, the reformers had to face the challenge by the conservatives. The abuses that had by then become widespread had already given powerful ammunition to the conservatives, who argued against rapid changes and strongly defended the status quo. As evidence of abuses of the system under reform mounted, the reformers were gradually put on the defensive.[17] Some sweeping theory was needed to justify the kind of apparent chaos in which the Chinese economy now found itself, and some ideological backing was clearly required to justify the continuing reform. That theory was furnished by Zhao in the name of the theory of the first stage of socialism. It was supposed to rearm the reformers with sufficient ideological ammunition to put through their agenda.[18] Backed up by the formidable support of Deng, the theory was endorsed as a blueprint for the development of a Chinese-style socialism in the 13th National People's Congress held in November 1987. It was a nicely formulated rationalization of the reform, but the fact that it was required at all indicated that the days of the reform were numbered.

The Runaway Economy and Back to Austerity

The situation would have been more bearable if the success in the rural sector could have been sustained. Unfortunately, however, the reformers, like their predecessors, looked at the rural reform as a ladder to rapid industrialization. Instead of building on success on the farm, they encouraged the growth of off-the-farm industries in the belief that the latter would spur industrial development as well as absorbing the surplus labor in the countryside. Indeed, the reformers were toying with the idea that by the end of the century, the proportion of the rural labor force would decline from its level of 80 to 85 percent in 1984 to only 30 percent, with the difference being taken up by rural industry, commerce and other sidelines. No wonder that the budget for agriculture, even in the peak of the boom, declined to a mere 6 percent of total state expenditures (Delfs 1984). After 1985, agricultural production began to show signs of stagnation.[19] By 1987, total imports of grain had increased to a level of 14 mn tons. What surpluses the farms accumulated during the boom years were siphoned off either into consumption, especially of a ritualistic kind or into the booming rural industries, both of which were not helpful toward agricultural production. Moreover, the rural industries gradually became linked with the urban industrial system and became increasingly dependent on the banking system. Instead of rendering support to the urban industrial reform by offering a continually abundant food supply to the cities, this rural industrial system competed with the urban industrial system for resources. As the two systems came into closer contact, the irrationalities of both were transmitted to each other and became amplified. On the other hand, the farm sector began to suffer from a rise in the prices of its inputs, especially chemical fertilizers. It too became the victim of the nationwide shortage phenomenon. On this subject, we will provide more detail later.

As shortages intensified and prices continued to rise, an increasing number of enterprises adopted the strategy of anticipating further shortages and price hikes. Instead of applying their resources to production, they retained them in anticipation of higher prices and higher profits. The enterprises that were compelled to part with their resources or materials were those badly in need of cash and finances. By this stage, it doubtless became quite clear to an increasing number of the economic participants that the situation could not last long. From their experiences of cyclical ideological swings in the past, many knew all too well that if they were to take advantage of the situation, they had to do it quickly. If they were to translate state resources into personal gains, they had to do it ruthlessly and before the others.[20]

With a strong motivation on the part of some sellers to hold onto their resources on the one hand and an equally strong motivation on the part of other sellers to realize their profits, one could explain why, in spite of all the publicity these speculative acts had attracted, the shortage situation was able to drag on for some period without becoming uncontrollable. What broke the camel's back came in fact from the indirect inflationary effects of such shortages on the prices of consumer goods and from the actions of the reformers in attempting to provide a stronger solution.[21] By early 1988, the reformers knew that the situation was getting out of hand. They realized that the shortages and the accompanying price rises were aggravated, if not directly caused, by the three-tiered price system. They were all aware of the different ways in which the system came to be exploited. They knew by then that the only rational move was to decontrol all prices. Unfortunately, the conservatives had by then mustered sufficient power and support to demand the restoration of order in the economy and a slowdown of the reform.[22] Intense debates ensued in the middle of the year as the party leaders gathered together in their coastal resort of Beidaihe to discuss the problems haunting the economy. Deng was still in favor of vigorous reform, and in an ill-fated public statement he made it clear that the price reform needed to be further pressed.[23] In August, a tentative plan was drawn up by the Politburo for reform over the next five years, calling for the decontrol of prices of the majority of goods except for a few important commodities and labor. It seemed that the reformers might still have their way. The delicate balance was disrupted as the agitated public, in fear of rising inflation, began to panic. A buying spree developed and became widespread, triggering some bank runs.[24] While Zao was still hailing the fact that China's first bankruptcy laws would take effect from November 1, henceforth allowing inefficient firms to be eliminated, in early September the State Council abruptly announced a package of measures, including, among others, the statement that China would take no radical steps in price reform and that the Politburo's plan was only tentative and was subject to revision.[25] Subsequent announcements made by the State Council indicated that a period of austerity was dawning on China's economy. The conservatives had won the day. What followed subsequently—austerity, turmoil and massacre—has already been covered in the first section of this chapter.

POST–JUNE 4 DEVELOPMENTS IN THE CHINESE ECONOMY

The most controversial question in the post–June 4 developments in the Chinese economy was whether the measures adopted by the hard-line leadership amounted to wiping out the fruits of the 10-year reform. Holders of the view that the 10-year reform had virtually ended except in name contended that under the conservatives, a large part of Zhao's reform measures were dropped, if not completely reversed. Opponents to this view held that, for one reason or another, the most important aspects of Zhao's reform still remained in substance, in spite of the changes made by the conservatives. Part of the confusion lies of course in semantics, for the word "reform" can refer to any change in policy. In the following discussion we will contend that one could distinguish two phases in the post–June 4 period. In the first period, the hard-line leadership was very much intent on reversing a large part of Zhao's legacy within the bounds permitted by Deng. Deng still held supreme military power, but he was very much discredited by the failure of the experiments of Zhao, his chosen disciple. As a result, he was compelled to make concessions to the conservatives and let the latter group manage the economy. Events that followed, however, persuaded the conservatives that a more pragmatic approach was necessary. The pragmatism that ensued was clearly founded on an eclectic mixture of their core policies and some of Zhao's reform measures.

A "De-Capitalized" Economy in Search of a Lower-Level Equilibrium

The Tiananmen massacre aggravated the problems of an economy that was already suffocating under the stern austerity measures introduced in late 1988. Even prior to that point, the economy had been suffering from severe shortages caused by speculation, hoarding and corruption, and the austerity measures amplified the shortage phenomenon. Apart from totally cutting off the supply of working capital that enterprises required from the banking system, they created intercompany liquidity problems and huge amounts of interlocking debts leading to further reductions in production and supply. The massacre further worsened the problem. Apart from drastically reduced foreign loans, tourist income and joint venture capital, it severely affected work morale by politicizing both the social and the work environment. In a generalized sense, the economy could be said to have undergone a process of "de-capitalization." The following are some of the effects caused by this process:

1. A large number of half-finished projects were scrapped. The capital embodied therein, or at least part of it, was lost.

2. Foreign capital inflows came to a standstill. International financial institutions, including the World Bank and the Asian Development Bank, postponed loans under consideration that would have amounted to up to $1.2 billion. Most Western governments froze loans at an official or unofficial level. Even Japan, which usually took an ambivalent position toward events in China, postponed a six-year $5.7-billion loan program that was intended to

finance 42 major capital projects including railways, ports, dams and telecommunication systems.[26]

3. Even before the turmoil erupted, a survey conducted by the All China Federation of Labor showed that 50 percent of the 210,000 workers interviewed were dissatisfied, mainly because of inflation, low wages and rampant official corruption.[27] Estimates were that the two months of unrest alone resulted in more than a $1-billion loss in man-hours and damaged properties.[28] The crackdown caused much resentment among the workers, many of whom were supporters of the students' cause. Moreover, after the crackdown, workers had to spend long hours studying ideological speeches. Suddenly finding themselves back in a politicized environment and having their bonuses drastically cut because of less work being available, the workers invariably responded in the form of work slowdowns. This amounted to an extensive loss of human capital.

4. The arrest of a number of reformers and the expulsion of a number of enterprise managers sympathetic to the reform cause represented an important loss of human capital. These people carried with them much experience from which invaluable lessons could have been learned. Those enterprise managers who remained in their office were much constrained, if not entirely reluctant, out of apathy, to freely apply their hard-won experience. They were partly constrained by the reinstated power of the party cadres stationed in the enterprises and by the now highly politicized environment in the workplace.

5. A severe loss of human capital was brought about by unemployment, as a result of the closing down of a large number of rural and township industries. When owners, entrepreneurs and workers in these enterprises were thrown out of work on a massive scale, what human capital they had acquired was laid idle indefinitely and

might, in time, be lost. A part of the effect of mass un-employment was manifested in the huge flow of rural workers into cities, a phenomenon that caused great concern in the central government because of its political ramifications.

6. We will deal with the subject of human capital in detail in Chapter 3 of this book. In the broadest sense, we might conceive human capital to include positive, mutual relations that facilitate transactions among economic actors, for example, the trust factor. The trust factor is appropriately taken as a form of human capital because its absence implies either increased inefficiency or higher costs of production. The post–June 4 economy was characterized by many questionable transactions which, by the standards set by the conservatives, might be considered as cases of corruption. As might be expected, a large number of enterprise managers engaged in destroying evidence, rectifying documents, or, in short, making efforts to protect their position. Emphasis on self-protection meant that tensions mounted among different enterprises. Together with rising intercompany debts, the trust factor, which was essential for smooth economic transactions, was seriously diminished. The result was a big loss in real production and effective work, as attention was increasingly drawn to these nonproductive activities.

The consequence of de-capitalization, both in the sense of physical capital and human capital, was that aggregate supply in the economy was drastically reduced. As intercompany debt affected overall liquidity and the trust factor, the level of business transactions between enterprises experienced a dramatic slow-down. Since they would now require cash payments or advance deposits, non-state-owned enterprises, especially the rural or township enterprises, were forced to cut back on production and business transactions. Given that there is a limit to the ability of an enterprise to cut costs (except through decreasing the bonuses of the workers), and given falling demand, these enterprises soon faced the threat of closure and bankruptcy. Some takeovers or mergers of these failing enterprises did take place in the case of spin-offs or subsidiaries of some parent enterprises, but those that lacked such backing were forced to slow down or cease operations. Depending on the particular conditions of their enterprises, the employees might continue to receive their basic salary or part of it, or might receive none at all.

The chain effects of these closures, as well as their effects on aggregate demand, could hardly be underestimated. According to the estimates of Guo Mantang, an Agricultural Ministry official, 30 percent of China's 18 million rural enterprises that had thus far managed to stave off bankruptcy, might go bankrupt during 1989 as a result of inadequate material supplies and tightened credit.[29] Were this the case, China's national output would be seriously affected, since the rural industries presently employ 90 million people, or nearly a quarter of the rural work force, and have a total output value of $162 billion.[30] This figure is not very much exaggerated, for a large number of privately owned enterprises in the rural and the urban sector alike would simply close down operations, regardless of whether they were in financial trouble. With the political climate changing fast, many people would, to play safe, gladly sell off their assets or inventories and adopt a wait-and-see attitude.

The state enterprises were better off in that they could count on the central government to bail them out eventually. However, in the meantime, they faced the same problem of shortages, credit squeeze, and intercompany debt. In Jiangsu province, for instance, the 10 largest enterprises under the Ministry of Machine Building were owed $123 million. They, in turn, amassed debts of $76 million and were short $91 million in working capital.[31] Meanwhile, they continued to accumulate unsaleable output, as the economy was fast plunging into a recession. By 1988, the total bailout subsidies incurred by the government had already risen by 18 percent to $18 billion. With business fast declining, more state enterprises are now going into the red.[32]

The grim situation described above would be much improved if the rural sector had been able to sustain its prosperity, but the myopic policies pursued by the reformers had negated such a favorable condition. Instead, the rural sector became a casualty in the wake of the failure of urban reform. To this point, we will revert in a later chapter. It suffices to say that as a result of lowered investment in agricultural infrastructure and the siphoning of farm resources to the nonfarm sector, namely the rural and township industries, the ability of the rural sector to sustain growth was adversely affected. Starting in 1986, farm production had come to a standstill. In the winter harvest of 1988, some localities, apparently in difficult financial positions, issued IOUs to farmers instead of paying them their due upon the procurement. This caused considerable alarm in the countryside.[33] It was also reported that some localities failed to observe the general practice of delivering the necessary chemical fertilizers and deposits to the farmers for their next season's crops, again causing much concern in the countryside. The central government, not unaware of the repercussions of these reactions, announced that these anomalies would not occur in the future. While it remains to be seen whether the government will continue to honor its promise, the confidence of many farmers has clearly been shaken.[34]

Realizing that the price of procurement was below the cost of production, and that farmers would be reluctant to maintain their present level of output if market prices should also fall in response to slackening demand, the government recently raised the procurement prices for grains and cotton. In spite of these moves, the farmers are still facing a profit squeeze as prices of agricultural inputs are on the rise, in particular those of fertilizers. What caused grave concern was that in some impoverished localities, farmers were required to submit to tax levies of different types, and there were occasional reports of them resorting to violence in their resistance to deliver their output. Under such conditions, and haunted by rising unemployment that was caused by the fall of many rural enterprises, the countryside is no longer enjoying the stability it used to have.

The Strategies and Predicaments of the Hard-Line Conservatives

When the austerity measures were first introduced in 1988, the conservatives, entrusted with the task of troubleshooting, were clearly employing these measures toward an economic purpose, namely, to bring the economy back under some kind of control. Taking unreined decentralization to be the cause of chaos, and deeply distrustful of provincial autonomy, the conservatives believed in the power of planning and supervision, which in their view were part and parcel of the socialist doctrine. The austerity measures were tools not only for dampening the overheated economy, but also for recentralizing economic power.

The June massacre and its aftermath brought a new dimension to these measures. The event represented a political triumph for the hard-line conservatives. It confirmed their view that decentralization was a destabilizing force, and that to eliminate such decentralized elements, the central government must recentralize not only its economic power, but its political power as well. Reactions to the massacre only hardened this attitude. On the international front, the universal condemnation of the massacre reinforced the conservatives' belief in the subversive power of an open-door policy. Although they had to take Deng's wishes into account in their rhetoric, they made it no secret that China was prepared to sever its links with the West if only to retain its style of handling its own affairs. On the domestic front, the massacre did not receive sympathy from a number of the provinces, some of which expressed dissatisfaction in the way the student movement was handled. These reactions naturally made the conservatives even more determined to strip, as far as possible, the provinces of their political as well as their economic autonomy. The large number of people giving support to the student movement must have also impressed upon the conservatives the need to root out the independent enterprises that gave their owners both the freedom and the material resources to oppose their authority. With these political considerations, the austerity measures took on new dimensions.

They became tools serving a political end, that is, to deal a blow to vested interests that were sympathetic to the cause of Zhao's reform. This theme of recentralization, it should be emphasized, ran through the policies of the conservatives. The reform measures initiated by Zhao that still remained in force were seen either as expedients or as something to be dealt with at a later stage after the recentralization was well accomplished. The dominance of political considerations explained in part the continued application of the austerity measures long after their colossal adverse impacts on the economy had manifested themselves.

If the conservatives had had their way entirely, they surely would have pursued their policy of recentralization as vigorously as possible. Economic reality, however, did not permit such a straightforward route. When asked about whether they would revert to some kind of commune system, the conservatives replied that they would not resort to force to make changes of this sort. In a similar vein, Li Peng confirmed that the financial contracting system with the provinces would remain, as would the contracting system with the nonstate enterprises.[35] From these reports, it was clear that the conservatives had been contemplating something more extreme but were finally compelled to make compromises for the time being. This was obvious from the ambivalent attitude of the conservatives on the issue of the rural and township enterprises.[36] At one point, they were anxious to reduce, if not to wipe out, these "unstable" elements, but on the other hand, they were fearful of the dire consequences of the massive unemployment that this would cause. In the case of things that were in their power to change without resistance or immediate negative consequences, the hard-line conservatives were not hesitant to act. The two major legacies of Zhao's reform pertaining to the enterprise, namely, the bankruptcy laws and the managerial responsibility system, were not totally discarded, but they were heavily modified. The bankruptcy laws were not discarded because there was a need to deal with the large number of collective enterprises that fell after the austerity measures, but these laws were not to be applied to the state enterprises, in spite of the fact that they were the real objects behind such legislation. The managerial responsibility system remained, but the party cadres in the enterprises were now given much greater power, at least over the political and ideological affairs of those enterprises.

The reform policies of the conservatives could be summarized as follows: (a) recentralizing political and economic power, (b) reducing the size of the collective and the private sector, (c) giving priority to state enterprises, (d) adopting a zero-inflation policy, (e) eliminating the multitiered price structure, (f) developing a new management system in enterprises with party cadres to play the leading role, (g) recollectivizing agriculture where appropriate and on a voluntary basis, and (h) eliminating "bourgeois cultural dregs" and "spiritual garbage." None of these reform measures, except for item (d) and to some extent (e), were compatible with those pursued in the days of Zhao. It was rumored in November 1989 that the Communist Party's Central Committee meeting to be held that month would map a radical economic program. Apart from pursuing the existing austerity program in order to curb inflation, it would, among other harsh measures, abolish the dual-price structure, seek a bigger portion of the revenues generated by provincial governments and the profits generated by the state enterprises, and deprive provinces of their autonomy to set prices and approve investment projects.[37] In effect, what the conservatives wanted was a more indivisible system with increasing irrationalities. Such a system, while serving to some extent as an antidote to the excesses of the runaway economy in Zhao's days, was also clearly turning back the clock.

It turned out, however, that the Central Committee meeting, while endorsing the overall austerity direction, did not press forward with the further measures that had been suggested by the conservatives. Several factors seemed to account for this. Probably the most crucial was the abrupt political change occurring in Eastern Europe. In a matter of several months, a democratic movement swept across these communist nations, bringing about the downfall of most of the existing regimes. This phenomenal change univocably demonstrated the power of the masses. The message was soon received, and the theme of the conservatives quickly turned to one of seeking stability and pacifying public sentiments. Mass unemployment was now seen as a potentially disruptive political factor with which to be reckoned. Private and collective enterprises were accepted after all as contributing importantly to employment and hence to social stability.[38] In a similar vein, stability in the countryside was perceived to be critical and essential to preserve even at a high cost. With this new orientation, the importance of agriculture was reemphasized, IOUs were stopped, and the raising of procurement prices of agricultural output was announced in order to restore rural confidence in the government.[39] It was reported that the Bank of China allocated $5 billion in short-term loans to pay for the autumn harvest with a view to pacifying the growing discontent of the farmers.

With the emphasis shifting toward the need to maintain stability, the destabilizing effects of the austerity measures, which were pushing the economy into a recession, were given a new interpretation. By October 1989, different economic indicators pointed to the fact that China was fast moving into a recession. The official State Statistics Bureau revealed that industrial output in September registered the slowest growth for that month in a decade.[40] Retail sales were falling sharply, while inventories continued to build up. In spite of slackening demand, consumer prices of many items continued to rise.

Fear of recession and its attendant destabilizing effects was not the only motive forcing the conservatives to take on a more moderate, eclectic approach. Another major problem that had been haunting the hard-line leadership was the country's deteriorating financial position. For many consecutive years the state budget had registered a deficit. As a matter of fact, the austerity measures had been supposed to bring the deficit under control. The budget for 1989 had aimed originally at reducing the state budget deficit of 8.05 billion yuans, which had been reached in 1988, to an estimate of 7.4 billion yuans. However, the events that ensued, instead of reducing the gap, enlarged it to 9.54 billion yuans.[41] It was forecast that for 1990, the deficit would stay in the region of 8.89 billion yuans.[42] If one were to properly take into account both foreign and domestic loans, the total deficit in 1989 stood in effect, at a staggering figure of 36.9 billion yuans.[43]

On the revenue side, widespread bankruptcies of collective and private enterprises contributed to the erosion of the economy's tax base, although the private enterprises did not contribute much to state revenue. Although the provinces were the first to bear the brunt of the financial pinch, the burden would ultimately be transmitted to the central government. Among the first casualty of the political repression was tourism, which had earned China $2.2 billion in foreign exchange in 1988. With hundreds of thousands of tourists lost, industry executives estimated that tourism-related losses would be at least $1 billion in 1989.[44] The contribution of foreign trade to state revenue also sharply declined as exports sagged in the same year. Among other factors, late deliveries due to shortages of inputs, deteriorating quality in export merchandise due to poor work morale and supervision, sharp decreases in the number of exporting organizations, and the refusal and inability of the trading organizations to settle quality claims because of liquidity considerations were important forces that adversely affected China's foreign exchange earning capabilities and indirectly reduced its tax base. This situation prompted the devaluation of the renminbi by 21 percent in December 1989, but experts believed that the effects would be minimal as the official rate was still far above the unofficial and black market rates. Besides, with an increasing number of state enterprises, which contributed importantly to state revenues, operating at a loss, the amount of revenue loss for government would be colossal indeed.

The financial contracting system between the central government and the provinces was also an important factor that negatively affected the government's revenue-generating power. Most of these contracts were made at times of lower inflation rates. Notwithstanding some built-in provisions for mild increases, the accelerating inflation experienced in the recent years meant that in real terms the central government received substantially lowered contributions from the provinces. There was also an additional problem: Since it would be embarrassing for the central government to admit the seriousness of inflation, it was forced to take an understated rate as the basis for its bargaining with the provinces.

While the revenue side was bad enough, the expenditure side was equally, if not even more, grim. The second largest item on the state budget (the first being infrastructure building) was subsidy to the ill-managed state enterprises. In 1988, the subsidy stood at 44.6 billion yuans. In 1989, it rose to 60 billion yuans. It was forecast to reach 65.7 billion yuans in 1990.[45] The fourth biggest state expenditure was price subsidies for food, housing, and transportation. In 1988, total subsidies stood at 31.7 billion yuans. In 1989, they rose to 37.0 billion yuans, and were forecast to increase to 40.5 billion yuans in 1990.[46] Together these two items accounted for one-third of government expenditures. With higher procurement prices of agricultural output needed to pacify an increasingly discontented rural population, and with more and more people losing their jobs, state subsidies, direct or indirect, would be on the rise. With domestic production jeopardized, China was facing an acute shortage in the supply of a number of strategic materials, and had to rely increasingly on imports. For example, the import of fertilizers grew to 14.7 million tons in 1988, representing an increase of 35 percent over 1987. With the devaluation of the renminbi, the import bill would continue to stay at a high level, in spite of improvements in reducing the spending power of trading enterprises via the austerity programs. To add to these burdens, China would start to service its foreign debts starting in 1990. It is estimated that China's total foreign debt at the end of 1989 stood at $40 billion.[47] With a debt of such magnitude, it was no wonder that the financial minister Wang Bingqian repeatedly emphasized on various official occasions the need for more austerity.

Such financial hardships naturally limit the options of the conservatives. In theory, the methods to meet such hardships may consist of the following: (a) raise more foreign loans, (b) raise more domestic loans, (c) print money, (d) coerce provinces to increase their contributions, or (e) raise taxes. With respect to the raising of more foreign loans, the June massacre cut off, at least temporarily, most of the available sources. Apparently a limit has also been reached insofar as the raising of domestic loans is concerned, as workers are already experiencing great hardships caused by cutbacks in bonuses, delays in salary payments, and price squeezes. Under the call for stability, this is no longer considered to be a feasible route. The same also applies to the raising of tax rates. Printing money is not very compatible with the style of the conservatives, although it appears that they are compelled to take on this route, albeit in a cautious way. The remaining route would be to coerce provinces to increase their contributions, but that would mean that the pace of recentralization would have to be compromised. In other words, the financial reality leaves the conservatives with no alternative but to adopt an eclectic approach.

Since November 1989, the government has decided to ease its austerity policies, but will not admit to this. The People's Bank of China announced plans to set up a fund totalling 100 billion yuans to provide relief funds or working capital for big enterprises in targeted industries, to pay farmers for their recent harvest and to relieve a portion of the staggering intercompany debts.[48] One targeted beneficiary was the sagging export-oriented sector, where many producers did not have enough working capital and the trading companies lacked the cash to finance such purchases. In January 1990, it was reported that the People's Bank of China released a credit amount of 30 billion yuans to the enterprises, although the results were by no means obvious, probably because the intercompany debt was so huge.[49] It was also learned that Li Peng, in a recent cabinet meeting in March, suggested "putting an end to sluggish growth by the end of June 1990."[50] To stimulate consumer demand, the Bank of China recently lowered the interest rate for savings deposits by a substantial margin. Indeed, these different moves prompted some economists to speculate that a new boom-bust cycle was already in the making.

Signals indicating that the conservatives are now subscribing to the more important objective of maintaining economic and social stability are ample. Repeated assurances have been made that the existing systems of contracting will remain, and that China will exploit and combine the best features of planning and of the market. There are hints that some kind of experimentation with share equity participation in state enterprises on a limited scale[51] will soon be resumed, and that price reform might take place in an "orderly" manner.[52] It has also been reported that China's National People's Congress is likely to approve some liberal regulations governing Sino-foreign joint ventures.[53] The announcement in May 1990 that a special economic zone will be set up in Shanghai, which was said to be supported by Deng, clearly indicates that a switch is being made toward a more pragmatic, moderate and eclectic approach. These rather abrupt changes also lead us to surmise that Deng, after his labor in restructuring the military, is reviving his interest in economic affairs, and his wish to see more economic reform is also confirmed by reports of recent meetings of economists who discussed the shape of the next five-year plan (1991–1995).[54]

CHINA INTO THE 1990s: SOME SPECULATIONS

With the conservatives forced to take on an unorthodox, eclectic approach in their struggle with a sagging economy, the questions to ask logically consist of the following: Will the conservatives be compelled by the force of circumstances to continue the eclectic approach to the point that they will eventually drop their orthodoxy? Will such an eclectic approach save the Chinese economy from collapse and its government from bankruptcy? If the conservatives should fail in their rescue of the economy, would second-generation reformers stand any chance of success? Finally, and equally important, what are the irreversible legacies, if any, of Zhao's reform that will persist regardless of changes of leadership, and what impacts will these irreversible features have on the future course of the Chinese economy?

In the analytical language we have been employing, the orthodoxy of the conservatives consists in restoring the indivisibility of the economic system. The policies of recentralization, more planning and regulation, reunifying the price structure, bailing out big enterprises regardless of their economic efficacy, and permitting political considerations to override economic benefits are intended to render the economic system more indivisible so that it can be centrally controlled or monitored from a minimal number of control points. The positive side of such an approach is that some of the irrationalities created or intensified under the reform regime of Zhao, for example, provincial protectionism, and the hoarding of resources for speculation, could be reduced. Such positive effects are clearly overwhelmed by the negative effects engendered. For reasons already given, an indivisible system of an arbitrary kind is an irrational system. In subjecting all economic actions or decisions to the interpretations and interferences of a central government, the important canons of economic rationality are made subservient to noneconomic criteria and considerations. Even less understood is the fact that an indivisible system of an artificial kind is a potentially unstable one, because irrationalities in one part of the system are liable to be transmitted to other parts and to be amplified or reinforced in the course of the transmission.

In the case of China, it needs to be borne in mind that a complete reversal to an indivisible system would even in theory be an impossible proposition. The apparently indivisibilities manifested in the old days of Mao were cemented by coercion, power and ideology, as well as by Mao's charisma. The lasting result of Zhao's reform is that the underlying cementing factors of the indivisibilities have been completely shattered. The reform has taught each individual the fruits of freedom and self-worth and, above all, the untenability of the command economy. In other words, the reform has unleashed the individualism of the Chinese people which had been previously put under the spell of a collective vision. When that collective spell was removed, and when the ills of the command economy became transparent and were acknowledged even at an official level, a full return to the previous system was no longer possible. This change has been unintentionally further reinforced by the single-child family policy, with its highly egoistic undertone and ramifications.[55] The hard-line conservatives might have contemplated restoring the commune system, but it soon became clear to them that short of a major catastrophe in the countryside—for example: famine—this would be an impossible policy to pursue. Recentralization, running against the grain of the now individualized social structure of China, would, if pushed to the extreme, meet with a resistance that the conservatives would hardly even be able to imagine.

Other lasting features of Zhao's reform might probably include the continuation of the flexible bonus system, the labor contract system, the increased autonomy of the enterprise manager, the application of the bankruptcy laws and the persistence of the private sector. All these features are presently facing different degrees of setback, but it would be difficult to erase them from the economic landscape because they are the logical outcomes of a more individualized system that characterizes China's social structure today.

The above discussion should help to explain in part why the conservatives are compelled to take on an eclectic approach and will have to stick to this approach with a slim chance of exit. Should this approach turn out to be successful, it will have self-reinforcing or self-fulfilling effects that will entrench and justify its further application. It is not unlikely that in the long run the success will turn the moderate conservatives into aggressive reformers. The critical question is whether the present eclectic approach will enable the present conservatives' regime to linger on, or whether it will bring about their downfall, to be replaced by a new breed of reformers. Although this is anybody's guess, let us construct hypothetical scenarios in order to more closely examine the respective possibilities. In constructing these scenarios, it is assumed that the political situation will remain more or less unchanged.

Let us start with a pessimistic model and then vary the assumptions as we go along. The present recentralization, reversing what has happened in the past 10 years, will have the effect of impoverishing the provinces should it be carried too far. However, the impoverishment of the provinces, unfortunately, will hardly result in the enrichment of the central government, just as, during the reform regime, the prosperity of the provinces was never transmitted to the central government. This is because resources that now go to the central government are continually being sucked, as it were, into the blalck hole of state subsidies, especially to the state enterprises and the urban consumers. As it now stands, both subsidies are on the rise, with few signs of relief in sight. Subsidy to state enterprises, which is the core of the conservatives' orthodoxy, will continue unabated. With the ascendency of the power of party cadres, the replacement of the more serious reform-minded enterprise managers, much lowered work morale, and lowered export capabilities, these enterprises, by virtue of their "structural" handicaps, will continue to bring in substandard performances. A temporary revival might come since the sluggishness of the consumer market is past but, stuck at low levels of productivity, the chances of state enterprises improving their cost and price structures to boost up demand would be very slim. The result is that, for those products over which they enjoy monopolistic positions, consumers will have to face persistently increasing prices. Collective enterprises that survive the present austerity regime and, therefore, have more rational structures will pose some threat to the state enterprises, and may offer more competitive prices to the consumers for some ranges of goods. However, since the former account for a relatively small share of the market, their effects are relatively insignificant. This is clearly a lock-in situation with little hope of escape, particularly as the gap between prices and costs will widen over time.

One type of state subsidy might help to relieve the hardship of the localities, namely, raising procurement prices to help the farmers. To its credit, the central government has moved in this direction and has temporarily restored some calm to the country-side. However, the new procurement prices are still lagging behind the increasing costs of production, and if one considers the meager share of agriculture in overall state expenditures, the statements made by Li Peng and others on giving top priority to agriculture are more rhetorical than reflective of reality. In any case, the increases in procurement prices will eat into the state budget, but will not help much to motivate the farmers to produce more. For that to occur, farmers must be able to count on a prosperous free market to absorb their above-quota production. Otherwise, the more they produce, the more they run the risk of a loss. Hence, one could expect rational farmers to pursue a cautious policy of keeping low levels of production under the present conditions. The result would again be reflected in higher market prices and more discontent among the urban workers and consumers, which eventually will push the government to step up its level of subsidy. Again, a vicious circle is clearly at work.

Not only will the farmers be relatively impoverished, the provinces themselves will also feel the pinch as the central government continues to drain away resources. At present, the central government has firm contracts with these provinces. When these contracts are to be renewed, the central government will likely demand much larger contributions. The provinces thus face a double predicament. On the one hand, they have to meet increasing demand from the central government. On the other hand, they are facing a dwindling revenue base as a significant portion of their rural and township enterprises vanishes. To make ends meet, they must cut their infrastructural programs as well as imposing more taxes. The former implies that the countryside will be in less of a position to provide more employment, while the latter implies that the better-managed enterprises and the farmers will have to bear a higher burden. Both factors clearly have destabilizing effects. Farmers in some counties were reported to be hard-pressed by the imposition of different types of levies, a point to which we will revert in a later chapter.[56] Should the central government decide to bypass the provinces in order to exert direct control over these affairs, it may run the risk of collecting revenues at levels below what the provinces themselves are able to attain. Apart from this obvious possibility, the resulting chaos and hostility that may be generated may trigger widespread reactions and violence, a phenomenon that the conservatives will be among the last to want.

If resources from the impoverished provinces dwindle and are slow to be transmitted to the central government, it may have to operate with a chronically inadequate cash flow. One solution is for the government to print more money. In this case, it will rekindle inflationary tendencies that are already reemerging because of low productivity and high production costs. If the government does not opt for this solution, it will have to reduce the rate of subsidies to the urban workers and consumers or bring back some kind of rationing system. This will stir up more discontent. Should such discontent coincide with rural uprisings, the chain effects that ensue may likely develop beyond what the government can contain.

The above is, of course, a very pessimistic scenario. More probably, the events that subsequently unfold will settle the system at some kind of low-level equilibrium without triggering any explosive situations. For example, the demise of many of the existing collective and private enterprises would mean that the state enterprises will absorb the business that had previously been taken away from them, reducing, after a certain point, the amount of loss they will incur, and thereby stabilizing the rate of increase of state subsidies at a steady level. The mass of unemployed people that swarm into the cities may eventually go back to their farms or take up work in the rural infrastructure.[57] This will reduce the level of state subsidies. Also with the passage of time, Western governments, for one reason or another, will normalize their relations and resume loans to China. With the injection of foreign loans, the central government will be relieved of many of its immediate pressures. With the passage of time, the resentment of many of its people will fade, and many will resume business as usual, provided the conservatives stop politicizing the work environment.

Just as the most pessimistic scenario will probably not materialize, the more optimistic scenario will not continue for long. At best, the economy will get stuck at some low level equilibrium. This is because the conservatives, entrenched in their belief that an orderly economy is a heavily regulated one, are highly distrustful of a decentralized order. Hence, there is a limit to how much they will allow the market to work. In other words, large numbers of indivisibilities and irrationalities will remain, and political considerations will always come before the economic interests of the state, let alone the interests of the individual. The eclectism the conservatives allow is, therefore, very much bounded by their ideology, fear and style.

Should future developments come close to the more pessimistic scenario that we portray, two possibilities may arise. If widespread revolt should occur, it would be difficult to predict the outcome and its repercusions on China's economy. More probably, change will take place within the party itself with the reformers regaining control of the state and the government. Should this be the case, a new wave of reform measures may be pushed through. How soon this may take place is, of course, unknown, but if the Chinese economy continues to perform poorly, the ability of reformers to once again dominate the economic scene will be enhanced, especially as the base of reformers still remains unshattered, and as there are still a huge number of reform sympathizers. In fact, if the conservatives are not able to lead the economy out of its predicament for some period of time, (even should it survive the worst part of it), the outcry for reform will once again heighten unless the conservatives themselves quietly transform themselves into reformers. In this regard, who dies first among the present group of aged leaders will be of critical importance.

The regaining of control by the reformers does not assure that the economy will quickly improve. It merely means there will be a more liberal political and economic climate. The same structural problems that inhibit the smooth working of the Chinese economy will still remain. Unless the new generation of reformers can introduce drastic measures such as allowing state enterprises to go bankrupt, prohibiting provincial protectionism, completely decontrolling prices, and permitting free labor mobilitiy, the new leadership is liable to face the same set of problems as the past generation of reformers did. Critical to their ability to introduce drastic reform is how much political capital they will command. Should their power remain constrained by the conservatives, thereby making their reform a partial one, the same pattern of decentralization and chaos will probably repeat itself, as the system is heavily overloaded by historical factors and structural constraints. Any decontrol, whether partial or comprehensive, will easily unleash familiar problems such as hyperinflationary tendencies, which are politically risky for whoever is in power. The paradox is a classical one. Partial reform under such a heavily constrained system will probably unleash imbalances in demand-side and supply-side factors, leading eventually to shortages, while an abruptly conducted comprehensive reform, albeit an economically tenable solution, is too risky for the reformers. To resolve this paradox, a new approach is clearly required.

To propose an effective agenda for reform, one must reexamine the first principles on which the Chinese economy was founded. China is at once a socialist country, a developing nation and a predominantly agricultural economy. To examine these first principles means that we have to look critically at the basic tenets of socialism, development economics and agriculture. To chart new paths for reform in China, it is important to know whether, as well as how far, these tenets are compatible with the Chinese condition. In the subsequent three chapters, we will cover these crucial aspects from a macroscopic stance. It is hoped that although the treatment will be brief, we can nonetheless cover the essential and relevant grounds.

NOTES

1. *Hong Kong Economic Journal*, 15 Dec. 1988.
2. *Asian Wall Street Journal*, 16 Dec. 1988.
3. *Asian Wall Street Journal*, 27 Dec. 1988.
4. *Asian Wall Street Journal*, 20–21 March 1989.
5. *Asian Wall Street Journal*, 1 March 1989.
6. *Hong Kong Economic Journal*, 14 April 1989.
7. This is congenial to Karl Popper's crude conception of the logic of the situation, but Popper (1957) himself did not give a detailed account of the methodology involved.
8. *Asian Wall Street Journal*, 29 Oct. 1988; Wu (1988).
9. Modern studies of the firm, however, reveal a lot of divergence. See, for example, Amihud and Lev (1981), Marcus (1982).
10. Savings in YMB might represent such a medium, but since there is a chronic lack of supply of goods, it acts at most as an uncertain, intermediate medium for the storage of value. Gold is another medium, and it is no accident

that a huge amount of gold is brought back into China via Hong Kong in the recent years.

11. *Asian Wall Street Journal*, 12 Oct. 1987.

12. *Asian Wall Street Journal*, 18 March 1986.

13. *Asian Wall Street Journal*, 12 Sept. 1987.

14. *Asian Wall Street Journal*, 3 Sept. 1986.

15. *Asian Wall Street Journal*, 30 July 1986, 29 Aug. 1986, and 20 Jan. 1987.

16. The State Council, however, forbade the public issue of state-owned enterprise bonds.

17. *Asian Wall Street Journal*, 4 Feb. 1987.

18. *South China Morning Post*, 2 Nov. 1987.

19. *Asian Wall Street Journal*, 22 Dec. 1986.

20. *Asian Wall Street Journal*, 16 March and 21 July 1988.

21. *Hong Kong Economic Journal*, 8 July 1988.

22. *Asian Wall Street Journal*, 25–26 March 1988.

23. *Asian Wall Street Journal*, 14 June 1988.

24. *Asian Wall Street Journal*, 19 Sept. 1988.

25. *Asian Wall Street Journal*, 22 Aug. 1988.

26. *Asian Wall Street Journal*, 3 Aug. 1989.

27. Ibid.

28. Ibid.

29. Ibid.

30. Ibid; see also *Hong Kong Economic Journal*, 25 Sept. 1989.

31. *Asian Wall Street Journal*, 3 Aug. 1989.

32. *Hong Kong Economic Journal*, 15 Oct. 1989.

33. *Hong Kong Economic Journal*, 23 July 1989.

34. *Hong Kong Economic Journal*, 4 Nov., 5 Dec., 11 Dec., and 30 Dec. 1989.

35. *Hong Kong Economic Journal*, 2 Sept. 1989.

36. *Hong Kong Economic Journal*, 2 Feb. 1990.

37. *Asian Wall Street Journal*, 4 Nov. 1989.

38. *Hong Kong Economic Journal*, 13 Oct. 1989.

39. *Hong Kong Economic Journal*, 23 Oct. 1989.

40. *Asian Wall Street Journal*, 21 Oct. 1989.

41. *Man Wei Po*, 22 March 1990. See also *South China Morning Post*, 21 March 1990.

42. Ibid.

43. The Chinese system of revenue accounting does not consider domestic and foreign loans to constitute part of the deficit. Hence, the official deficit figures have been consistently understated.

44. *Asian Wall Street Journal*, 3 Aug. 1989.

45. *Man Wei Po*, 22 March 1990.

46. Ibid.

47. *Hong Kong Economic Journal*, 10 July 1990.

48. *Asian Wall Street Journal*, 29 Nov. 1989.

49. *Ming Pao*, 24 March 1990.

50. *Asian Wall Street Journal*, 12 March 1990.

51. *Hong Kong Economic Journal*, 26 April 1990.

52. *Hong Kong Economic Journal*, 3 May 1990.

53. *Asian Wall Street Journal*, 29 March 1990.

54. *Hong Kong Economic Times*, 9 June 1990.

55. The spoilt children of the single-child family become egoistic but not necessarily individualistic. Their ramifications for the future of China will be colossal, and should not be underestimated.

56. *Hong Kong Economic Journal*, 10 Feb. 1990.

57. See *Ming Pao*, 17 Dec. 1989, and *Hong Kong Economic Journal*, 5 Feb. 1990.

2

The Bankruptcy of Practiced and Theoretical Socialism

Although by now it has become clear to us that socialism is hardly compatible with human progress and economic development, we should guard ourselves against the complacency that this hard-won understanding will never be lost. In China we have already witnessed such a reversal, and should the reforms in the Soviet Union and Eastern Europe turn sour, conservatives and ideologists in these places will have every reason to advocate a return of socialism in purist forms.[1] Socialism, being semantically associated with altruism, fraternity, and the alleviation of human suffering and poverty, is always morally appealing. The bureaucratic control of resources made amply possible under this system is oftentimes an irresistible proposition to many politicians. In spite of the fact that it is an inefficient economic system, socialism does possess the capability to act as a stabilizing agency and to effectively muster and redistribute resources during extreme and turbulent periods (see Nove 1986). Given the enormous power of socialism to enslave and victimize humanity by way of concentrating and abusing power, no effort should be spared to dispel any lingering conviction regarding its claims of economic viability and moral superiority. Although it might seem out of date to reexamine the negative aspects of socialism, it is still important to remind policymakers in China and elsewhere that turning the clock back to the days of a command economy relying fundamentally on central planning and administrative guidance is nothing less than a great leap backward. In this chapter, we will launch a critique on both practiced socialism and theoretical socialism on both economic and ethical grounds. Given the purpose of this book, we have to be very brief with respect to familiar arguments. Instead, we will concentrate selectively on arguments that have been relatively neglected.

THE BANKRUPTCY OF PRACTICED SOCIALISM

Primary versus Secondary Characteristics of Socialism

It is not the purpose of this section to give a historical account of the kind of socialism that had been practiced since its inception in the Soviet Union some 70 years ago. We choose to focus on the major shortcomings of some of the practiced socialist systems, as well as the difficulties involved in some of the attempts to reform them. By way of illustration, we have selected the Soviet Union, Hungary and, to a lesser extent, East Germany.

First let us delineate the essential components of socialism, not so much to arrive at a definition, but rather to clarify the essential relations between the different aspects of socialism so that semantic confusions can be kept to a minimum. We consider socialism to consist of two essential properties, namely, public ownership and distributive justice. Different writers or theorists give different emphases to these respective properties. For our purpose, we need not be bothered with the question of their relative importance. Our concern rather is to distinghish the primary characteristics of socialism from its secondary ones, and to demonstrate the logic and structure of the instruments employed in the management of a socialist economy. Taking public ownership to be an essential feature of socialism, it follows that, to be consistently impartial, the most appropriate form of management should be one discharged with the aid of a preset and preapproved plan. To achieve distributive justice, the best route should be for this very feature to be preincorporated in some explicit way prior to the stage of actual production, and should preferably be taken into account in the planning phase. Hence, master plans designed by a central agency are a logical and integral feature of a socialist system. For these plans to be easily executed and monitored, it is desirable to keep the number of organizations responsible for executing the plans to a minimum. For these plans to be executed as impartially as possible, it is desirable that socialist organizations be of a big scale. Hence, one finds that state enterprises are invariably of mammoth dimensions.

Under the regime of distributive justice, it is desirable that everyone should be able to enjoy a higher standard of living as quickly as possible. This dictates that the planners should aim at achieving the highest possible growth rate for the economy. For this to be possible, the planners may well adopt the strategy of maximum capital formation through compulsory savings and repressed consumption. Equipped with apparently solid plans, apparently sound strategies, and apparently powerful and controllable state enterprises, and seemingly in a position to mobilize both physical and human resources at will, the socialist government is invariably led to have great confidence in its power to effect positive changes. The rhetoric of distributive justice also leads it to believe that it is in a position to stir the altruistic instincts of people on a collective scale and to overcome what inertia may exist among the masses during the course of change.

The Planning System in Crisis: The Soviet Experience in a Nutshell

Thus, the economic instruments of socialism consist of central planning, state enterprises and vigorous capital formation. Together they form the conceptual core of Soviet socialism, a model copied by the Soviet Union's satellite nations in East Europe, other communist countries and, to different degrees, many developing nations. In reality, the inception of Soviet socialism was not deliberate or well planned. As is well known, Karl Marx and

Friedrich Engels did not have much to say on either the blueprints of communism or the transition to that system. According to them, the transition would be brief, and steps in the direction of communism could be taken immediately. The classical scholars of Marxism, too, conceived of the future society romantically as a system in which everything would be obvious. There were some discussions of the economics of a possible socialism before 1917 by scholars like O. Neurathe and E. Barone, but at the time of his seizure of power, Vladimir Lenin obviously had little idea about either the problems of allocation or the methods of planning under a socialist regime. It is still a matter of controversy among historians how far the state of affairs that Lenin adopted, which came to be known as "war-communism," was due to either war or communism, or explicable by ideolgical enthusiasm (Nove 1986). Whatever the major cause, at the end of 1919, in the midst of civil war, hunger and disease, Soviet socialism emerged, taking on some characteristically extreme features, for example, an almost total nationalization, centralization of planning and control, a ban on private trade, partial demonetization, and so on.

No more than war-communism was New Economic Policy (NEP), the succession to war-communism since 1921, a consciously sought model. NEP was generally seen as a forced compromise made by Lenin in response to the excesses of war-communism. In essence, it was a kind of mixed economy, permitting small private enterprises to operate freely and allowing the peasants to grow and sell what they liked. The real offensive in the development of socialism did not therefore come about until Stalin took control and adopted the first Five Year Plan (1928–1932). It was clear that Stalin strongly believed that under a command system, the virtues of socialist instruments such as planning and state enterprises could be fully and fruitfully unleashed. To him, the command system would be ideal for fostering rapid industrialization and expansion of the economy's capacity because the system is able to control and shuffle resources efficiently and effectively. To foster rapid industrialization, the most profitable strategy in Stalin's view was to cut back sharply on the resources that traditionally went to agriculture, light industry and the consumer, and to siphon off these savings into the heavy industrial sector. One corollary of this strategy was the idea of primitive socialist accumulation, namely, to transfer as many resources as possible from the private sector (predominantly peasants) to the growing socialist urban sector through some form of unequal exchange. To do so, collectivization of agriculture would be necessary and justified. In a nutshell, this approach has come to be known as the Stalinist model.

To its credit, in the first phase the Stalinist model achieved what was expected. It did bring about the industrialization of a backward country in record time. In the first period, the power of the command system to mobilize and shuffle resources proved to be remarkable. By the 1930s, the Soviet Union was achieving rates of industrial growth that surpassed those of many other countries at the time. According to official Soviet statistics, Soviet national income by 1937 had increased by almost fourfold since the start of the Five-Year Plan in 1928, a rate of growth that continued into the 1950s. The national income, according to official Soviet statistics, increased by 14 times from 1913 to 1953. Many of these figures turned out, upon scrutiny by some scholars, to be exaggerated claims (see Bergson 1978). However, even if one were to discount these claims substantially, the Soviet performance was still impressive. Apart from achieving rapid growth, unemployment was literally eliminated and inflation was said to have been kept to a minimum. No wonder the Stalinist model came to be taken seriously by many a Western scholar. Indeed, some of the early development economists (for example Paul Rosenstein-Rodan), who were inspired by the apparent feasibility of the Stalinist model in overcoming the inertia of development, embraced strategic concepts like "big push," which bear much affinity to the industrial strategy of Stalinism.

When the "miracle" was over, the shortcomings of the Stalinist model became apparent. These shortcomings were nothing if not familiar to us. Among these, the cardinal features included acute shortages of materials coexisting with extensive waste and the stockpiling of resources; the inability of the plans to respond to consumer preferences; heavy subsidies on inefficient enterprises; the proliferation of unfinished projects; rigidities of planning, with the mentality of the planners causing stagnation in product innovation and technological development; and increasing inefficiency due to a growing bureaucracy and the lack of private incentives. Of these problems, inefficiency, shortages, and bureaucratic mismanagement were the most destructive. To make matters worse, the ills of the system apparently took on a life of their own, defying the efforts made by Soviet leaders after Stalin to wrestle with them. Until the 1970s, Soviet leaders, while admitting their problems and initiating different reforms to overcome them, had never in their rhetoric questioned the superiority of the socialist system. By the end of the 1970s, however, it had been acknowledged by most economists and finally conceded by politicians in the Soviet Union that its economy was plagued by a long-term slowdown. The slowdown was first attributed to the oil crisis in the early 1970s, but soon it became clear that while the West as a whole was able to rebound from the crisis, the entire Soviet bloc was never able to reemerge from it. The recognition of the seriousness of the situation led to what is now called a period of "new revolutionary reforms" (Galbraith and Menshikov 1988, p. 20).

The decade of the 1980s was an epoch of crisis and reform for the Soviet Union and for Eastern Europe as a whole. Some theorists, rather than accepting the fundamental weaknesses of the socialist system, advanced the view that cyclical movements in the economy are as inherent to socialism as they are to capitalism (Bauer 1981, Brody 1967, Kaleczki 1972). To this end, Tamas Bauer developed a theory of state socialist cyclical crisis, contending that in the West, tendencies toward economic crisis are the result of overproduction and insufficient demand, whereas crisis in the socialist system is characterized by over investment and an excessive demand for goods. Other researchers, notably Wlodzimierz Brus, however, contended that such a comparison is too superficial, for the current crisis that plagued the Soviet and East European economies lasted too long, and was too deep and broad to qualify as just another cycle in socialist economic growth (see Szelenyi 1985). This was in sharp contrast with the capitalist countries, which have reemerged into prosperity since 1982.

Needless to say, the chronic stagnation cast doubts among many people in the community of socialist countries over the validity of the socialist claim of superiority in economic production and organization. It stirred researchers to wonder whether state socialism in the way it was practiced had already exhausted its growth potentials. I. Szelenji, for example, proposed a theory of the general crisis of socialism (1985). His basic tenet was that previous socialist development was characterized by the adoption of extensive growth, for example, converting agricultural surplus labor into industrial workers and employing conventional mass production technologies. The potentials of these strategies have now been exhausted. The economy has entered the "intensive" stage of growth, where growth is possible only through increases in productivity and the development of new technologies. Since the state socialist system is bureaucracy-laden, the proper conditions for intensive growth are lacking. Hence, the current stagnation is a traumatic experience because the successful transition from the extensive to the intensive stage requires a restructuring of the whole socialist economy. Central planning which, in the extensive stage, dealt with a few thousand agents, must now predict and take into account the behaviors of millions of consumers. In light of these irreversible "structural" changes, Szelenji wondered if the whole system of central planning might have to be scrapped.

Stanislav Menshikov, a renowned Soviet scholar and staunch defender of the virtues of socialism (insofar as he believes that socialism is the only system capable of producing a just society), openly admitted that the main reasons for the slowdown of the economy were internal, and that the Soviet leaders had only themselves to blame (Galbraith and Menshikov 1988). Menshikov believed that the chief reason for the deceleration of the Soviet economy was the bureaucratic mismanagement of industry. The system is overcentralized to the extent that the central authority has been attempting to control all aspects of economic life down to the last detail, leaving scant incentives or discretion to the enterprises. Agriculture suffers all the more because there is an additional layer of intervention imposed by the local authorities, which have the power to intervene but do not bear the responsibility for the results. On the supply side, increasing difficulties are experienced with the dwindling supply of the essential factors of production. The Soviet economy is suffering from an increasing shortage of manpower, a phenomenon Menshikov held to be in stark contrast to the high level of unemployment prevailing in the West. This shortage, in his view, could be attributed to the inherent tendency of enterprises to stockpile labor, to the dwindling flow of labor from the countryside, and also to changes in demographic structures. Furthermore, the proportion of the gross national product available for capital investment is declining as real income received by the average household is on the increase. Meanwhile, the bureaucracy, which is a system with a built-in tendency to perpetuate its self-interest, has gradually grown out of proportion to the rest of the country. At present, 15 percent of the total Soviet labor force works within the country's bureaucracy, which has mushroomed since 1964, ironically following the reforms that were meant to put an end to centralization. Over time, these supply-side problems have manifested themselves in features that we commonly witness in a socialist economy, namely, corruption, black market operations, and a shadow economy. Menshikov, in fact, has honestly admitted that these have become characteristic features of the Soviet economy, particularly since the 1960s.

The Soviet Union is not, of course, the only nation that has been experiencing these predicaments. Each and every nation in the East European bloc, following the footsteps of the Soviet Union in adopting the Stalinist model, experiences the same difficulties to a different extent. To overcome these problems, reforms have been initiated by these countries, but without much success. In the following section, we will look at the reforms pursued in East Germany, Hungary, and the Soviet Union itself.

Fine-Tuning the Planning System: The East German Solution

One direction toward reform in the socialist system has been to improve the planning system itself. This reform direction reflected the received wisdom of the late 1950s and early 1960s, and served to guide the reform measures taken at that time. Its popularity was supported by the then-prevailing belief in the feasibility of social engineering through the sophistication of planning and control techniques and by the mushrooming of a new array of techniques after World War II that were believed to be effective for such purposes. These included, among others, econometric models, linear programming, input-output analysis, and computer programming. Planning, by way of controlling and directing the "rationalistic parameters" of an economy, and designed to be backed up by the computer and the promise of a developing information technology, not only became the fashion in the socialist countries, but was also held out as an ideal tool for development in the Third World. Within the Soviet bloc, East Germany and Czechoslovakia stood out as the most eager to embrace and apply these tools. The vision of socialism, to these planners, was that of a scientifically planned, rational order. East Germany, in particular, is the paradigmatic example of such "scientific-technical" socialism. During much of the 1970s and early 1980s, East Germany consistently reported itself to have maintained an impressive growth record, which was apparently achieved without the cost of inflation or increased social inequity. The East Germany leadership boasted of its successes in maintaining steady increases in labor productivity and economic growth without introducing fundamental reforms in economic structures and organizations.

By the early 1980s, the East German economic "miracle" had evaporated. Not only was growth slowing down, but the competitiveness of East Germany's products in the world market was much in question. In response to the economic pressures of the early 1980s, the government introduced an austerity program and a campaign to increase labor productivity. The growth in labor productivity was said to be achievable both by harder work on the part of the population and by the "socialist rationalization" of the production process. The latter entailed organizational changes as well as greater energy efficiency and automation in the production processes. At the highest level, the ministerial structure was streamlined, with ministries surrendering much of their power to newly formed "combines." In these "combines," research and development functions were grouped directly with production with a view to minimizing the time lag between technological innovation and industrial application.

Organizational changes notwithstanding, energy conservation was also intended to play an important part in boosting the East German growth rates. Toward this end, robotics and microelectronics were viewed as important components of its industrial strategy in the 1980s. In fact, East Germany boasted the most advanced computer industry in Eastern Europe, as well as the highest level of robotics in industry.

East Germany's reported success in meeting targets and maintaining steady rates of growth into the 1980s might have contributed in part to the leadership's open confidence in holding onto their mode of socialist engineering. This stands in marked contrast to the self-criticisms of the Soviets, the soul-searching experiences of the Hungarians, and the inquisitive openness displayed by other reform movements throughout Eastern Europe. Ironically, many ailments such as shortages and queues still exist in East Germany in spite of its claims of superiority.

Recent events need little elaboration. The democratic revolution sweeping Eastern Europe led in East Germany to the downfall of the party chief, Erich Honecker; to the dramatic demolition of the Berlin wall; to the vote for a noncommunist ruling government and for rapid economic integration with the West; and to plans to unite with West Germany. As a result of these dramatic changes, East Germany becomes part of a united Germany and will never be the same. Among these shocks, there is an insidious one that is specially worthy of mention and reflection, namely, the enormous, long-standing discrepancies between the official propaganda spread by the East German government and the reality as perceived by its people.

The "Second Economy": The Hungarian Experience

Another route of reform has been pursued in Hungary since 1968. The "New Economic Mechanism" introduced by Hungary's general secretary János Kádár employed economic regulators such as credits, exchange rates, taxes, and market prices (to a limited extent) to supplement production targets as guides to economic activity. Such measures were designed to reduce inefficiency and to shorten lead times in responding to marketplace demands. In addition, a kind of second economy was officially rendered legitimate. The second economy encompassed activities that fell outside national plans, for example, rural activities, private retail trade and certain services. By the mid-1980s, 70 percent of the households in Hungary were earning income from the second economy and about one-fifth of the country's income earners was reported to receive one-third to one-half their income from private business activities. The result was a "reform by default." It represented the pragmatic outcome of compromises between different factions and interest groups in Hungary that were anxious to avoid repeating the tragic incident of 1956. As a result of the reform, significant improvements were made in the realm of provision of foodstuffs, consumer goods and services, regardless of the fact that according to official statistics the overall growth rates registered by Hungary in the 1970s were not as high as those reported in some other Eastern Bloc countries.

In the early 1970s, the reform came under pressure from the conservatives, who feared both the loss of central control and the long-term political effects of the growing disparities in income that were gradually developing between different social groups. The reformers also supported efforts by the government to protect the economy from the escalating oil prices of 1974 and 1979. As a result, subsidies and price supports were introduced to maintain the living standards of the bulk of the population. As might be expected, such subsidies reduced the impact of the economic regulators. As a result, growth slowed and trade deficits mounted. By 1985, Hungary began to register zero or even negative growth.

The emergent economic crisis reflected, in a nutshell, how a stagnant state sector gradually weighs down a relatively small second economy. Prosperity in the second economy raised consumer expectations that the bureaucrat-ridden industries of Hungary could hardly satisfy. The result was that a substantial national debt was incurred in the import of consumer goods. On the other hand, the second economy was too limited, too consumption-oriented and too deficient in both vertical and horizontal linkages to become an independent system, let alone a force that could bail out the increasingly bankrupt state sector. In addition, the part of the population that was left out of the second economy and had no private income became relatively impoverished, causing increasing social and political tensions in the system. Even those who were participants in the game gradually discovered that opportunities were diminishing, while newcomers found it difficult to face the cut-throat competition in a system that provided little room for rapid expansion. Thus, for all its progress in creating new institutions and moving toward a market economy, such as fledgling stock and bond markets, loans for private entrepreneurs, and privatization laws, serious problems persisted in the Hungarian economy. While its reform went as far as the passing of a bankruptcy law in 1986, it still controlled prices, taxed the populace heavily and continued to erect bureaucratic roadblocks that discouraged entrepreneurs.

In response to the deteriorating situation, in 1987 a group of leading Hungarian economists and scholars presented two interesting proposals entitled *The Turnaround and Reform* (Antal et al 1987) and *Social Contract, Precondition of Political Rejuvenation* (Kis et al 1987) to their government in an attempt at reform. The former proposal called for a more restrictive monetary policy, a reform of the taxation system, liberalization of imports, devaluation of the domestic currency, certain degrees of liberalization of property rights, (for example, turning some state enterprises into joint stock companies), and creation of more possibilities for private enterprises and foreign investment. Its philosophy was to provide a better structural framework within which individual rewards would be pegged to performance and to enable Hungarian products to compete in the world economy. The latter proposal, on the other hand, called for radical changes in the political system in order that more effective economic reform could be formulated.

With the recent political upheavals sweeping through Eastern Europe, Hungary quickly embraced more radical political changes. By June 1989, party reformers had successfully pushed Communist Party Chief Károly Grósz to accept a multiparty political system, independent trade unions and a new constitution that no longer reserved a leading role for the Communist Party. In the ensuing months, the Communist Party voted itself out of existence. The stage is now set for more aggressive economic reform. Whether subsequent developments will be favorable now depends on how far the market will prevail and how far the existing bureaucracy stands in the way of the former.

Gorbachev's Reform

The most dramatic of all reforms has come, surprisingly, within the Soviet Union itself. Everything considered, one might venture to say that what Mikhail Gorbachev is embarking upon amounts to no less than a revolution. Insofar as the economic side of the reform goes, its aim is to free the economy from the burden of bureaucracy and to do away with the country's shadow economy, with its different types of corruption and black marketeering. Alternatively stated, the reforms aim to make room for personal and collective initiatives within a broadly socialist framework in such a way that the advantages of central planning can be maintained and exploited.

Briefly, the reform measures consisted of the following. Enterprises were allowed to retain part of their after-tax profits for capital investment. Capital for investment was to be either internally generated or derived from loans by banks, but was no longer to be supplied by the government. Each enterprise now had the power to decide what and how it would produce, following satisfaction of certain contracts handed out by the central authority (on a competitive basis). The enterprise had to become more market and consumer-oriented. It had to find its own supplies of materials and machinery from other enterprises instead of just applying to the central authority. It was supposed to be free to choose its own suppliers and to market its products to different consumers or enterprises. Joint ventures between enterprises and foreign capital, subject to certain conditions, were also allowed under the reform. The enterprise managers were to be elected by the workers of the enterprise and to have full management responsibilities, although workers' councils would still supervise the work of the management and their appointments were to be subject to approval at the ministerial level. Additional income earned by the enterprises was to be distributed as bonuses to the workers, with a view to raising their efficiency and upgrading their performance. In agriculture, the reform took the form of contracting out to each family part of the authority to decide what it should produce and how it should sell its products after complying with the state contracts. A large range of tractors, fertilizers and other inputs was to be made available in the market from enterprises that produced and sold them. Needless to say, these measures bore much resemblance to those introduced in China's 10-year-reform.

Since Gorbachev put forward his blueprint for *perestroika* in June 1987, the situation in the Soviet economy has unfortunately deteriorated. Judging by the results so far, Lenin's famous phrase "one step foward, two steps back" seems appropriate in describing what has actually happened. Subsequent plans for reform unleashed a paper blizzard of new laws, regulations, slogans and resolutions, many of which were confusing and contradictory. Many proposals have never been put into practice. In some key areas, policies adopted to decentralize the Soviet economy have been watered down or abandoned. In agriculture, production at state and collective farms remains wasteful and shortages continue to grow. The new State Agro-Industrial Committee, known as *Gosagroprom*, formed by merging five farm-related ministries and several other organizations does not seem to have done much to reduce the bureaucratic red tape: it was reported that each instruction issued by its leadership went through 32 layers of administration before reaching the farmer. The 1987 Law on State Enterprise, giving factory managers greater control over production and wages, was supposed to reduce the power of bureaucrats. In reality this has not been the case. In most areas, the ministries have continued to force factories to hand over their entire production. Moreover, with the shortage of most consumer goods increasing, the old command system has remained in force in spite of the reform rhetoric.

Similar to the case in China, Gorbachev allowed private-sector cooperatives to mushroom in the hope that they would bring competition, entrepreneurship and badly needed consumer services to the Soviet Union. Also as in the case of China, corruption has flourished on the heels of such liberation, with racketeers either running many of the new small businesses or threatening them. Instead of pegging rewards to performance, many factories were authorized to fix pay rates. This meant that, similar to the Chinese situation, factories were rewarding their workers with pay increases that were unmatched by improvements in productivity. Gorbachev was keenly aware that his reforms could work only if the nation's artificially set prices were revamped, but given the continued power of the state industrial monopolies and the lack of a wholesale trade market, the government had second thoughts in introducing a complete price decontrol. The new Five-Year Plan unveiled at the end of 1989 suggested that the state's grip on the economy was to remain unchanged. Together with price reforms, other ambitious measures such as a broad sell-off of state enterprises, privatization of property rights, and an aggressive monetary policy were also ruled out. Such a setback was, however, short-lived. To clear the way for radical economic reform, in early 1990 Gorbachev successfully rammed legislation through the Congress of People's Deputies to give him sweeping power to govern by decree. At the time this book was written, radical measures were again redominating the reform scene. It remains to be seen whether these measures can take root and whether Gorbachev can survive, among other factors, the political impact of these reforms.

Toward a Theory of Crisis of Partial Reform

One interesting question to ask is, in the context of the Hungarian and Chinese experiences, will the "partial" reform being conducted in the Soviet Union share the same fate? Employing the kind of argument we developed in Chapter 1, our answer tends to be in the negative. Indeed, by generalizing the Chinese and Hungarian experiences, a more abstract framework can be formulated. The upshot of this framework is that a partial reform in any structurally indivisible or rigid economy, instead of achieving the intended results, is even more likely to generate potentially explosive disequilibrium situations that challenge the existing political framework. It will invariably unleash irrational economic behaviors in certain subphases of the reform until a crisis emerges, at which point either the reform will be brought to a halt or the existing political framework will undergo dramatic changes.

The first phase of reform is characterized by a controlled unleashing of incentives and initiatives at the individual and enterprise levels. During this phase, both supply-side and demand-side factors are expanded. Incentives are unleashed by way of giving more autonomy to enterprises and more or better consumption goods to workers and consumers. Conspicuous unleashing of quick results on the supply side is made possible by the fact that under a command regime the socialist system actually stockpiles a considerable amount of idle resources. Workers and consumers, on the other hand, need little prompting when they are tempted with the promises of material benefits. The result is that sharp increases in production or productivity can be realized within a relatively short period. Such an initial success will give the reformer the credibility and support to press for more reform, but very soon, such successes will reach their limits. These limits are set either by historical factors or by institutional rigidities, the liberalization of which would be either too slow to take effect or simply too radical ideologically to be palatable to the orthodoxy which still holds its grip on the reformers. Whereas the expansion of supply-side factors soon comes to a bottleneck under a partial reform, demand-side expectations, however, pick up their momentum if they are not checked. Increased income on the part of the beneficiaries, together with demonstration effects, rapidly and qualitatively alters the nature of consumer demand, which can no longer be satisfied by the existing framework of supply. This is to be expected, partly because the socialist production system, being suppressive of entrepreneurship and product innovation, has a natural propensity to expand in a linear direction, and partly because the producers, in their hurry to capture the rising demand, often fail to take into account changes in consumer taste. The result is that the demand for imported consumer goods will soar, thus intensifying, via some rounds of demonstration effects, the gap between what the system can produce and what its consumers want.

In contrast to the unchecked growth of demand-side expectations, eager producers and workers who invest more effort for a reward become frustrated as the gap between effort and result widens and as the constraints on supply-side factors turn out to be more tenacious than expected. Under such circumstances, reformers are forced to make more demand-side concessions to sustain the enthusiasm of their followers, while more economic actors see that it pays them better to circumvent the existing rules than to make more efforts to improve real production and productivity. Rewards thus begin to be transferred to rent-seeking or directly unproductive profit-seeking (DUP) activities, activities that aim to escape the discipline of competition or to earn abnormal gains using less-than legal means (see Colander 1984). During the earlier rounds when there are relatively few parties engaged in rent seeking, these activities tend to reward the practitioners with handsome profits. One could thus say that the second phase of partial reform is characterized by the joint escalation of demand expectations and rent-seeking behaviors which have mutually reinforcing effects on each other.

The third phase emerges as the negative effects of rent-seeking behavior begin to intensify. As more economic actors are drawn into rent-seeking behaviors and as more capital investments are drawn into producing consumer goods that are unwanted or projects that are never completed, more and more resources go into the hands of unbridled economic activities and become translated into demand for foreign goods and foreign currencies. On the other hand, real production begins to suffer as overexpansion causes shortages and as costs of production escalate. At this point, dissatisfaction from different quarters begins to set in. Those who find hope in more radical reform will start to challenge the existing political system, while those who believe that the chaos and the "evils" that are emerging on the scene are the direct results of reform will turn to the side of the conservatives. These conflicts will grow in intensity until they become political in character, thereafter requiring a political solution with highly unpredictable results. Moreover, should this line of argument hold, the present reform adopted by Gorbachev may likely experience the same sad ending as the reform in China has recently experienced.

The failure of a partial reform, as in the case of China, might mean a comeback of the conservatives, who feel comfortable with, or benefit from, a command system. Although it is doubtful whether the conservatives could ever put the clock back to the old days of a pure and complete command economy, they might, with legitimacy on their side and backed up by military power, stick to and defend a rotten system for an indefinite period of time. Furthermore, they could always argue that the existing ills of socialism represent malpractices caused either by human error or by the subversive acts of their enemies, and do not in any way mar the theoretical soundness of pure socialism. It is to this theoretical question that we now turn.

THE BANKRUPTCY OF THEORETICAL SOCIALISM

In this section, we would like to briefly revisit the most devastating critiques of socialism, as well as the most powerful arguments in its defense. It is hoped that any remaining illusion that readers may still have toward the feasibility of theoretical socialism will be dismissed.

The Impossibility of Rational Allocation of Resources under the Socialist Regime: The Challenge of von Mises

A leading opponent of socialism was the Austrian economist L. von Mises. He posed the challenge that under socialism, rational economic calculation is not possible. Briefly, his arguments are as follows: Since public ownership of the instruments of production does away with a market for capital goods, there can be no prices for these goods. Without prices, which serve to indicate the relative importance of the factors of production, economic calculation is out of the question. Market prices are important in two respects. First, they signal relative scarcities. Second, they guide producers to use less of the expensive inputs within a range of substitutes and to use more of the cheaper items. Deprived of these two essential functions, a socialist economy is inevitably bound to experience the kind of gluts and shortages that we witness in the socialist economies. With such gluts and shortages, the socialist economy cannot be anything but inefficient.

In other words, what von Mises attempted to show is that the socialist economy lacks the fundamental conditions for economic efficiency. Without private property rights, without the conditions of exchangeability of goods and without a general medium of exchange, "all production by lengthy and roundabout processes would be so many steps in the dark" ([1922] 1981, p. 101). This is because

> no single man, be he the greatest genius ever born, has an intellect capable of deciding the relative importance of each one of an infinite number of goods of higher orders. No individual could so discriminate between the infinite number of alternative methods of production that he could make direct

judgements of their relative value without auxilliary calculations. (p. 101)

As a consequence, "in societies based on the division of labor, the
distribution of property rights effects a kind of mental division of
labor, without which neither economy nor systematic production
would be possible" (p. 101). In fact, it is only under very simple
conditions that it is possible to dispense with money calculations.

> Without calculation, economic activity is impossible. In small
> and insignificant things, rational action might still exist. But
> for the most part, it would no longer be possible to speak of
> rational production. In the absence of criteria of rationality,
> production could not be consciously economical. (p. 103).

Von Mises elaborated further:

> Under a system based upon private ownership in the means
> of production, the scale of values is the outcome of the actions
> of every independent member of society. Everyone plays a
> two-fold part in its establishment first as a consumer, secondly
> as a producer. As a consumer, he establishes the valuation of
> goods ready for consumption. As a producer, he guides produc-
> tion-goods into those uses in which they yield the highest
> product. In this way all goods of higher orders also are graded
> in the way appropriate to them under the existing conditions of
> production and the demands of society. The interplay of these
> two processes ensures that the economic principle is observed
> in both consumption and production. And, in this way, arises
> the exactly graded system of prices which enables everyone to
> frame his demand on economic lines.
> Under socialism, all this must necessarily be lacking. The
> economic administration may indeed know exactly what
> commodities are needed most urgently. But this is only half
> the problem. The other half, the valuation of the means of
> production, it cannot solve. . . . But it cannot assimilate them

to a common price denominator, as can be done under a system of economic freedom and money prices. (pp. 103–4)

One might contend that improvements in technology might close at least part of the gap. For von Mises, however, such improvements could hardly be of any avail, for they miss the point that technology itself cannot solve the crucial economic problem which is a different one altogether.

Technology tells us how a given end could be attained by the employment of various means which can be used together in various combinations, or how various available means could be employed for certain purposes. But it is at a loss to tell man which procedures he should choose out of the infinite variety of imaginable and possible modes of production. ([1949] 1966: p. 207)

The only instrument qualified for this calculating job, he concluded, is the price system. What the price system does, in effect, is to transform, for each decision-maker, the otherwise overwhelmingly large number of technologically feasible ways of producing things into the relatively much smaller number that appear economic—that is, that appear to more than repay their costs. Without the guidance provided by price signals, each producer is likely to engage in a project which, were it the only goal of society, could probably be carried out (technological feasibility), but which, since it is not the only goal, finds itself running out of scarce resources which have been used up by other producers (economic infeasibility) (Lavoie 1985, p. 54).

The Case for Socialism: The Rebuttal by Oscar Lange

Against von Mises' challenge that rational economic calculation is impossible in a socialist economy, Oscar Lange in 1938 launched his seminal work *On the Economic Theory of Socialism* ([1938] 1964). According to Lange, the economic problem of rational allocation of resources is fundamentally a problem of choice between alternatives. To solve this problem, he believed that three types of data are needed: (1) a preference scale that guides the acts of choice; (2) knowledge of the "terms on which alternatives are offered"; and (3) knowledge of the amount of resources available (p. 60). Lange considered that a socialist economy may regard the data under (1) and (3) as given, at least in as great a degree as they are given in a capitalist economy. The critical question is whether the data under (2) are accessible to the administrators of a socialist economy. Whereas von Mises denied that (2) is available to socialist planners, Lange held that if prices are looked at not in the narrow sense as exchange ratios on a market, but in the generic sense of "terms on which alternatives are offered" after, say, P. H. Wicksteed (1933), then there would be little difficulty for socialist calculations. This is because the absence of a market does not prevent the setting up of "accounting prices" or provisional valuations for the purpose of allocating resources.

Anticipating the criticism that accounting prices are arbitrary and therefore cannot guide rational calculations, Lange contended that the equations of economic equilibrium can be solved in a socialist economy by trial and error, just as prices are actually determined by trial and error in a competitive market. Using E. Barone and F. Taylor's analysis as the basis of his argument (Barone [1908] 1935, Taylor 1938), he attempted to show that there is no fundamental qualitative difference between a socialist economy and a competitive market economy, as long as the former adopts valuations of its production factors, however arbitrary they may be, at the very start. This is because the "right" accounting prices will reveal themselves in "unmistakable ways" after the first round of operation. The right accounting prices are

> simply found by watching the quantities demanded and the quantities supplied and by raising the price of a commodity or service whenever there is an excess of demand over supply and lowering it when the reverse is the case, until by trial and error, [thus] the price is found at which demand and supply are in balance. (p. 89)

The Central Planning Board of a socialist country can thus perform functions similar to those of the market, monitoring such discrepancies and taking appropriate corrective actions. It establishes the same essential conditions and rules in determining the combination of the factors of production and the output of an industry as those of the market, namely, the parametric use of prices in accounting, the minimization of costs and the equating of marginal cost with the selling price of the product. In this way, the Central Planning Board enables the socialist economy to ascertain the relative importance of different factors of production and to arrive at a rational allocation of resources.

In addition to his assertion that a socialist economy that is managed in the above way is "functionally" equivalent to a market economy, Lange further contended that a socialist system so managed is superior to a market economy in several important ways. First, a socialist economy is more liable to reach the right equilibrium prices through a much shorter succession of trials than a competitive market. By corollary, it will be less subject to the fluctuations of the business cycle, for the Central Planning Board has a much wider knowledge of what is going on in the economic system as a whole than any private entrepreneur can possibly have under capitalism, and the board also has the power to contain local mistakes before they are amplified. Second, being capable of effecting a more even distribution of income within the socialist economy, it is in a better position to satisfy the "relative urgency of the needs of different persons," in sharp contrast to the market economy that is alleged to consistently distribute in favor of the preferences of the rich (p. 100). Third, a market economy in the mature stage is characterized by the existence of monopolistic or oligopolistic large-scale enterprises that are no longer compelled to introduce innovations and that have every incentive to artificially preserve the values of their old investments. As a result, profitable investment opportunities will be exhausted and chronic unemployment will follow. All these ills, in Lange's view, could be avoided by the central planning system, in spite of the fact that the system must also employ an arbitrary rate of capital accumulation.

Lange might well be right with respect to some of the flaws of capitalism, but he clearly failed to anticipate the way in which an evolving capitalist system gradually acquires the capability to correct many of the flaws he mentioned. The story of Western capitalism should well refute many of Lange's allegations. Of special concern to us here, however, is whether Lange was correct in asserting the functional equivalence between the capitalist economy and the socialist economy, and in particular whether the socialist system is truly capable of equilibrating its demand to supply and vice versa. The history of practiced socialism shows that the system is not capable of such an automatic adjustment. First, while the system can easily register oversupply in the form of inventory buildup, it can hardly gauge the extent of over-demand without first allowing prices to fluctuate in a spontaneous manner. Even if such assessments should occur, the system possesses no spontaneous mechanisms with which to make corrections. Without spontaneous adjustments such as those provided by the market system, the estimates on the demand side could only be very incomplete and at best would indicate only broad magnitudes or directions. There is no guarantee that the next round of accounting prices would ever come near a better match of demand and supply.

There is another important reason for the absence of an adjustment mechanism in the planning system, namely, there is a lack of incentive on the part of those who are in charge, as well as a lack of effective surveillance on the part of their superiors. Whereas incentive and surveillance problems, which contemporary economists term agency problems, exist both in capitalist and socialist economies, there are qualitative differences in their nature and effects. In the capitalist economy, the force of competition and the absence of a bailout system will eventually drive firms that produce at costs persistently exceeding market prices out of the market. In this very process, the firms in question first suffer a loss of profit, then experience a diminution of their working capital (income effect) and finally go bankrupt, leading to a depreciation or a complete write-off of their capital (wealth effect). In the socialist system, where bailouts are guaranteed and where incentive and surveillance problems are serious, an enterprise may respond to the situation in which its prices persistently exceed the equilibrium prices in three ways: (a) accumulate unsold stock under the disguise of investment, necessitating more working capital or subsidies from the state; (b) cut production and maintain the price; or (c) lower the quality of the product. In these cases, the income is still flowing to the enterprise in question and the purchasing power of the enterprise and its employees remains intact. Alternatively put, the capitalist system is able to eliminate its inefficiency and waste by eliminating the purchasing power of individuals responsible for those problems. By contrast, the socialist system does not possess such a self-regulating mechanism. Whereas inefficiency and waste can become rampant in the socialist system, the growth of purchasing power is not held in check. Over time there is more income in compensation for relatively less goods. In other words, aggregate demand chronically rises faster than aggregate supply. This explains, in part, the phenomena of chronic overinvestment and shortage characteristic of the socialist economies. To deal with these phenomena in more detail, we will address J. Kornai's criticisms in the next section.

Whereas prices could be conceived in the broad sense of "terms on which alternatives are offered," Lange clearly failed to grasp the role played by specific prices as opposed to prices in the abstract meaning of opportunity cost. He failed to appreciate the general reliance of economic actors on specific prices (the narrow sense of prices) for making their decisions. He was not aware of the fact that whereas the value of goods is generally reflected in their prices, it is also the case that an existing system of specific prices is capable of imposing on consumers some pattern of value, which they will employ to judge the new supplies available to them in a second round.[2] In addition, an existing system of specific prices also serves to guide suppliers in their guesswork as to what opportunities might come up in the next round. In other words, there is more to prices than the abstract idea of opportunities forgone or alternatives offered (the broad sense of prices). A system of fluctuating specific prices reflects, therefore, an intricate interplay between subjective valuations and evolving social conventions. It could hardly be replaced by a set of arbitrary accounting prices incapable of such spontaneous and subtle evolutions. The functional equivalence between accounting prices and market prices therefore breaks down, and von Mises' argument remains unaddressed.

The Knowledge Problem and Its Coordination: The Impossibility of an Omniscient Planner

Lange stated rather flippantly that the socialist economy could take care of consumer preferences without any difficulty. He asserted, "that part of the subjective equilibrium condition of a competitive market applies also to the market for consumers' goods in a socialist economy" ([1938] 1964, p. 75). As a result, he misinterpreted F. A. Hayek's argument against socialist economic calculation (Hayek 1935) so seriously that he thought Hayek agreed that a rational allocation of resources is theoreticaly possible in a socialist state but could not work out in practice. Such a misinterpretation blinded Lange from seeing the importance of Hayek's challenge to the theoretical feasibility of socialism. Indeed, Hayek's conception of the operation of an economy as a coordination problem as well as a knowledge problem remains today the most devastating criticism of central planning, which is so essential to the socialist system.

Like von Mises, Hayek ascribed two important functions to the price system: the signaling of the relative scarcity of resources and the coordinating of the plans of the individual economic actors (1935, 1948). Pointing out that the ruling orthodoxies in economics (both Marshallian and neo-Walrasian economics) neglect the information problem and the "causal processes" inherent in economic activity, Hayek drew attention to the importance of the division of knowledge, which should at least be ranked on a par with the division of labor. In his view, this is "the really central problem of economics as a social science" (1948, p. 50).

The price system, in Hayek's view, is the system on which we should focus in our study of the coordination problem in economic activities. The price system registers not only the effects of changing objective conditions and the reactions of transactors of these changes, it also registers the ever-changing expectations of market participants. Of special importance, too, is the fact that the price system is the least costly system of resource allocation. In the socialist calculation debate in the 1930s, Hayek pointed out that the price system, with its relatively cheap communication network, is the best possible method of allocating resources (1935).

The reason Hayek put forth was that while a planning agency may collect mountains of data, it is doubtful whether it is capable of collecting relevant data that are needed to uncover a modern economy's interesting empirical realities which reside deeply embedded in and dispersed among the separate minds of the economic actors. In other words, the knowledge relevant to economic decision making exists in such a dispersed form that it cannot be fully captured or even meaningfully extracted by any single agency in society. However, such an extraction is precisely what would be required for planning to be feasible at all. Knowledge in this sense is not and cannot be equated to data.

A very slightly different but congenial interpretation of Hayek's position is this: Hayek's conception of knowledge is one in the "inclusive" sense. Knowledge includes not only academically proven theoretical knowledge, but also what we would call information about particular situations in a particular environment, as well as opinions, hunches and skills of all kinds possessed by different economic actors. The kind of knowledge used in an economic action thus ranges from the objective to the subjective and the overt to the tacit as well as from the general to the specific. As can be expected, much of this kind of knowledge cannot be passed onto a central planning agency. The epistemic status of such knowledge, especially that of how to exploit a particular situation, does not permit such a possibility. Indeed, given that the knowledge being used in economic actions contains a large element of intuition or momentary impressions, such knowledge could not be used without a particular context and without being guided by the particular values and motivations of a particular person or firm in a free market society.

To further elaborate, the epistemic status of an important part of the knowledge employed in economic activities goes beyond the directly conscious realm of the economic actor. In line with M. Polanyi (1958), who showed that even in the realm of scientific activity a scientist employs knowledge that carries an essentially personal component and a tacit dimension, Hayek showed that the kind of knowledge relevant to economic decision making must contain such tactic dimensions in substantial proportion. Being tacit and unconscious, much of the knowledge employed by the economic actors in a practical way is not and cannot be fully articulated. Indeed, the unarticulated components of our knowledge and the unconscious rules we employ, Hayek further pointed out, guide much of our social activities. Law, for example, has been a necessary institution even for the survival of the primitive societies, but it has only been articulated in modern times. In a similar vein, the market operating with prices is an ordering and coordinating mechanism. It developed for a long time without anybody wholly understanding it, but it nonetheless effectively enables us to utilize widely dispersed information about the significance of circumstances of which we are mostly ignorant. Only in a free market consisting of freely associating individuals can such knowledge be brought into the open and occasionally used. Needless to say, such knowledge could not be captured and would be completely lost in a planned, socialist economy. Hence, it cannot be of service to economic calculations for the socialist system.

One recent route by which Hayek proceeded to criticize socialism is through analyzing the moral development of humanity (1988). Hayek posited that our socialist propensities arose from some of our deep instincts dating from humanity's early days; these instincts still govern and dominate our emotions, and are deeply ingrained in our moral constitution. For example, our duty to serve the visible needs of our known friends, and our activities in joining others in a common effort for common ends in a primitive society clearly underline our innate search for socialist ideals. These instincts are so pervasive and compelling that Hayek could not help but admit that

> in a sense we all are socialists. We are still governed by feelings that are based on what was necessary in the small group of known people among whom each had to aim at fulfilling the needs of persons he knew; where he had to collaborate with a definite group of fellows, who were given to him and whom he could not choose, to pursue common purposes. (1983, p. 41)

However, humanity evolved, and so did human rules. Hayek contended that the

> rules on which the growth of civilization is based are very largely rules that told us we could disregard these primitive instincts. By following instead certain abstract rules of conduct we could do more good—not by aiming at the satisfaction of the needs of known people, but by following the abstract guides of market prices that led to the formation of modern society. (pp. 38–39)

It was, actually, this gradual evolution of a new morality, of new rules that were opposed to natural human instincts, that enabled us to build a worldwide society based on exchange, in which each of us did more good by serving the abstract symbols of the market than could have been done by devoting energy to the needs of known and familiar fellows (p. 39). Gradually, these new traditions of abstract rules became the basis of a civilization embracing the Western world, until about 150 years ago when a reactionary development took place. At that time there emerged a "rationalistic" philosophy that made people doubt a discipline of rules whose significance they did not understand. The market system was, unfortunately, far too complex for their articulation and comprehension. As a result, appeals to our innate, primitive moral instincts were once again triggered, and together with the rationalistic tradition, they provided the background conditions leading to the rise of modern socialism.

Hayek believed that in obeying the rules of the market and in relying on the purely formal rules of law without any central direction, we can achieve more than if we were to return to a system in which we were all working for known purposes in harmony with our familiar fellows and aiming at the same specific ends. The development of human civilization clearly speaks of the superiority of the spontaneous order of the market and its rule-governed characteristics. In Hayek's view, we are living in a society that exists only because we are capable of serving people whom we do not know and of whose very existence we are ignorant, and we in turn constantly live on the services of other people of whom we know nothing. From this perspective, socialism is an abberation in the process of cultural evolution, rooted in the false belief that humanity can, by conscious efforts alone, direct and use resources in the most efficient way, and that it is in our power to put everyone on the level at which we would wish them to be by way of redistributing income.

An Insider's Critique of Socialism: The Economics of Shortage

Hayek's arguments against socialism could generally be viewed as a conclusive demonstration of the theoretical unfeasibility of socialism. By the 1970s, more and more details about the failings of practiced socialism had become evident, and more economists inside the socialist system undertook soul-searching researches to uncover the theoretical problems of an operating socialist system. Among them, J. Kornai ranks as one of the most important contributors.[3] Since the late 1950s, Kornai has been engaged in searching for a more comprehensive framework to explain the inefficiencies and shortages in a socialist economy. His first work, *Overcentralization in Economic Administration* (1959), attempted to explain such phenomena in terms of overcentralization. However, he soon came to realize that this is an inadequate explanation, for the experiences of decentralization clearly showed that the decentralization of economic decisions failed to arrest the recurrence of shortages. In a subsequent work, *Rush versus Harmonic Growth* (1972), he noted another important property of the socialist economy, namely, that socialism has an inherent tendency toward rushed, accelerated growth and over investments, along with the phenomenon of shortage. All these questions and analyses culminated in his masterpiece, *The Economics of Shortage* (1980), which offered a more comprehensive explanation of the tendency in the socialist economy toward overinvestment and the reproduction of shortages, regardless of what system of prices it adopts.

According to Kornai, the shortcomings of the command system consist of the following: Enterprise managers tend to disguise their capabilities in order to avoid ambitious, difficult-to-fulfill targets. They tend to leave a wide margin to allow for the ample contingencies generated within the bureaucratic production systems. Insofar as they are compelled to fulfill "unreasonable" targets, they will do it at the expense of quality and to the neglect of equipment maintenance and other hidden costs. Since the plan is generally calendar-based, the pace of production lags behind in the beginning and tends to accelerate toward the end. As a fall-back strategy to make up for late or unreliable delivery of inputs from other enterprises, these enterprises invariably hoard large quantities of inputs, including labor. Thus, a large portion of resources that could have been actively used are forced to remain idle, and shortages coexist with wastes. Predictably, too, the adaptation of production to changing demand and new technological possibilities is slow, for the risk of taking on these innovations is not worthwhile from the stance of the enterprise manager, whose primary objective is that of fulfilling planned targets, no more and no less.

From the Hungarian experiences, Kornai further analyzed the shortcomings of the socialist mixed economy, namely, a planned economy that permits the coexistence of a market sector. According to Kornai, state enterprises, or indeed any publicly owned enterprises, operate with "soft budget constraints." That is, these enterprises are permitted bailout by the state even if they operate at a loss for an indefinite period of time. Without clear-cut ground rules to penalize these enterprises or enforce these rules (even if they exist, the enterprises concerned can easily put the blame on factors beyond their control), managers of enterprises are inclined to expand their production capacities and, thereby, their demand for capital goods, if only to expand their bargaining power or influence. Also under the regime of shortage, enterprises will have to settle for second-best substitutes to carry on their production. The result is inferior quality and decreased competitiveness in an increasingly sophisticated world market.

In a mixed regime, the price system is inconsistent, blending arbitrary prices with relatively rational prices. Since prices are interdependent, the arbitrariness of some prices is transmitted throughout the system. Moreover, a mixed regime is characterized by a complex system of taxation and subsidy. In theory, a firm's expenditure should be limited by what it earns from sales. In practice, its budget may be altered at will by the authorities, who can revise the pretax, presubsidy profit as much as they want. An important characteristic of the soft budget constraint is "leveling," which means that enterprises that perform well usually have their extra profits taxed away while their poorly performing counterparts have their losses compensated. After fiscal redistribution, the extremes are eliminated and the distribution moves closer to the medium, usually concentrating around low levels of profit. This means that profits depend as much on success in the market, that is, "horizontally," as on the generosity of financial authorities or the enterprises' ability to bargain with them, in other words, "vertically." A vicious circle is thus brought about. Because the price system is partly arbitrary, fiscal redistribution is needed for compensation. Since fiscal redistribution is inherently arbitrary, so are the resultant prices. On the whole, the budget constraint of the enterprise is too soft to respond rationally to prices. New formulae that are introduced to harden the budget constraint usually fail to function properly because they cannot eliminate the fundamental arbitrariness at the root of the system, although hardening of the budget constraint might, through tougher financial discipline, improve profit incentives and accountability (Kornai 1987).

Additionally, because internal financial resources from retained earnings cannot cover all investments, enterprises use either credit from the banks or investment subsidies from the central government. Again, however, the allocation of finances is not strictly pegged to the profitability of the enterprise, which is also arbitrary due to the leveling involved. In other words, there exists a strong vertical dependence for the enterprise's investment on the financial authorities. We have already seen that state-owned enterprises are prone to overinvestment because they are not fearful of the consequences of the failure of their investment projects, due to the variety of instruments for softening the budget constraint, for example, subsidies, tax exemptions, postponements of debt service, adjustments of the selling prices to the cost overrun of the investment project, and so on. Hence, demand for credit persistently exceeds supply. Under such conditions, the only way for the central authority to control investment is through arbitrary administrative means. Such arbitrariness, too, enables central planners to cover up their wrong decisions. With such ample room to cover up mistakes, the central planners, in turn, cannot effectively check the drive for expansion that the enterprises crave.

In spite of these shortcomings, Kornai is of the opinion that the mixed regime is superior to that of the pure command economy, and his suggestion is to move toward a healthier combination of planning, central control and market forces. This is, of course, an eclectic position that has yet to be proven tenable even in theory. What Kornai has in mind seems to be a fundamentally market-driven economy, guided by macroeconomic parameters and controls, and supplemented by state welfare programs. How much macroeconomic control he advocates, how these controls enable his ideal regime to be free of the problems experienced by the kind of partially reformed regime we have so far analyzed, or how far they are different from those employed in the contemporary industrial countries of the West, remains unclear. One thing, however, is certain. Whatever the controls are that will be spelled out in his blueprint, they are unlikely to be of the very specific type.

TOWARD A MORAL CRITIQUE OF SOCIALISM

Hayek is insightful in his observation that socialists today can preserve their position in academic economics only by maintaining that judgments about the relative merits of capitalism and socialism are value statements about which science and facts cannot conclusively decide. To expose the weakness of such a position, Hayek launched a "scientific" exposition of the changing moral systems of humanity. To him, socialist ideals and, by extension, traditional moral values, albeit rooted in our primitive instincts, turn out to be incompatable with the development of human civilization. Regardless of the truthfulness of such a hypothesis, Hayek's stance appears to be detrimental in that it unnecessarily makes too many concessions to the moral foundation of socialism. Worse still, it is liable to lead us to neglect the fundamentally immoral nature of such a system. I will contend that whereas a capitalist system, contrary to popular belief, has the capacity to turn private vice into positive moral qualities, a socialist system unleashes nothing but the vicious parts of human nature. In these discussions, I shall adopt a commonsense conception of morality and take it for granted that qualities such as a sense of responsibility and mutual trust are desirable, while qualities such as envy and suspicion are not.

Moral Order and Economic Order

Whereas the phenomenal development of the modern economy seems to be partly founded on the dissociation of economic activities from moral allegations and prohibitions (such as the question of usury in the Middle Ages), an interesting parallel exists in the fact that economics has also successfully developed a domain of its own upon freeing itself from ethical issues since the days of Adam Smith. Economic laws, one might be tempted to infer, must operate independently of moral considerations and imperatives. After all, Marx has convincingly shown that moral orders are merely superstructures reflecting the shape of economic laws that reign in certain epochs of history. Lest moral issues should adversely affect the status of economics as a science, "scientifically minded" economists took pains to label the part of economics that could be studied independently of moral issues as "positive" economics, as opposed to "normative" economics, which is alleged to deal with the kind of economic means that should be employed to attain certain economic or noneconomic ends.

Not all economists, however, agreed to the banning of moral discourse outside the domain of economics. Max Weber ([1922] 1976) had persuasively shown that a particular religious order promoting certain moral qualities is able to yield positive economic results that otherwise would not be possible. His specific hypothesis was that the rise of modern capitalism could be explained by the pursuit of virtues that constituted the Puritan system of morality, for example, a sense of self-responsibility, frugality, and so on. In spite of the obvious causal relations between the moral order and the economic order, mainstream economists to date have been complacent in confining their attention to positive economics. This is so probably not because they fail to realize that moral qualities matter in economic discourse, but because they know well that morality must involve values that are essentially pluralistic (for example, Sen 1987) and thereby might create intractable problems for a unified economic science under the banner of positive economics. This state of affairs, however, seems to be gradually changing. In the sphere of development economics, the relevance of traditional moral values of certain societies to economic behaviors is increasingly being recognized. In a recent work, Sen pointed out that to the degree that human conduct is shaped by moral considerations, moral qualities matter not only for normative economics, but also for positive economics as well.

Whereas it is generally recognized that a particular moral order has causal effects on economic behavior, it is seldom pointed out that a particular economic order tends to nurture certain types of moral values and codes of behavior, which in turn will shape or reinforce certain types of economic behavior. In other words, causation is multidirectional rather than unidirectional. To presume that positive economics alone is adequate for the understanding of the most important parts of economic phenomena is a false illusion, for no economic order fails to yield moral qualities which, in turn, will have important effects on economic phenomena. In the following discussion, we will show the way a planned economy produces degenerative moral qualities that ultimately defeat the system itself.

Apparent Superiorities of Comprehensive Plans

The reasons why comprehensive planning is appealing are manifold. From the cognitive viewpoint, a comprehensive plan presents the qualities of solidity and vision. From the moral perspective, it displays the qualities of impartiality and fairness. As an individual, we require some kind of plan in managing our daily affairs. These plans in general serve us well. It thus seems logical that the more comprehensive a plan, the better it should serve us. It also seems logical to say that since individual plans are generally useful, comprehensive plans for society should be superior to ad hoc plans. With distributive justice being the major pillar of the socialist ideal, a comprehensive plan making explicit such results in advance would seem to be the perfect instrument to ensure the attainability of such justice. Even if the preset results fail to materialize, the explicitness and comprehensiveness of such a plan would still assure us that some kind of moral integrity has been preserved throughout the process of implementation. Thus, the more comprehensive a plan, the better it appears to equip us to be masters of our fate.

However, the above logic is seriously flawed. Experiences tell us that the plans we use for personal affairs are mere working devices that do not always match reality in every detail. Indeed, the more comprehensive our plan, the more often it will not materialize. In fact, if we were to pursue a plan, a cruder one would seem to be more flexible. With a comprehensive plan, it is not easy to design fallback positions. This is because changes in one part of the plan will affect many other parts of a comprehensive plan, and small changes may result in many different versions altogether.

A central comprehensive plan in the hands of policymakers is clearly something more than a working device, for if a central plan is perceived to be nothing more than a set of working guidelines, the purpose of the plan will easily be belittled and its status may be debased. Should it be merely a loose set of reference points, people will no longer take the planned targets seriously, and the purpose of setting up the master plan will be defeated in the second round. Hence, a central comprehensive plan has to go beyond the instrumental dimension. It is compelled to contain an inherent moral imperative demanding that it be fulfilled, at least on face value. Uncompromisingly, it has to be an indivisible system requiring a complete or near-complete fulfillment to sustain its credibility.

The Moral Consequences of Subordination to a Master Plan

A central plan backed up by the socialist ideology once inaugurated thus becomes the Plan, an entity that quickly generates a cult of its own. Lest the plan settle for less than its complete fulfillment and lest subsequent plans lose their credibility and appeal, it requires a class of "guardians" whose role is to make sure that the plan is fulfilled, if not in substance, at least in appearance. In other words, upon inauguration, a central plan inescapably takes on a moral imperative, legitimatizing its guardians to adopt any means they see necessary to keep the Plan in good shape. The guardians, on the other hand, are quick to assume the role because it confers on them the power to interpret the course of events and to intervene whenever they choose. Given less-than-perfect knowledge of individual preferences and resources, the central plan is unrealistic at the very start, but since the moral imperative of the

Plan requires it to be fulfilled as far as possible, it follows that reality has to be compromised and that everyone concerned must do something to make up for the discrepancy. Such a supervising task becomes the specific job of the guardians.

As can be expected, readings by the guardians in the course of monitoring the execution of the Plan are characteristically arbitrary, particularly if they are related to the fulfillment of arbitrary results. Apart from being arbitrary, these readings usually carry a moral undertone, for the underfulfillment of state plans can easily be taken as undermining the socialist cause or betraying the collective interest. In other words, economic actions in the socialist system, being indivisibly related to the Plan, take on a "public" character and thereby open themselves to moral interpretations and allegations. Under the name of collective interest, any economic action can be morally labeled.

Not only are economic actions indivisibly related to the Plan, but all other actions of the individual are, by corollary, also indivisibly related to the collective interest of the socialist system, and can thereby be given moral labels. Legitimately, the collective "good" penetrates the entire life of the individual, subjecting all behavior to moral interpretations and intimidation. In this regard, the socialist system is not only an economically indivisible system, but more horrifyingly, it is also a morally, socially and politically indivisible system that is intricately fused into a whole. In this system, the ruling class is vested with legitimate, complete and unlimited power, in the name of the interests of the whole, to intervene in any action of any individual down to the last detail. In a sense, the socialist society is, insofar as indivisibility goes, structurally similar to some primitive societies where the leader has complete control over the members of his tribe. As far as the economic aspect is concerned, this represents a great leap backward, for we know very well that until human economic actions are liberated from close moral supervision, and until the pursuit of private interests no longer entails the possibility of public condemnation and penalties, the vitality of the capitalist forces cannot become unleashed. Subsuming economic actions under a moral framework means that private incentives, even if they bear positive results in the interest of the public, stand the moral hazard of being accused of subverting the public interest.

The consequences of moral reading and arbitrary control of economic actions on the social life of the individual are far-reaching. To protect himself from intervention and penalty, the executive of a plan is compelled to fulfill any planned target that is imposed on him, regardless of the real state of affairs. This means that if he fails to meet the stipulated targets in real terms, he will either make up something or point the finger at others. The executives of the plan are not the only parties compelled to become dishonest under such a regime. No other economic and social actors can escape from this process of moral degradation which is caused by the spread of the protectionist mentality. Planners and guardians of the plans, needless to say, are open to corruption because of the infinite power vested in them. Since it is inherently difficult to identify the sources of many mistakes in the collective system, all economic actors who have long been exposed to that system become accustomed to shying away from admitting the mistakes they made. As they deny themselves to be the sources of these mistakes, one would hardly expect them to take such mistakes seriously or take them into account in their future actions. Hence, economic actors in the socialist system are generally prevented from learning from their errors.

Distributive Justice and the Suppression of the Rule of Dessert

One cardinal feature of the socialist system is that it advocates a conception of "end-state" distributive justice. A society is considered to be just only if it arranges the distribution of its output on a basis that is as egalitarian as possible. In this conception, the rule of dessert, namely, the rule of attributing rewards to individuals commensurate with their effort in conjunction with their "entitled" resources, is considered to be unjust, because such a principle is alleged to generate over time an uneven pattern in the distribution of income and, as a result, to lead to the increasing impoverishment of certain members of society. Regardless of the truthfulness of such an allegation, it is obvious by now that the conception of distributive justice itself is a false ideal and incapable of realization. The strongest objection to this conception is that it is an "unhistorical" principle. It is unhistorical in that it holds that past circumstances or actions of people that created differential entitlements should be ignored or evened out. Unhistorical principles cannot provide the foundation for creating an economy with vitality and dynamism, because in wiping out the entitlements conferred by past efforts, they remove the primary motive of economic actors to expend their present efforts in order to build up their entitlements for the future. By corollary, denying the historical principle implies that arbitrariness will rule. With arbitrariness dominating, the possibility of justice and, thereby, the possibility of a civil society, is out of the question (see Nozick 1974).

A system that emphasizes end-state, distributive justice also is not in a position to consistently select conscientious performers, for these can only be nurtured within frameworks of historical principles of justice and individual motivation and incentive. Similarly, the system is not able to produce the most innovative workers. In place of the rule of dessert, which alone can provide the necessary framework for talent formation, the socialist system relies on promotion and selection criteria that yield opposite results. The logical corollary of abandoning the rule of dessert is that the degree of ideological purity on the part of its managers becomes the principal selection criterion. Apart from the question of relevance, this is a highly arbitrary criterion that has serious moral repercussions. Those who are eager to demonstrate their ideological purity are liable to take on extreme positions and deliberately violate canons of efficiency. Emphasis on ideological purity easily breeds hypocrisy, for one need not have a true command of the socialist ideology or a genuine belief in that ideology to appear to be ideologically pure. Without a simple rule to delineate those who truly understand the ideology from those who do not, the hypocrite can pretend indefinitely to be ideologically pure without running much risk of being discovered. On the part of the superior, it is also not in his interest to select competent subordinates. Having gained and maintained his position by manipulation or through personal relations, he will clearly know that subordinates of mediocre capabilities pose a lesser threat to him and better serve his long-term interests.

The moral predicament of the socialist planning system goes beyond the fact that it embraces an untenable principle of justice. Ironically, it subverts its own manifest goal. On the surface, a socialist economy seems to arrange the distribution of its product on a relatively even basis. In reality, however, the guardians of the plan or the politicians who back up these guardians invariably exact intangible compensation by virtue of their power or position. Although nominally they seem to be sharing an equal part of the economic pie, they are more than equally compensated by an intangible package that includes, among other privileges, unchecked power, special access to "public" amenities, and the freedom to abuse rules and laws. In fact, equality of distribution in "real" terms such as the socialists hope for cannot exist as long as the socialist system must be hierarchically organized for economic effectiveness. Since economic effectiveness demands that the socialist system, like any other economic system, has to rely on the division of labor, specialization and managerial competence, the possibility of absolute equality in real terms over a long stretch of time for people with different talents and levels of competence is nothing but a myth, given human nature.

Thus, it turns out that the command system, lacking a natural "selective mechanism," is compelled to adopt arbitrary rules in filling its offices. Though avowing itself to be egalitarian in principle, the central plan, operating in conjunction with the principle of distributive justice, is actually suppressive of responsible and honest individuals. As arbitrariness rules, the hypocrite and the manipulator are rewarded. The economy will suffer not only because it loses the services of its best people, but also because it is ruled by the morally corrupt (compare Hayek 1944).

Asymmetry in the Moral Orders of Capitalism and Socialism: Discrepancies between Demand-Side Expectations and Supply-Side Capabilities

Superficially, the capitalist system appears to be morally inferior to the socialist system. Whereas the latter can boast of solidarity, humaneness, altruism, and so on, the capitalist system, which is built on personal avarice and greed and distinguished by the indifference of its members toward the sufferings of others, is apparently indefensible as a desirable moral order. This superficial asymmetry, curiously enough, turns out to yield the opposite results over a long stretch of time. Whereas the capitalist order does stem from and is sustained by egoistic motives, it is able to foster a set of moral qualities that turn out to be compatible with human progress and the unleashing of individual potential. The possibility of self-realization under the capitalist regime for a large proportion of its members means that many manifest inequalities at a particular point of time are gradually dissolved or ameliorated as the percentage of responsible persons rises. On the contrary, the socialist system, which was supposedly founded on our most treasured virtues, turns out to be suppressive of them in the long run. Such a serious reversal of the asymmetry, we contend, is caused by an inherent regulative moral mechanism that exists in the capitalist system but is absent from the socialist system.[4]

We posit that in all economic systems, demand-side expectations on the part of the economic actors act as stimulant to improving their supply-side capabilities. In the capitalist system, the latter perform a unique regulative function. Since the economy is a fluid system and opportunities are generally available to people with rare talents or skills or with something special to offer, it will pay an economic actor to make efforts to augment his supply-side capabilities by way of, say, attaining a higher qualification, developing his own business, or changing to a more sophisticated job. Provided that he works hard enough, makes a sufficiently large number of attempts or learns well from his failures, he stands a good chance of realizing much of what he first aspires to in the long run. This kind of hope, backed up by a sense of realism and made possible by the market, acts like a kind of self-regulating mechanism in the mind of the economic actor. On the one hand, it acts to suppress his highly unrealistic demand-side expectations. On the other hand, it lures him to make efforts in a progressive and realistic manner. Thus, a process of self-actualization is nicely combined with material progress for the aspiring individual. With such open prospects, one naturally finds that many economic actors in a capitalist economy concentrate single-mindedly on augmenting their resources and capabilities.

The consequence of concentrating on the improvement of his supply-side capabilities is that the economic actor will gradually develop a set of positive attitudes. He will develop realism in his aspirations, accept responsibilities and consequences for his actions, develop a respect for the rule of law, and practice self-restraint in his present consumption in exchange for the hope of a better tomorrow, and he will accept in a detached manner the success of other people, even if that success has a large component of luck. In stark contrast, there is hardly any mechanism in the socialist system that serves to regulate the relation between demand-side expectations and supply-side capabilities among its economic actors. Since to materalize one's expectations, whether existing or newly gained ones, is largely out of an individual's means and control, an economic actor in the socialist system can hardly develop any realistic criteria to rank his expectations. Without any realistic basis to order his expectations, his craving remains raw and unchecked. Given the opportunity, he will seize whatever he can lay his hands on. Without the right to claim resources, coupled with a protectionist, moralistic mentality, the economic actor in the socialist system is in no position to make sustained efforts to build up his supply-side capabilities. To this extent, he is clearly not in a position to check his demand-side expectations.

This asymmetry could be further explained by the following: In the capitalist system, the status of an economic actor is determined as much by the level of his conspicuous consumption as by his supply-side capabilities. Quite often, the demand-side performances of an economic actor are considered secondary indicators. In extreme cases, frugal but capable entrepreneurs are often objects of admiration and legendary interest. In the socialist system, since one cannot or even will not want to be explicitly measured by his supply-side power (since the fulfillment of a plan is something that is to be expected, and since it would be counterproductive to the individual to persistently overperform on what a plan prescribes), the only way to demonstrate that one is different from, or superior to one's compatriots, is through the route of conspicuous consumption (when it is permitted). Moreover, for those who are deprived of such consumption, their responses are typically ones of envy or jealousy, qualities that are not only unhelpful in promoting their capabilities, but are obviously detrimental to others making such efforts.

Economic participants in the capitalist system are, of course, as greedy and avaricious as their counterparts in the socialist system. This remains a fundamental condition of humankind. The difference in the two cases is that over time the economic actors in the capitalist system come to realize that their efforts will lead to an increase in the total economic "pie" and thereby in the sizes of their respective shares, if and only if most other people follow the same set of ground rules. Conversely, they will become aware of the fact that naked avarice unleashed in a ruleless manner will not pay off for anyone in the long run. In other words, in the capitalist system, moral values are gradually seen to be compatible with utility, and justifiable even solely on utilitarian grounds. In contrast, since participants in the socialist system are forced to be concerned with the relative shares in the pie, regardless of the fact that such concerns will hardly increase the pie's total size over time, the system is gradually sapped of the vitality even to maintain itself.

Let us assume that we subscribe to Hayek's view that the socialist system was originally founded on the ideals of altruism and solidarity. If an individual becomes more concerned with protecting his own position, whatever sense of altruism and solidarity he might have in the first place will gradually be dissipated. In the same vein, if he is no longer accustomed to taking on responsibility for the results of his actions, and instead acquires the habit of pointing his finger at others, no genuine altruism and solidarity will follow. Genuine and enlightened altruism requires the backup of material resources on the part of the economic actor, as well as moral resources demonstrating that he is psychologically mature and independent. Ironically, socialism in practice effectively extinguishes the very qualities on which the ideals of socialism are said to have been founded. In a similar vein, the important moral quality of mutual trust among economic actors, which clearly has positive effects on economic efficiency, hardly exists in the socialist system. To the extent that mutual trust prevails, the overall overhead in the operation of an economy will be lowered. This advantage is denied to the socialist system, where the ruling mentality is protectionist in character and where distributive equality is the key concern among its economic actors.

As much as altruism, solidarity and mutual trust are not achievable under the regime of socialism, the moral imperative of efficiency and its attendant rejection of waste, which we take for granted in the capitalism system, is alienated in practiced socialism. Although socialism does talk about the need for efficiency and at times gives special credit to this virtue, the individual pressing for efficiency under the command system will have to risk moral condemnation. Efficiency on the part of a producer in a capitalist system which results in extra production or lowered selling prices may provoke moral reactions by competitors in the first round. However, these competitors will soon find that moral condemnation is futile and that the only effective way to deal with their problems is to beat the producer on his own terms. The result will be a continuing, overall improvement in productivity and product innovation. In a socialist system, however, suppliers facing the same challenge need not respond in a forceful way. They can afford to ignore the aggressive supplier who aims at improving efficiency because their own well-being will hardly be affected as long as they fulfill their own part of the plan. Moreover, even if they do face a decline in demand for their less competitive products in the (occasionally) open market, they have little worry over their financial position, knowing too well that they will eventually be bailed out by the state. As a result, the increased output made by the small handful of aggressive suppliers may backfire because it does not trigger positive responses from the overall system.

The above analysis also throws light on why partial reform of the kind practiced in China fails to attain its avowed goals. Since over time socialism produces nothing but a population of morally unrestrained economic actors, the lifting of the command economy and its conferring of new freedoms on its economic actors would no doubt unleash previously suppressed desires and all the attendant undesirable immoral qualities. Once set free, the long-suppressed egoism will manifest itself in envy, greed, corruption, unscrupulous attitudes, a scramble for conspicuous consumption, disrespect for the law, and ruthless rent-seeking behaviors. The emergence of these qualities alone creates untractable problems for reform and implies that subsequent developments will be chaotic and out of control.

The kind of moral argument we have employed in the above discussion is not entirely new. As we previously mentioned, Max Weber long ago pointed out the affinity between religious precepts and the self-discipline of mundane conduct, and described how theoretical ideas and religious fervor unwittingly promote secular successes. In his classic *The Protestant Ethic and the Spirit of Capitalism* ([1904–5] 1976) Weber insisted on the precedence of inner spiritual and cultural preconditions over all external economic forms. The Protestant teachings, especially in the Calvinist tradition which Weber emphasized, state that a believer's behavior is not subject to sanctions by any external spiritual authority but only to the inner dictates of one's own conscience. Such an attitude undoubtedly lends strength to the virtues of responsibility, self-control and spiritual independence, virtues that prove to have the positive effects of enhancing the material well-being of whoever espouses them. Weber's project was, however, global in scope. He was concerned with the relation between religion and society in different civilizations, and how the ethics of different religious doctrines affected the rationality of economic life. From this broad framework, he aimed to throw light on the question of why capitalism developed in the way it did in the West and why other cultures failed to follow the same developmental path.

Weber's project was an all-encompassing one. A work of such scope naturally left out the many subtle ways in which an economic order might engender certain codes of conduct or unleash certain moral values, as well as the ways these moral "products" affect the economic order itself. In this regard, our present thesis that an economic order can be studied in terms of its attendant moral values and with respect to how such values affect its very operation serves to fill part of the gap left by Weber. With this new theoretical framework, let us now summarize the moral predicaments of socialism.

Socialism is an immoral system.[5] Its immorality lies in the fact that its operation unleashes moral qualities that subvert its very ideals. It undermines the essential human moral values which are needed to maintain a lawful society by injecting the element of arbitrariness into all aspects of economic and social life. It denies the very capacity of humanity to attain the goal of self-realization, and calls for outright dishonesty to cover up any failures. It undermines the value of responsibility and ignores the blatantly irresponsible. It creates envy, suspicion and mistrust among its economic actors and leads to deep tensions within the system, thereby adding a great burden to the economy's overhead. All these factors have clearly formidable repercussions on economic rationality and efficiency. Socialism's continued existence, therefore, depends on the use of coercion as well as fear-inspiring and distrust-promoting instruments, rather than on grounds of economic feasibility. In gradually developing a population of economic actors who are powerless to restrain their raw, primitive desires, it produces in effect a dangerous population capable of ruleless acts and unscrupulous behavior. In short, if morality consists of building a system of consistent rules to guide behavior, what socialism produces is a moral vacuum, reducing humanity to the state of sullen, egoistic brats, for whom the end fully justifies the means.

NOTES

1. Admittedly, a complete reversal of the sweeping changes in Eastern Europe is highly unlikely. In this regard, one should not underestimate the impact of the June 4 massacre on the changes there.

2. Woo (manuscript).

3. An interesting though similar analysis was made by Jan Winiecki in his work *The Distorted World of Soviet-Type Economies* (1988). He argued that

> while actions of individual agents are rational at a microeconomic level, the resulting aggregate behavior is inefficient. Thus shortages arise as a result of excessive pressure placed on enterprises to produce at high levels. These shortages create an atmosphere where enterprises must protect themselves from input uncertainty. Vertical integration and underspecialization in production result as enterprises try to protect their input sources. Similarly, investment cycles are created when risk-averse managers find that it is costless to request additional capital. Initial overfunding leads to midcourse corrections and failure to complete all planned projects. Inflation is explained as part of a profit-push process where management and labor press against the central planners for higher wages. The wage bill rises at a rate that reflects productivity growth in the highest productivity sectors. The rapidly rising wage bill generates inflation which is sometimes open, sometimes hidden, and sometimes repressed depending on whether prices rise, quality changes hide the inflation (or aggregate measures of inflation are distorted), or price controls create shortages.

Both Winiecki and Kornai are diametrically opposed to the views of some conventional economists (notably Richard Portes, a macroeconometric modeler) that comprised the "disequilibrium school." Briefly, this school held that a chronic, persistent and sizable imbalance between demand and supply is impossible, or alternately put, that disequilibrium cannot be a chronic feature of the centrally planned economies. In this view, correct price policies are sufficiently powerful to regain macroeconomic balances. (See Christopher and Charemza 1989; Portes 1981, 1989). Portes's approach clearly suffers from a number of methodological drawbacks; moreover, his research results squarely contradict well-known empirical facts, and need not be taken too seriously (see Brabant 1990).

4. Hans-Hermann Hoppe, in a recent work titled *A Theory of Socialism and Capitalism* (1989), contended that capitalism is morally superior to any form of socialism in the sense that capitalism respects, whereas every form of socialism violates, property rights belonging to some members of the society. He did not,

however, give convincing arguments about why private property rights itself are morally defensible, which would be necessary to prove the validity of his thesis.

5. While this assertion is generally true, we are confining our discourse to the realm of economics.

3

Vision, Capital and Development: The Tenets of Development and Feasible Strategies

THE PROBLEM OF DEVELOPMENT AS THE PROBLEM OF CAPITAL AND ANTICAPITAL IN THE INCLUSIVE SENSE

If central planning together with reform carried out only partially, the way it has been done in China, could not lift China out of its predicament, we have to look to other approaches for a tenable solution. Given that China is predominantly a developing country, it is natural that we should look at the host of existing development theories to see if there are promising strategies applicable to China's condition. Because it is possible that, in a hurried attempt to solve their immediate problems, policymakers in China will embrace any expedient or be lured into seemingly persuasive models of development without considering their full consequences, we will attempt in this chapter to review the fallacies of major approaches in development economics and to show the kind of considerations a tenable theory of development must take into account. Upon these foundations, some feasible strategies will subsequently be recommended.

The Changing Conceptions of Steering Resources in Development

Most accepted theories, especially those set forth during the early phase of development economics, operate with a narrow and "economistic" definition of capital. Early development theories could be said to draw their intellectual resources from the neoclassical and Keynesian growth models or from some blends of them. Among these early theories, the Harrod-Domar model served as a popular point of departure (Harrod 1939, Domar 1947). Characteristically, these theories conceived steering resources for development to be tangible capital and capital aggregates. Abstracting themselves from any institutional context, these theories and models implied strongly the "engineerability" of people and society. The general view shared by these theories was that development should and can be quickly attained by supplying what a developing nation allegedly lacks the most, namely, capital and technology. In these theories, the first question in development planning becomes, "How much total investment is needed to produce target increases in per capital income?" (Arndt 1987, p. 55). By corollary, incremental capital/output ratios are taken as the standard tool of development planning.

Shortly afterwards, these crude models were replaced by more sophisticated ones. While macroscopic parameters were still taken to be steering resources for development, structural factors that inhibited development or rendered the necessary conditions of development deficient were taken into account.[1] Dual economy models, of which Arthur Lewis's (1954) was a pioneering and paradigmatic one, represented this line of development. In these structural deficiency assumptions, development became a matter of choosing the right strategic designs to make up for these deficiencies. For example, the structural assumption that factors that contribute to economic growth, like demand and investment infrastructures, do not increase smoothly but rather are subject to sizable jumps or indivisibilities, justified big push strategies in development design (for example, Paul Rosenstein-Rodan 1943). In the same vein, the assumption of disguised employment in the agricultural sector logically suggested that the proper strategy for development is to transfer the surplus labor from the agricultural sector to the industrial sector. Whereas these structural assumptions appeared at first glance to be insightful, they were either generally lacking in micro-foundations or turned out to be false in their postulates of microeconomic behavior. In other words, they were not rooted in a careful analysis of the properties of the economic actor, in particular his motivational structure and perception of reality.

In the 1960s, a new awareness gradually dawned, shifting the conception of development resources as the tangible kind toward the conception of the less intangible human resources. In 1961, H. W. Singer declared that the fundamental problem of development was no longer the creation of wealth but rather the capacity to create wealth. That capacity was believed to reside in the people of a country, and to consist of brain power. This shift in thinking was, to no small extent, influenced by the economists' discovery of the importance of the "residual factor" responsible for economic growth. Economists, notably Moses Abramovitz (1956), Robert Solow (1957), and Edward Denison (1962, 1967), in their empirical studies of the aggregate production functions, first of the United States and then of other industrial countries, concluded that the explanation of economic growth and of the differences in the rates of economic growth among different countries had to be sought in the residual factor, which they identified with technical progress, or more generally, with advances in knowledge, chiefly those resulting from education. Development, in this view, became the way in which human resources could be stimulated, expanded and used to the fullest.

Human capital and, by extension, education, as a factor in economic growth were further developed by Schultz and Becker, who were also first concerned about the economic growth of the industrial countries. The ideas quickly spilled over to thinking about economic development in the Third World. As a consequence, they fostered the revival of interest in technical assistance from the industrial nations to the developing countries, and gave impetus to development strategies such as manpower development and planning. Such developments engendered the optimistic view that it was possible to define the optimal levels of the education budget in attaining specified growth targets. A large literature proliferated, extending the same mode of analysis to those aspects of human capital investments that lent themselves readily to aggregation and quantification, for example, the level of investment in health services. Being selectively concerned with aggregates and quantitative aspects, the advent of the idea of human capital did not, however, bring about a quest for a deeper understanding of the role of the subjective order underlying development. Hence these analyses generally lacked causal depth. As a matter of fact, the "human capital school" did not even challenge the prevailing orthodoxy of capital formation or the conventional objectives of development.

Once human resources were recognized to play a crucial role in economic development, the logical direction of enquiry would be to understand how human motivation driven by self-interest and material incentives is related to socioeconomic institutions. This, in part, spurred renewed interest in how the free market or the private enterprise economy unleash human incentives and direct the efficient allocation of resources. A "counterrevolution" was thus said to have taken place, with economists, notably Peter Bauer, vigorously contending that economic development is essentially the unleashing of market forces and individual incentives. By corollary, foreign aid, government intervention and redistributive measures are counterproductive because they negatively affect the decision making of atomistic individuals and because they negate the benefits that privately organized markets bring to a developing country. Convergent but not congenial to this position is another popular view that social institutions fostering certain types of cultural values, for example, Confucian ethics, play a crucial role in initiating and sustaining rapid development; however, the market is just one such social institution, and not necessarily one of the most efficacious. In this view, development consists in building the proper social institutions that foster cooperation among individuals and reduce transaction costs in the operation of the economy.

From the above account, one might discern that the idea of capital has gradually been expanded from the level of concrete, tangible capital goods to the less tangible level of human techniques, and then to the intangible level of human incentives and motivation. By corollary, one might also discern changes in policy recommendations with changes in how capital is conceived. As the idea of capital is expanded to embrace less tangible qualities, the recommended policies become less rigid and specific. One might refer to development designs consisting of concrete projects, specific plans, and so on, as "hard" designs, and refer to designs that aim to indirectly influence results by laying down ground rules and principles as "soft" designs. Hard designs are "constructivist" in nature, while soft designs are "cultivationist." As the conception of capital was broadened to embrace intangible dimensions in the history of development economics, hard designs gave way to soft designs and, by corollary, the role of government and planning was gradually deemphasized. With the recognition that the changes in the conception of capital have a decisive effect on the type of development strategies that are preferred, one might surmise that as we arrive at a more sophisticated conception of capital, we will be able to hammer out a completely different set of strategies for development.

The Ontology of Capital and Causal Depth

In spite of the above advances in the broadening of the conception of capital, one could still say that development economics has not gone far enough in this direction. The quest for quantification and aggregation and for the building of models based on measurable variables, driven by a false image of the scientific nature of the discipline, remains a stumbling block in taking bolder views. As a result, subjective qualities that are causally primary to human action and thereby to economic results are still very much neglected. However, subjective qualities are important because they occupy the initial section of the chains of economic events that give rise, in due course, to quantifiable results. We have shown in our analysis of the socialist system how moral values embedded in the economic actors affect economic performance. We can

further generalize this position by saying that the subjecfive qualities of the economic actor in general, for example, his self-image,
his perception of the future, and his desire for material gains, be
these of an ethical or a nonethical nature, are causally primary to
economic performance. In a broad sense, the subjective qualities
that promote positive economic performances could be conceived
as some kind of "capital" discharging a function not dissimilar to
that of physical capital or human capital (in the conventional sense
used by many economists). Such "subjective capital," lying at the
root of the causal chains of human actions, clearly affects the
quality of human capital (in the conventional sense), for how
people perceive themselves, how far they are prepared to make
sacrifices for future gains, what means they accept as proper for
attaining certain ends, and so forth, doubtless have a bearing on
how they will perform, in spite of the fact that there is no easy way
to quantify this kind of capital. In a similar way, it can be easily
demonstrated that subjective capital has an important bearing on
the efficacy of the employment of physical capital. We all know
too well that with different degrees of vigilance on the part of the
economic actor, the same set of equipment or machinery may yield
very different results in different production units. As a matter of
fact, misfits between physical capital and the human factor are a
big and common problem plaguing the socialist countries as well
as the developing nations. Hence, to say that subjective qualities
matter in development is more than a truism.

At the risk of oversimplification, we may say that the more a
theory of development is founded at the level of subjective capital
or takes such subjective dimensions as primary, the more causal
depth it can be said to possess. Conversely, a development theory
that takes its main variables from the later part of the causal chain
of events or that ignores the mediating factors at the level of the
subjective can be said to be lacking in causal depth. The methodological case for adopting the canon of causal depth is, however,
not obvious, and requires some elaboration. One advantage of a
causally deep theory is that it is less likely to omit the more
important factors in the necessary process of abstraction in theory

building. To this end, it might be objected that whereas the idea of causal depth is sound, it does not specify how deep one needs to search in order that no important variables be missed. In other words, one needs to establish why a particular level of discourse is inadequate in producing a theory powerful enough for a particular purpose. In our case, when we set out to explain differences in performances in economic development, we need to demonstrate why a strictly economic level is insufficient to provide the necessary causal variables to enable us to produce theories that satisfactorily explain differences in performance across different developing nations. To this end, one could easily point out that many countries that are less well endowed in respect to quantifiable capital unambiguously outperform many others that are much better endowed. Anomalies of this sort therefore suggest that the level of discourse at which these aggregates reside lacks adequate causal depth and that we should look to a deeper level for a more satisfactory explanation. By corollary, we should continue to dig deeper until our theory embraces sufficient causal depth for its explanatory purpose.

Another methodological justification of causal depth is this: Economic development in the prescriptive sense entails the assumption of the engineerability of people and society. However, it is clear that there is a limit to such engineerability. To understand this limit, we need to know what features in people and society are subject to engineering and the pace and degree of feasible engineering. This implies that any development theory, in order to generate the right kind of development strategies, inescapably demands an accurate diagnosis of the nature of humanity, in particular motivational structure and cognitive makeup. Hence, even in theory, one cannot escape the subjective level when developing a tenable theory of development and designing feasible strategies.

We have seen in the preceding chapter that some subjective qualities of the economic actor—for example, mutual distrust and suspicion—have clearly negative impacts on economic performance, both on an individual and a collective level. We might term these qualities as "anticapital," an antithesis to the idea of capital. Methodologically speaking, the importance of the idea of anticapital is twofold. First, it lends further justification to our methodological case for seeking more causal depth. Since these qualities cannot be captured by aggregates, they are inescapably omitted in a strictly "economistic" framework. Hence, the extension of the idea of anticapital beyond the economistic level is likely to be a fruitful approach. Second, certain subjective qualities—for example, desire for material gains—being neutral in themselves, are capable of being converted into either capital or anticapital depending on the specific socioeconomic conditions under which they operate. Therefore, one can hardly tell from aggregate facts the relative components of capital and anticapital for any economy, nor can one easily infer the existence of the latter. Hence, causal depth beyond the level of the manifest aggregates is necessary to isolate these capital components and endowments for a particular economy.

Anticapital and the "Hazard" Theory of Development

The significance of the idea of anticapital goes beyond providing the justification of the methodological canon of casual depth. It contributes importantly to our understanding of the causal complexities of dynamic systems, largely of an irreversible or not-so-easily reversible type, which characterize the modes of economic development in many developing nations. Development implies of necessity the replacement of an existing order by a new one. It implies the dismantling of structures in the old order, as well as the erection of new structures. The dismantling of the old order means that the new order under development is exposed to hazards of different kinds, for example, conflicts between different interest groups (see Perroux 1983). An adequate theory of development thus needs to consider the plausible range of hazards wrought by development. Only upon considering these possibilities can development policies be realistically designed with a view to forestalling such potential hazards. By the same logic, since no developing nation starts with the same set of physical, social and institutional endowments, a development theory should be able to identify what kinds of endowments pose obstacles to development and what endowments are helpful. A tenable development theory should therefore contain a subtheory about obstacles to development as well as about their removability. It should also posit the essential conditions that must be present for development and, if these endowments are missing, how they can be nurtured or cultivated.

The idea of anticapital, relating subjective qualities that hamper development to their sociocultural origins, helps to throw light on the nature of obstacles or potential hazards that the typical developing nation faces in the process of development. It is untrue to say that existing development theories entirely ignore the question of hazards. One important family of development theories focuses on the role of trade as an instrument for economic development. At the dawn of development economics, Paul Prebisch and Gunnar Myrdal already contended that far from acting as an engine of economic growth, international trade was responsible for hindering development (Prebisch 1949). The main argument made by Raul Prebisch was that because of inelastic world demand for primary products and a combination of monopolistic pricing of manufactures with competitive markets for primary commodities, the "periphery" tends to transfer a part of the benefits accruing from its technical progress to the "centers," while the latter retain their own benefits for themselves. Gunnar Myrdal, on the other hand, posited that international trade, contrary to what the equilibrium theory would seem to suggest, does not work toward equality in the remuneration to factors of production and consequently to income. On the contrary, the underdeveloped countries find their traditional industries ruined by cheap imports and their skills becoming impoverished (1956).

Partly inspired by these conceptions, a host of "dependency theories" evolved, harping on the theme that the relationship between the center (the host) and the periphery (the developing countries) is one not only of unequal sharing of the benefits of development, but also one of dependence involving domination and economic exploitation. The result is "peripheral capitalism," a kind of parasitic and flimsy capitalism incapable of providing the necessary basis for proper development. In the hands of Osvaldo Sunkel, this thesis took on a broader perspective, positing that such dependency is an inescapable manifestation of the historical process of global development of the international system leading to increasing polarization in different spheres (1969). In a more radical version advanced by A. G. Frank, the thesis asserted that it is capitalism, both world and national, that produced underdevelopment in the past and that continues to do so (1971).

The center-periphery thesis and its attendant dependency theories are not bona fide "hazard" theories in our sense because they are not founded on a dissertation of the nature of anticapital and its mode of operation. The more radical versions in particular are macroscopic and long-view theories that make relatively little reference to the micro-foundations of human incentives and disincentives. Congenial to our view, but theorizing on a less macroscopic and dynamic basis, are the host of "structuralist" theories that dissect the weaknesses of the price system, or more precisely put, the nature of market failures. The key elements of the price system, namely the signaling component, the response component and the mobility component, were all called into question by these theories. They were found to be malfunctioning in the context of the developing country characterized by monopolistic or oligopolistic markets, by economic actors that are lukewarm to the profit motive and by the low mobility of both the labor and the capital markets. Paul Rosenstein-Rodan (1951) and Tibor Scitovsky (1970), for example, emphasized the inadequacy of prices as a guide to investment decisions. Gunnar Myrdal and Hans Singer, on the other hand, stressed that the free play of market forces generates unacceptable social costs and aggravates inequality both nationally and internationally (see Myrdal 1957, Singer 1950). The result is that the proper kind of development we expect may not be forthcoming in the developing nation. Because of the general poverty that prevails in developing nations and because the government has limited scope for policy interference, "even short-term changes are continuously liable to start a development toward some sort of public disaster" (Arndt 1987, p. 125).

On the whole, structuralist theories deal with the level of cost and price structures and emphasize supply-side rigidities that distort them. Implicit in their metaphysics is the view that in the developing nation, the supply of most things is inelastic. This, together with the corollary that the price system functions defectively there, is said to adequately explain the phenomenon of structural inflationary disequilibrium that prevails in much of Latin America. On the whole, the contribution of structuralist thinking is that it alerts us to the defective properties of a developing economy, how these defects limit policy options, and how the choice of improper policies may lead to disasters. In this regard, they could be looked on as some kind of "hazard" theories of development and are helpful in our understanding of the nature of underdevelopment. However, existing structuralist theories, stressing the relation between economic variables and institutional parameters, seldom reach out to the level of human resources and motivation, and still less to the level of human cognition and value systems that in turn mould the shape of economic motivation. Human visions of the future, moral qualities that affect personal commitments to work and collective values that affect interpersonal relations in team work (for example, envy and suspicion) are seldom explored. Thus, while these hazard theories of development have more interesting explanations than conventional development theories in accounting for the diversity of development experiences, they have not as yet, partly by virtue of their relativist outlook, been able to give an adequate account of development hazards based on a comprehensive analysis of the notions of capital and anticapital.

With the above discussion, one may attempt to reformulate the problem of development. If a deeper understanding of the underlying mechanisms of development and its hazards is conditional on a deeper and broader understanding of the conception of capital, a tenable theory of development that enables us to reach sufficient causal depth and to become sensitized to different aspects of hazards clearly has to embrace an encompassing theory of capital and anticapital. The problem of development becomes how policies should be designed upon our proper knowledge in the broadest sense of capital and its antithesis, anticapital, as well as of the mechanisms and conditions for generating or harnessing such steering resources. The problem of development, in a nutshell, is the problem of capital in the generalized sense.

Toward an Inclusive Concept of Capital and Anticapital

The relevance of an expanded conception of capital to a tenable theory of development means that we should further explore new dimensions of the notion of capital. The task of this section is to explore different levels of capital in order to arrive at an inclusive concept. It is hoped that the exercise will shed light on the essential ontological properties of capital and, by extension, those of anticapital. Together, the properties of these complementary concepts constitute the main thrust of the problem of development.

Accepting the methodological canon of causal depth and causal primacy means that for explanatory fruitfulness, we have to consider the concept of capital from the level of the mind. At this level, we posit that the vision of the future held by the economic actors together with their moral values are the most outstanding factors, because together they govern their motivations as well as their interpersonal relations. We have already pointed out how moral qualities affect economic performance. In a subsequent section, we will examine the way in which visions of the future held by economic actors affect their economic plans and decisions. While we acknowledge deep relations between human visions of the future and moral values, we will pass over them at this time. Suffice it to say that since human motivations and interpersonal relations have clear effects on economic performance, we can say that human visions of the future and our moral values constitute the thrust of capital at the intangible, subjective level.

Above the strictly intangible stratum of human capital residing at the level of the mind, one might consider a semitangible level consisting in the specific skill and knowledge possessed by the economic actor. This is the level at which economists conventionally define human capital, although their interest lies more in the quantitative indicators of such capital than in the internal mechanisms governing its generation.[2] Beyond this semitangible level is the level of concrete, tangible capital familiar to the economic theorist, in the form of physical objects such as equipment and machinery, or in the form of financial assets that make claims over other forms of capital. Within this level, we can discern two sublevels, one consisting of capital owned by individual economic actors or agents (including the firm), while the other consists of public capital owned by society as a whole.

There is a wide array of factors and socioeconomic conditions that induce or discourage the formation of the different components of physical and human capital mentioned above. Among others, one can include, for example, the commitment of the government toward providing the necessary legal and constitutional framework, and its commitment to enforcing the rule of law, building infrastructural projects, and so on. One could also include factors at the societal level, such as society's legal tradition, its overall ethos and values that foster conditions that favor or reject free competition, promote or inhibit investment in education, approve or disapprove of team work and cooperation, or value work over enjoyment (or the other way around).

One important question is this: Should we consider the above-mentioned societal factors and conditions as exogeneous to the idea of capital or should we include these factors as part of an all-inclusive conception of capital? By all accounts, the latter seems to be an odd proposition. On the philosophical plane, it is also questionable whether such an all-inclusive concept of capital consisting of different layers of discourse would not commit us to making the so-called "category mistake." On the other hand, there seem to be compelling reasons for taking on an all-inclusive concept. First, like the idea of value, capital is essentially a "relational" concept.[3] A set of equipment does not by itself constitute capital, unless there is the right kind of skill to use and monitor it. An individual's vision of the future will be a meaningless concept if it is not related to the visions of other economic actors or to the collective vision of society as a whole. Similarly, the sense of responsibility of any individual would never function as a kind of capital in a world of unscrupulous economic actors on whom no standard codes of conduct are binding. In other words, neither a subjective attribute nor physical equipment will count as capital unless it stands in some definite relation either to other kinds of capital or to certain socioeconomic factors and conditions.

This relational property is even more outstanding in the case of anticapital. This is because there is no easily identifiable counterpart for anticapital at the level of the physical and the concrete. Anticapital—for example, mutual distrust, envy, and irresponsibility—resides largely at the level of the intangible and only manifests itself as results at the level of the concrete. Physical capital that has no use or has zero value, or that incurs debt that exceeds its face value might in some sense be called anticapital. However, these are rare cases and are relatively insignificant in comparison with the noticeably destructive effects of anticapital at the level of the intangible. Also of importance is the fact that certain intangible attributes of the economic actor, like greed, only count as anticapital under certain socioeconomic conditions. The same property could function as capital under an entirely different set of socioeconomic conditions. This means that without an all-inclusive conception of capital or anticapital embracing the level of social values and institutions, we will not be in a position to distinguish between capital and anticapital in some cases. Failure to identify anticapital in an economic system means in turn that we will not be able to deal with potential hazards that beset an economy and will handicap our understanding of the dynamic pathways that lead to disequilibrium situations.

Another justification for the case of an inclusive concept of capital is this: If we take socio-institutional factors and values as part of the concept of capital that we can call "social" capital, the concept's multifaceted and multilayered nature would render it more fruitful and powerful. We can now legitimately speak of the formation of capital at this macroscopic level. We are consequently compelled to be more attentive to the multifarious relations between the different layers of capital, namely social capital, tangible capital and intangible human capital. It will become necessary for us to uncover laws and regularities that govern the relations between these layers, to ensure that the assertions we make are "interlevel-compatible" and to eliminate policies that may arise from the incompatibilities. It will also become necessary for us to appraise policy designs more comprehensively in terms of how far they promote or discourage capital formation in a generalized sense.

An additional advantage of espousing an "economy-wide" conception of capital is this: Once the development of an economy starts to depend critically on the division of labor or the requirement of using more than one factor of production, a fruitful concept of capital as the productive resources commanded by an economy, as well as the efficiency of a particular kind of capital, has to depend on the relations between a multiplicity of economy-wide factors that affect, ultimately at the level of the economic actors, how such factors promote or impede the desires and capabilities of these actors. A "generalized" conception of capital cutting across different levels of human reality is, therefore, in line with the fundamental characteristic of capital in a multifactor production system. Capital, in the ultimate analysis, is inescapably a relational and holistic concept.[4]

The understanding of the ontological properties of capital, that is, its foundational, structural characteristics, is crucial not only to arriving at a fruitful definition of the notion of capital, but also to deepening our understanding of the supply-side characteristics of an economy, as well as to designing policies to promote development. If what count as productive resources are to be extended to how these resources are organized, then as Marx rightly observed, the way the economy is organized socially and politically will have important ramifications for any set of tangible capital. If capital is defined in an inclusive, economy-wide sense, it can no longer be taken as exogeneous to an economic system. The total stock of capital possessed by an economy in a second round must necessarily be affected by the very products of its capital in the first round, because the distribution of that product can no longer be considered as neutral to the incentives of economic actors. In other words, capital in the inclusive sense will compel us to look at how capital in a particular phase will affect both the level and the quality of capital at a subsequent phase. Such complexity probably explains why it proves so difficult to strictly relate the physical capital endowment of an economy to its performance. The holism of the concept of capital does not mean that we will end up with the truism that everything depends on everything else. The requirements of causal depth and causal primacy necessitate that we take the level of the human mind as the first level of discourse. Within this level we have to further identify a set of core concepts as the point of departure for positing a theory of development. Within this core, the primacy of the human vision of the future stands out clearly.

Human Vision of the Future as Capital: Cognitive Foundations

The reason for studying the nature and structure of human visions of the future in theories of development is that we consider it a fundamental thesis that human plans that lead to human actions, of which the generation and allocation of resources are a part, are critically dependent on human visions of the future. As a matter of fact, human visions of the future could be taken as the distinguishing mark of humankind. Whereas both people and other animals possess the capacity of visualizing what is real, the possession of extensive nonreal visions, namely "imaginations," may be said to be unique to humans.[5] This special property of humankind could be conceived to be the logical development of the human brain and a necessary extension of our representational capabilities. While most animals can form mental representations in some analogue with reality only when reality as such is present, the enormous brain size that makes room for the development of the human memory has enabled us to possess a powerful capacity to store mental representations and to retrieve them at will, even when reality as such is not immediately present. A further corollary of this power to form images without the corresponding presence of reality is that we can produce them in sequences that need not have any analogue in reality. The possession of representational powers of this dimension means that we can freely form images in anticipation of events, namely, visions of the future. These constructions may have some corelations to the subsequent unfolding of events or may just be mental inventions without an analogue to what will happen later.

In relatively simple animals such as insects or fish, perception is driven entirely by sensory information. The way information is interpreted is determined by the innate organization of the neural circuits involved. By contrast, mammalian perception depends not only on sensory information, but also on other activities in the brain. In this regard, learning plays a major role in the interpretation of sensation. As a result, mammals are able to bring additional sources of information to bear on the interpretation of sensation, and they become increasingly adept interpreting the kinds of sensations they normally experience. This not only gives them a more powerful and flexible kind of perception, it also provides the essential conditions for imagination. Once perceptual activities become sufficiently automatic, it is possible for them to be triggered by internal events alone without any input from the senses (see Taylor 1983).

An important subset of human imagination is the individual's vision of the future, and this turns out to be of great causal relevance to the evolution and progress of humanity. Of far-reaching importance is the fact that visions of the future provide, together with other factors, the foundation of our conception of values and meanings, for the ability to anticipate what will happen in the future is the necessary condition for the meaning we attribute to a large part of our actions. With the invention of a "conceptual future," we can calibrate and compare the relative values of our present and future actions as well as the values of our present and future pleasures. Upon this foundation, the important ability of humans to postpone our innate craving for immediate gratification has been developed, whereas this craving is characteristic of lower creatures (Bronowski 1973). This ability to postpone present gratification in exchange for bigger potential gratification in the future in turn provides the essential causal basis of our willingness to work toward material improvement.

Not all human visions of the future direct us to postpone our immediate craving for gratification. Some of these visions are whimsical or are only dimly related to reality. Visions of this type are studied in psychology, and they have little relevance to economic actions. For visions of the future to have bearing on economic results, they must somehow be pegged to reality and to the level of resources possessed by the economic actor. In other words, they have to be plausible and reachable. Realistic human visions of the future are, therefore, generally characterized by a sequence of subvisions, each of which is linked to a subset of the economic actor's plan in deploying his resources. In turn, these plans are rooted in the individual actor's repertoire of skills, experiences and material resources, and connected voluntarily or through contractual relations with the plans of other economic actors. Given their essential openness, these visions are generally volatile and are subject to revision along with changes in reality. While they are causally primary in the sense that they direct human plans and actions, they are nonetheless also causally affected by changes in the human reality. A kind of interactionism therefore appropriately describes the two-way traffic between human visions of the future and human reality.

If what happens in reality is able to augment, sustain or diminish human vision, we need to posit the essential features in these happenings that have these respective effects. It sounds like a truism, but it is the case that the more these visions correspond to what really happens in the course of time, the more likely it is that they will be sustained. Should reality turn out to match a previously held vision nicely, the holder of that vision may further augment the span of his subsequent visions. This in turn may prompt him to shuffle more present resources to invest in that "extended" future or to substantiate his already made plans. However, if reality turns out to only poorly match his vision for a sustained period of time, the rational actor will have to curtail the span of his vision, either to avoid further loss or to restore some kind of psychological balance to such a chronic mismatch. In other words, one can detect a kind of self-fulfilling process in the augmentation and closure of vision, with reality setting off either a virtuous or a vicious circle in the vision formation and vision maintenance of an economic actor. Since reality is generally of a continuous nature and acts to regulate changes of these visions in small steps, the latter are generally of an incremental character, capable of fine-turning and continual revision.

Apart from their links with reality, the visions held by an economic actor are also sustained by their links and bonds with the visions of other economic actors, as well as by the "collective vision" held by the community as a whole. The latter, in turn, is shaped by the cultural heritage, social ethos and ideological biases transmitted through different generations in society. Indeed, individual visions in the same community are often holistically and intricately bound with one another, to the extent that a community as a whole can be said to possess a rather uniform span of vision. By corollary, different communities often command divergent spans of collective visions. Apart from institutional features such as the rule of law, the existence of private property rights, and so forth, which are crucial to the maintenance of a long-range vision of a society, there is the fact that there exist among economic actors highly diverse spans of visions which are complementary to one another. The plans of economic actors with longer-range visions provide the very frames within which the visions of others are structured or materialize. In turn, the former will be able to form even longer-range plans, knowing that others will follow them. These expanding visions thus have the self-fulfilling effect of shuffling society's resources toward building the future. The reverse also holds. A society plagued by inflation that closes down vision, that disproportionately rewards rent-seeking activities, and that allows corruption to distort the direct relations between reward and effort will inescapably lead to the self-defeating processes of vision-closure. The result is that resources that are intended for investing in the future will be reshuffled toward present consumption. A society thus becomes "visionless" if a predominant number of its members resort to present consumption, refuse to postpone their craving for gratification to some future date, possess no resources to back up any long-range visions they may have, or lack feasible plans to mediate between their visions and reality.

From this perspective, the socialist system, both in theory and in practice, can be interpreted to suffer from a kind of fatal "schism." At the level of the individual, the span of vision is typically very short, since the individual possesses no material resources of his own with which to make any long-term plans. Neither is he motivated to augment his intangible human capital because, economic results being largely predetermined, the returns to such investments are indeterminate, if not negative in some cases. Ignoring this crucial fact, the socialist government invariably attempts to set up long-range collective visions as blueprints for development by using fixed time-frame instruments such as five-year plans. However, these grand visions are hardly shared by the individual actors because they are too remotely related to the latter's short-range visions. The existence of such a schism means that the grand visions entertained by the political authority lack support from the masses.[6] Hence, socialism is a contradiction in itself.

Feasible and action-directing visions are strongly related to and interdependent on the moral qualities of the individual. Without a sense of responsibility for one's actions on the part of the individual, or the willingness to accept the verdict of nonarbitrary rules, his visions would easily become subject to the vagaries of reality, making long-range plans no longer practicable or feasible. On the other hand, an economic actor would not have the opportunity to learn about the very idea of self-responsibility nor be able to accept the consequences arising from such actions if he himself does not possess some disposable resources. Without the back-up of disposable resources, these actors would not have developed sensible and practical ideas of what risk-taking entails, and thereby would not have nourished the moral courage to accept the results of his risk-taking actions. Without such experiences, it would be inconceivable that he could learn from his failures or stage any comebacks. All in all, a moral economic actor has to be a visionary actor in the first instance, and an actor can only become visionary if he possesses disposable resources that he can call his own. The idea of private property rights can thus be theoretically justified at the deeper level of intangible capital, that of human visions and morality.

Without individual actors willing to hold themselves accountable for the results of their own actions, the trust factor will not play a significant role in improving the efficiency of economic transactions and in reducing the "overhead" in the operation of some economies. More explicitly formulated, one might say that the trust factor can only be operational in a society of responsible individuals with long-range visions, and in a society with explicit rules of the game as well as long-range collective visions. No wonder economists find that this factor is very much lacking in, say, Latin American countries which are plagued by inflation and forced to operate largely on a cash basis.

In summary, we might say that human visions of the future are causally a primary part of economic development in that they constitute the fundamental part of capital in a generalized sense. Visions are fundamental in that they direct our plans regarding the allocation and shuffling of resources toward investment for the future, give meaning and value to present acts of abstinence, nurture the proper kind of moral values that underpin an effective economic order, and motivate the acquisition of knowledge that is necessary to the tapping of opportunities. "Opportunity signal," conventionally considered by nonorthodox economists to be essential to entrepreneurial activities, will be a more fruitful concept if it is supported by the view that visions are primary economic inputs.

The ramifications of taking human visions as primary economic inputs that are essential to economic development are multifold. First, since human visions are sensitive and elastic to institutional arrangements, research should emphasize how visions can be effectively nurtured under different institutional regimes. Second, since development designs should be directed toward the nurture of visions, the effectiveness of designs can now be appraised in terms of the scope and quality of the visions that they nurture. Third, since human visions can be at once volatile and rigid (depending on what types of institutional backgrounds are presumed), and invariably take time to nurture, soft designs that operate in longer time frames are, as a rule, more effective. This probably explains why hard designs, which are largely concerned with directing physical resources, are less appropriate than soft designs for the unleashing of vision centered human resources, which take much longer time to materialize. Development, in this view, can be seen metaphorically as associated with the expanding pictures of the future held by individual participants, and effective designs of development can be seen as designs that expand these visions.

ANTICAPITAL AND THE HAZARDS OF DEVELOPMENT

Anticapital, Vision and Hazards of Development

If human visions of the future are to be conceived as primary economic inputs, any theory of development or any development policy can be fruitfully appraised in terms of its vision-augmenting or vision-closing effects both for the short run and for the long run. Factors such as rent-seeking behaviors, corruption, and inflationary pressures (beyond a certain point) are known to have vision-closing effects, and hence constitute part of anticapital in the sense in which we have defined it. They are vision-closing in that they distort the rules of the game, the sense of value on which these visions critically depend or the relations between reality and expectations embodied in such visions. As a result, resources earmarked for the future are shuffled back toward present gratification, diminishing the total capital stock of the economy in question. Expectedly, these effects operate in a self-fulfilling or self-reinforcing process. A vision-closing system would direct the attention of its economic actors toward short-term gains. Apart from channeling resources away from long-term investment, and hence depressing the system's total level of investment, such a mentality easily triggers actions that violate existing rules of the game or propensities that bias toward corrupt and rent-seeking behaviors. The latter, as we have noted, have self-reinforcing effects, triggering a scramble for further short-term gains, and hence speeding up the rate of collapse of the originally held visions and their embodied expectations.

Of special significance is the fact that vision-closing effects are accompanied by emotions and fears that have deep demoralizing effects on existing value systems and moral codes. Fears once triggered will have contagious effects and will set off protective strategies on the part of the economic actors, for example, the strategy of minimizing maximal loss. Once these strategies are universally adopted, they will become self-defeating, leading to a new round of fear and protection. In other words, vision-closure and anticapital causally reinforce each other. On the one hand, the closure of vision spurs the formation of more anticapital—for example, irresponsibility and envy—as economic actors rush to realize their gains or protect their positions by minimizing loss. On the other hand, the proliferation of anticapital has important vision-closing effects by way of disrupting existing patterns of reward-effort relations and thereby the returns to investment in the future.

Being self-reinforcing by nature, anticapital is reproducible under certain sets of socioeconomic conditions and institutions. Beyond a point, its reproduction will impede the operation of existing capital, as well as those institutions that produce capital, by way of reducing the span of vision held by the economic actors in question. As a metaphor, one might liken anticapital, as far as its function is concerned, to cancer cells in the human body. Just as cancer cells, through their proliferation, prohibit the normal functioning of other cells, anticapital, upon proliferating, will de-capitalize the capital base of the economy. This in turn will reduce the range of feasible options open to the economy's policy-makers. Thus, the hazards posed by anticapital to development are similar to the way in which cancer endangers the life of the human body through the process of first ousting the resources, both tangible and intangible, and then reducing options of its economic actors. The results are the same in both cases. Both the body and the economy are set off on a dynamic path of impoverishment. However, we should not carry the metaphor too far, for the economy will still survive, no matter in what wretched form it ends up. Indeed, in the case of the economy, as circumstances worsen, the increasing impoverishment of its resources may trigger a mentality of self-preservation among its economic actors. Not only will their readiness to expand their human capital in terms of accumulating knowledge and skill be negatively affected, but the social capital of the economy in question in terms of mutual trust and coopera-tion among economic actors will also be badly shattered.

By way of illustration, we will briefly examine some mecha-nisms that have the effect of anticapital formation. These include (a) the engendering of demand-side expectations among the eco-nomic actors outstripping their supply-side capabilities, (b) the proliferation of rent-seeking behaviors, and (c) the polarization of resources among the economic actors. In the preceding chapter, we have already discussed at some length how the supply-side capa-bilities of the economic actors in a capitalist system serve to regulate their demand-side expectations by enhancing their moti-vation to better their skills and knowledge while keeping their expectations in line with their capabilities. Unfortunately, as in the case of the socialist country, such a self-regulating mechanism is absent in a typical developing nation. On the side of demand-side expectations, its economic actors acquire painlessly and almost instantaneously both the desires and the superficial knowledge about consumer goods produced by the West via demonstration effects. On the other hand, there are, as a rule, formidable structural rigidities in such a system that inhibit its economic actors from acquiring the know-how needed to earn the spending power they want.

This asymmetry is nothing but natural. Improvement of supply-side capabilities takes time to achieve. It requires on the part of the average economic actor either the willingness to abstain from current consumption or the willingness to exert extra efforts, backed up by a strong conviction in a future that rewards those who continually exploit opportunities. Clearly, in the developing nations, the relations between return received and effort expended by an individual are governed by a large number of contingencies beyond the individual's control. Typically, most economic actors find it difficult to attain the minimum resources needed to exploit the opportuniites that exist in this kind of economy.

On the demand side, consumer goods are always available in small denominations. The piece-rate system and the weekly pay system that one usually finds in developing countries serve to nurture and reflect such a short-term mentality. Cultural institutions prevalent in many developing countries—chiefly the extended family, which provides a kind of insurance system for the individual—also make immediate consumption a logical proposition. As we have previously pointed out, economic actors who have scant resources under their control and who find the buildup of supply-side capabilities irrelevant to their life-style tend to identify themselves psychologically with consumption, especially conspicuous consumption. Owing to the rigidities of the system in question, such rising expectations usually have a minimal effect on the economic actor in improving his capabilities. On the contrary, they tend to give a higher premium to present values, thus further discouraging both the willpower and the effort necessary to make investments for the future.

Once converted to the values upheld by the West, a developing country will embrace more and more goods of Western origin, to the extent that even the idea of basic needs will gradually extend its scope. For example, it is now considered necessary by many to use Western drugs and medicines, infant feeding formula, and so on. Embracing such Western-type goods either out of a changing conception of basic needs or out of the desire to imitate the Western life-style means that a developing country will soon find its ability to pay for such imports very much in question. To cope with such rising demands or for fear of the political consequences of sup- pressing them, a developing country is invariably compelled to incur chronic trade deficits and debts, a subject we will address in a later section.

As in the case of a socialist country, the government in a developing country is eager to see speedy and concrete results. As a result, it will hardly be able to resist the temptation to engage in massive development projects, chiefly infrastructural ones, regard- less of the long-term consequences of these "top-down" measures and regardless of the initial endowment of the economy in ques- tion. Since a developing country is typically short of the right kind of skills and expertise, and since a lot of these imported projects involve state-of-the-art techniques, their implementation will fall to the small group of the country's elites, including government officials, in spite of the fact that this group may not be qualified for the projects. These elites, usually lacking the right expertise but occupying the key managerial positions, will rely heavily on expatriates and foreign corporations, preferably those that were connected to them in the colonial or early postcolonial days. Out of self-interest, this group of elites will naturally exploit these projects to their own advantage. A portion of such acts are, of course, blatantly illegal. Where they fall within the margin of the law, they are inescapably rent-seeking in character, earning profits that have little relation to real effort, improved productivity, pro- duct innovation or creative marketing.

The result of having such handsomely profitable projects thrust upon this group is that the people most qualified to perform the entrepreneurial functions in a developing nation are lured to the most counterproductive activities. Corruption and rent-seeking behavior, as we have pointed out, distort the ground rules essential to the sustaining of visions. Corruption on the part of those who hold the key to power means that the stipulated rules of the game are rendered nonsensical. The result of more people becoming engaged in corruption means that the cost of corruption will increase as its effectiveness declines. Beyond a point, only a few can afford the game or play it successfully. The proliferation of rent-seeking behavior means less people are interested in real production activities and, as less output is produced in subsequent rounds, more players will become losers. Under such a regime, it is no longer profitable to invest in human capital formation. With huge rent heaped upon a group of elites, the man in the street will have to bear not only the burden of the government's spending spree and the mistakes of many a white elephant project, but also the interest cost required to service the debts so incurred. In other words, the present assets of the average economic actor are reduced and their future assets are mortgaged as these become redistributed to the small group of elites and their foreign connections.

The effects of such polarization are devastating. We have said that the ownership of a minimal level of assets or resources to the extent that the economic actor can shuffle some of such resources for investing in the future is instrumental to the nurturing of his visions of the future, from which his other motivations arise. Such minimal holding, enabling the economic actor to survive the present and to spare resources to build for the future, is essential to his continued will to struggle and ability to vest meaning and value in the future. Polarization of resources will, beyond a point, have a mass vision-closing effect on economic actors at the grass roots. We have also said that the individualistic system of morality, upon which capitalism flourishes, depends on the possession of some minimal resources on the part of the individual sufficient for him to make autonomous and responsible decisions (as opposed to the cases where his actions are compelled by the force of circumstances) and to learn to bear the consequences of his decisions and actions. A deep sense of responsibility cannot, therefore, truly develop without a material base that permits such autonomous decisions. In reducing such a material base, polarization and impoverishment may, beyond a certain point, demolish an existing moral order that is productive of human capital and replace it by a moral order (or disorder) of extreme egoistic individualism fostered by the mere concern of survival.

One might, however, contend that whereas large industrial or infrastructural projects initiated by the government may breed corrupt or rent-seeking behaviors, they are still needed to create employment for the masses and give them the opportunity to acquire the proper skills in a modern economy. It is also hoped that a more skillful labor force will attract more investment from multinational corporations. This hope, however, is not necessarily well-founded. Many of these government projects require the importation of foreign skills, leaving the low-level work to the local people. While it is possible that over time, the local labor force, at the supervisory, junior managerial, or junior technical level, will acquire better skills on the job, the rate at which these skills build up will depend very much on local conditions. Developing countries with diverse cultural backgrounds will experience different rates in the buildup of their stock of skills. This means that not all developing nations benefit equally from upgrading their labor force. As a matter of fact, a process of natural selection takes place, with the countries that manage to forge ahead earlier attracting a disproportionately higher level of foreign investment than the others. The result is that countries that fail to create a highly adaptive work force quickly enough will lose out, setting off a vicious circle that renders them less competitive and less attractive in the international investment scene.

In the first round, these government-initiated projects may provide employment to a considerable number of workers, probably drawing an exodus of labor from the countryside. However, the nonprofitability of many of these projects will be gradually rendered obvious and will not last indefinitely. The eventual scrapping of some of these means that many workers will lose their jobs, and, in time, the skills they have acquired. With prolonged unemployment, workers who have deserted their homelands to settle in the urban centers will be thrown into despair, contributing to the political instability characteristic of many developing countries. Attempts to pacify these unemployed people through welfare schemes in turn means that the government will be compelled to incur further deficits which it has little hope of repaying. Development in these countries, instead of unleashing supply-side resources, often has the unintended effect of stripping many of its human actors of their basic capacity to look after their own needs. Moreover, unless the kind of structural deficiencies here analyzed can be made up for or forestalled in development designs, chances are that a developing country with a rigid supply-side framework may end up being trapped in a vicious circle.

Interlocking Vicious Circles of Deficit and Inflation, and Anticapital Formation

Most developing nations on the miserable pole of development face, either separately or jointly, the twin problems of inflation and deficit. In many instances, these two problems reinforce one another, moving the economy in vicious circles and eventually leading it either toward a low-level equilibrium trap or a phase of explosive disequilibrium before plunging it into a lower-level equilibrium.

Very much opposed to the views held earlier, inflation as a development strategy is now generally perceived as too hazardous to be considered tenable. In the earlier days of development economics, a number of economists, such as Robert Mundell (1965), held the view that an inflationary policy could be beneficial to development. They contended that inflation enables government to control a larger share of resources and use inflationary credit to redistribute income from wage earners who save little to capitalists with higher rates of productive capital formation, as well as enabling the economy to move toward full employment and channel resources from traditional sectors to the rapidly growing sectors.

Whereas there are still controversies over the empirical relations between inflation and growth, the negative impacts of inflation on development should be nothing but obvious.[7] One negative impact is that inflation tends to distort the real rates of return between different sectors and different types of financial assets (see McKinnon 1973). Another argument against inflation and the inflation tax is that they can easily get out of hand. Great caution is needed to contain them to the level where they will stimulate growth, especially if one considers the fact that monetary and fiscal instruments in a developing country are usually too weak to contain inflation without sacrificing real income, employment, and social welfare programs. Furthermore, inflation increases the prices of domestic goods relative to the prices of foreign goods. This adversely affects the competitiveness of domestic goods in the international markets and usually leads to current account deficits. Inflation also discourages the inflow of foreign capital by eroding the real values of investment and future repatriated earnings. Large international deficits which often come with rapid inflation can further increase debt burdens and limit "essential" imports.

In a mature market economy, mild inflation usually signifies up-and-coming opportunities, enabling producers to step up their supply of goods. These opportunities, however, are not readily accessible to producers in a developing country that is immersed in structural rigidities and haunted by uncertainty in cost structures. Uncertainty in cost, owing to corruption, government overregulation, and similar factors, also reduces the amount of opportunity signals available while at the same time raising both the subjective and the objective probabilities of risk.

The negative impacts of inflation go beyond the manifest levels. Inflation strikes at the very root of development by inducing extensive anticapital formation. We have analyzed how the dominance of demand-side expectations erodes the sense of self-responsibility among economic actors, how the proliferation of rent-seeking behavior reduces exploitable opportunities and how polarization of wealth and income forces the masses to focus on present values. Inflation is both the cause and the effect of these phenomena. By reducing the future value of money and, by corollary, the value of present abstinence, inflation compels economic actors to give up investing in the future and to scramble for whatever is available for exchange at the moment. Conflicts among different interest groups will prevail as a protectionist mentality is being fostered. What mutual trust and cooperation exist will therefore evaporate in a regime of escalating inflation. Another familiar result is that people will have to spend a disproportionately large part of their time and attention to cope with the administrative burdens imposed by fast-changing prices.

As much as a developing country is inflation-prone, it is also deficit-prone. We have already seen how the chronic excess of the demand of a developing country over its exchange-earning capacity leads it inescapably into chronic balance-of-trade deficits. Such chronic trade deficits, on the other hand, are caused to no small extent by the relative composition of its exports and imports. Typical of a developing nation, a larger proportion of its imports are manufactured goods characterized by prices that are relatively inelastic compared to those of its exports. Besides, inflation and deficits are interlocking phenomena. At the risk of oversimplification, their dynamic relations can be represented in the following: inflation tends to discourage the inflow of foreign capital and frighten away domestic capital, unless very high interest rates are maintained. However, maintaining high interest rates means that new opportunities for profitable investment in the economy will be drastically reduced and existing investments will have to bear high financial costs. This means that in the next round there will be less domestic production and fewer exports, leading to a further deterioration of the balance of trade. The prevalence of a regime of high inflation means that the economic actors will have to resort to hoarding goods or inputs and to managing their affairs on a cash basis. Both imply that transaction costs will rise and that the economy will lose a significant part of its efficiency. In turn, the increased inefficiency will lead to lower and less competitive levels of production and export, which will be manifested in further balance-of-trade and payment deficits. Clearly, these interlocking relations will, after a point, develop into a runaway situation as both inflation and the service costs of debts build up at compound rates. What has been happening in the Latin American countries is a classical manifestation of these vicious circles at work. The result is a severe polarization of wealth and income, as inflation redistributes the resources of the economy in favor of the more powerful groups, causing degeneration in the average standard of living among the masses.

THE MARKET/GOVERNMENT CONTROVERSY AND SOME FEASIBLE DEVELOPMENT STRATEGIES

The Visionary Theory of Development and the Market/Government Controversy

It is not the intention of this work to give a detailed account of the debate concerning the market/government controversy with its enormous literature. However, the discussion of development as conducted in the above does compel us to rethink the fundamentals of this controversy. The following brief discussion, with the aid of the inclusive conception of capital and the conception of vision as primary economic inputs, will attempt to reformulate this controversy in some broader terms and to show that an eclectic position founded on these ideas may be a tenable one. We have reformulated the development problem as a problem of capital and anticapital formation. The task of development is to foster the formation of capital (in the broad sense) while preventing the formation of anticapital. The latter task, as we have shown, is important because the typical developing country is beset with conditions that favor the flourishing of anticapital.

The presence of supply-side rigidities and a skewed distribution of resources and economic power means that market failures are characteristic of a developing economy. The question for development is how these different market failures are to be identified and made up for. It is recognized by now that there are many types of market failures, even in the developed countries (see Greenwald and Stiglitz 1986). It is therefore not surprising that market failures are widely prevalent in the developing countries. Theoretically, on the assumption that the dessemination of knowledge and information is less than perfect in an economy, its markets, by corollary, cannot be perfectly competitive. Earlier entrants will tend to enjoy monopoly rents. If a market is not sizable enough, manipulative activities backed up by monopoly rents could well perpetuate the situation, accounting for the persistence of income differences as well as differences in the pace of innovative activities. Market failures thus can be matters of temporary disruption caused by occasional blockages in information flow, or in the case of developing countries, matters of persistent structures caused by imperfect features of the market. As a result, most firms in a developing economy face downward-sloping demand curves for their products as opposed to the perfectly elastic demand posited in the classical theory (Stiglitz 1989). In certain respects, persistent market failures can be perpetuated by initial conditions that exist in the market. In this regard, history becomes fate.

The capital market is particularly illuminating. Problems of adverse selection, moral hazards, and contract enforcement imply that even in developed economies, capital markets do not look like the textbook models of the perfect capital market. Even competitive markets may be characterized by credit rationing (Stiglitz and Weiss 1981) and equity rationing (Greenwald and Stiglitz 1988). New share issues result in sufficiently large decreases in a firm's market value that few firms resort to new equity issues as a way of raising capital. Not only do these informational imperfections lead to credit and equity rationing but, more important, the institutional frameworks for dealing with these capital market imperfections are probably less effective in the developing countries, partly because of the smaller scale of firms within these economies and partly because the institutions for collecting, evaluating and disseminating information are likely to be less well developed.

Failures of the market lead some theorists to advocate strong government actions. There are a number of familiar arguments for government actions, such as problems of scale and externalities, the problem of invisibility of group preferences, the impossibility of excluding access, or in short, the existence of group indivisibilities. They will not be repeated here. In the case of a developing nation, there seems to be additional justification for government action. No matter how hazardous government action may be, it seems that as long as there is a need to move an economy out of a lock-in situation, we need an agency powerful enough to give it the necessary impetus.

Needless to say, government actions are seldom effective substitutes for market functions. Indeed, it is often the case that in terms of magnitude, government failures turn out to be more disastrous than market failures. In general, the government faces informational and incentive problems of an order far surpassing those faced by the market. Owing to factors including its size, its rigid reward-effort system, its need to accommodate short-term political sentiments, and its natural propensity to expand its bureaucracy and therefore to overregulate, even a relatively well run government is insufficiently sensitive to its capabilities and weaknesses. In a developing country, where the government lacks the self-discipline in its exercise of power or where there is an absence of a mature political environment that would serve to check its power, such insensitivity is often compounded. To aggravate the problem, a lot of resources in a developing country tend to concentrate within the government or go through government channels. Concentration of resources easily creates the false illusion among policymakers that resources are easy to come by and reinforces their impulses to embrace immediate and visible results without considering the long-term cost-effectiveness of the projects on which they embark. Convinced of the seriousness of government failures, some researchers hold that, left to the market and adhering consistently to its rules, economic actors can ultimately evolve strategies that collectively overcome at least part of the known market failures without enlisting the help of the government. The validity of such an argument, however, remains to be demonstrated.

As may be expected, market failures generally trigger more government intervention. Owing to the characteristics of the developing economy, increased government intervention usually leads to failures that are worse than market failures. Subsequent efforts to correct such failures lead either to more government intervention or, alternatively, to more dependence on market forces. Since in the formative stages human visions of the future are highly elastic to institutional stability, human capital that is initially stimulated by either the market or by the government in the first phases of development will be abruptly truncated should these two types of failures occilate and reinforce each other. The result of such swings in policy and the reinforcement of failures of different types is that individual economic actors are likely to adopt a protectionist strategy that clearly discourages any willingness to invest in the future. Since bad habits, once formed, are difficult to eradicate, successions of different rounds of market failures and government failures will entrench rent-seeking behaviors while discouraging human capital formation.

If market failures and government failures tend to reinforce each other, then it should be obvious that reliance on either of these two agencies by a developing country is hardly a feasible way to lift itself out of its predicament. To make up for these respective failures, a mix of market incentives and government action in some proper proportion seems to be required. However, to say this amounts to endorsing a kind of naive eclecticism is not very helpful. Clearly, until the appropriate magnitudes of the market and the government solutions are defined and the sequences in which they should occur are delineated and ordered, the thesis remains a tautology. To render it more satisfying, the debate might be coached in terms of the respective vision-augmenting and vision-closing effects of these two agencies. The market is clearly a superior agent to nurture visions, because the visions generated are of a natural kind. While government does help in inculcating artificial and temporary visions by way of, say, planting visionary landmarks via its infrastructure-building time table, its many other actions may have vision-closing effects, especially its mindless changes in short-term policies. However, this does not mean that the disruptive effects of the government could not be ameliorated, nor that the positive effects of the market could not be well exploited. After all, the "natural" vision-augmenting function of the market requires as its precondition the role of the government as a guarantor of justice.

If public policy is to be appraised at the level of vision formation among the economic actors, individual government actions could be separately evaluated in terms of their contribution to vision formation or vision closure, and there would be no need to categorically write off government action as a whole. For example, we could now ask whether, in a particular phase of development, certain types of government policies could supplement market forces in the latter's vision-augmenting functions without themselves having significant vision-closing effects. We could also ask whether, in a stagnant situation where the market is dominated by a small number of large players, government could effectively alter the rules of the game in order to mobilize potential actors into competition. Similarly, we could ask whether government could move into those areas where the market situation is fast deteriorating in order to prevent the closing of the vision of its actors, or intervene where anticapital formation is proliferating so fast that vicious circles of vision closing are being set off. It may, of course, be contended that vision-closing or vision-augmenting effects are not directly measurable and therefore may not provide solid ground on which policies may be formulated. However, while direct measurement is out of the question, there is no lack of indirect indicators by which broad patterns of the spans of vision held by economic actors could be qualitatively defined and ordered, and hence objectively compared. What is needed, therefore, is the positing of the multifarious relations between different types of government actions and different types of ground rules and their respective vision-augmenting or vision-closing effects.

We will have to leave the study of these multifarious and deep relations to future research. At the risk of oversimplification, we might conjecture that the following assertions might be worthy of serious attention and further study. First, since familiarity with ground rules is liable to breed visions among economic actors, these rules should be made as explicit as possible. By corollary, short-term policy changes need to be related to and made consistent with such ground rules. Second, where possible, the nurturing of visions should be left to the market with its natural vision-creating capacity, with the government left to lay down ground rules for market operations. More important, these ground rules should specify how much intervention they will permit so that all players can be well aware of the limits in advance. Third, active government actions to promote the vision-nurturing function should be justified only upon a demonstrated ability that vision nurturing can be sustained for a stipulated period and on the grounds that there is no market to do the job. Fourth, while infrastructural time tables can be useful for planting collective visionary landmarks, their real effectiveness in promoting the range of individual visions should be carefully spelt out beforehand, lest the gap between collective visions and individual visions turns out to be too big to fill. From the perspective of vision augmentation and hazard avoidance, one could restate, in a nutshell, that the role of government is to monitor the hazards of development, to steer the economy clear of potential hazards, to lift it out of a hazardous path as early as possible by removing or rooting out the causes of anticapital formation and to prevent itself from being a cause of anticapital formation.

With this, we come to a bifurcation of the respective roles of the market and the government in development. The market should be prepared as far as possible to nurture the capacity of the economic actors to the extent of their range of visions and thereby to maximize human capital formation, while the government should aim at preventing the proliferation of anticapital and its destructive effects on vision formation, with the condition that its actions should not be demonstrably vision-closing. The market should be assigned the positive role of inculcating human capital, while government should take on the "negative" role of minimizing the potential hazards in development, and if necessary should take actions to lift an economy out of lock-in situations through non-hazardous measures. There is a clear-cut, "natural" boundary between the functions of these two agencies, and a kind of mutual fine-tuning seems to be possible. The resultant eclecticism becomes sophisticated because in appraising any development policy, the question becomes, apart from prima facie reasons for and against the market or government solutions, how far vision formation and disruption will be caused by the respective solutions in both the short term and the longer term. Government actions would be permissible if they could have demonstrably positive effects on vision formation while at the same time having no effects to the contrary. Where possible, however, government actions should be restricted to the realm of hazard control. Indeed, once we step beyond the "natural" functions of the market and the government, we should be extremely wary of their unintended consequences, for while such cross-boundary functions can at times be useful contributions, there is no easy way for us to gauge the degree of their potential hazards. Hence, extreme caution should be exercised once these respective agencies step beyond their natural boundaries.

Some Plausible Strategies for Development, and Their Rationale

Having explained the plausible roles of government and charted the realm where it could contribute to development, we propose, by way of illustration, to examine a few development strategies that take these principles into account. Before proceeding, a few disclaimers should be made. First, the strategies proposed here are intended to illustrate the principles we have discussed so far. As such, no claim is made that they will exhaust all possibilities. Second, these strategies are generally "negative" in character. They aim chiefly to reduce the formation of anticapital and, by corollary, the potential hazards besetting development. Third, whereas we believe that these strategies will be of use to a developing country, we make no claim that they will be applicable to a mature market economy, and therefore more research should be done before any changes are made. Needless to say, important but familiar factors such as anticorruption measures are too obvious to be included in this discussion.

One plausible strategy concerns the problem of scale. Given what we have said about vision formation, the important role of small-scale enterprises in development needs little elaboration. One direction of development, in this view, is to provide the right kind of environment whereby small-scale enterprises can be induced to develop and conditions that suffocate such development can be removed. We will skip other factors that pose obstacles to the development of small-scale enterprise and will confine ourselves to the question of scale.

In mature market economies that have reached a certain size, some kind of balance seems to exist between the proportion of large-scale and small-scale firms. This is a complex issue, and space does not permit a lengthy treatment here. Briefly, we can say that different opposing forces are at work that bring about some kind of equilibrium. On the one hand, centrally directed manipulative activities such as image building, advertising, and to some extent, research and development activities enable a big firm to grow bigger because of the economies of scale inherent in these activities. In this regard, the overall optimal size of the firm appears to expand over time, particularly with improvements in marketing technologies. On the other hand, however, the existence of diseconomies of scale in management compels the big firm, in order to keep up its efficiency in production and so forth, to either break itself up into smaller profit/cost centers or farm out a part of its work to subcontractors. This strategy will be required if the big firm considers it important to maintain its vitality and its market share. Even without severe competition among the big firms, there is always competition among the small subcontracting firms that vie for work contracts with the big ones. Thus, not only is there always scope for the existence of competitive small-scale enterprises, but the symbiotic relations between the small firm and the big firm are also well established in a competitive market.

Unfortunately, such a "self-regulating" mechanism to keep the proportion of small and big firms in some balance barely exists in the immature economy that is characteristic of a developing country. With only a few big firms dominating the market, there is little check to the growth of a manipulative firm that flourishes on rent-seeking activities and enjoys windfall profits of such an order that the disadvantages caused by diseconomies of scale can be dismissed lightly. Without a significant proportion of small-scale firms that foster competition in the market or that develop symbiotic ties with the bigger ones, the human capital formation essential to vigorous development will be severely restricted. Moreover, should the bigger firms continue to grow at the expense of the smaller ones, the effect on human capital formation may even become negative.

Two types of policy options immediately present themselves. One type consists in introducing de-scaling or scale-limiting measures. The other type consists in measures that deliberately favor small-scale firms. Considering the difficulties in executing control measures in a developing country, and the contention that control of scale may seriously handicap a developing country in adopting state-of-the-art technology or management techniques, it seems that the second type of option, namely those measures that benefit small-scale firms, is more preferable. However, some kind of intermediate design also seems to be available. The idea is to develop some kind of legal framework that promotes "intrapreneurship" within the larger-scale firms. Briefly, our proposal is to encourage the emergence of certain types of legal corporations, the original founders of which know in advance that they will have a significant part of their equity shares transferred to the management or their working employees after a certain stipulated period. Entrepreneurs who opt for this kind of corporation will initially enjoy special tax and credit privileges in return for ultimately giving up the lion's share of their equities. Employees who join these corporations will know in advance that if they perform properly, they will eventually become owners through some kind of financial arrangements that are, say, to be guaranteed by the government. The starter-owner will stand to benefit because in return for giving up part of his equity, he will have a highly motivated management as well as substantial tax benefits and expansion possibilities (such as better credit terms).

The only serious objection to this proposal would be that this scheme would put other types of firms on an unequal footing in competition. However, it is precisely because there is an inherent bias favoring existing and bigger firms in the developing nation that a design of this kind is required to correct the imbalance. Since the operation of the system is supposed to be rooted in some explicit ground rules, the economic actors involved will have no confusion about what they should expect. The economy as a whole will not stand to lose because the tax benefits and other privileges given to those firms will likely result in the emergence of more firms, and thereby a wider tax base, as new entrepreneurs and intrapreneurs move in to exploit such advantages. In the long run, it should be a positive-sum game for every party concerned, for even the ordinary firm will benefit from the expanding base of the economy. There remain, however, many technicalities to be resolved about this new type of corporation, for example, the flexibility and liquidity of shares among the management, and the time table and mode of transfer of equity between the starter-owner and the working management, and it is not supposed that these problems will have easy solutions. Solutions of this kind, however, will be left to future research.

We have previously mentioned that one potential hazard to development is the explosion of demand-side expectations and their asymmetrical relation to supply-side capabilities. The result is that both the people and the government spend more than their earning power allows, thereby leading to trade deficits and inflationary pressures. Obviously, some institutional designs are needed to restore a balance between these two sides. One conventional policy that has been adopted in developing countries is to impose import restriction measures such as tariffs or quotas while permitting the quiet functioning of demonstration effects. These measures are of dubious value, because reduced access often has the countereffect of enhancing the perceived value of such imports. Fearful of further increases in prices caused by increases in tariffs and so forth, consumers are likely to be induced to step up their spending as fast as they can.

Another conventional strategy to discourage present consumption is to preserve the purchasing power of the consumer by maintaining a high interest rate for savings. Conventional wisdom has it that positive real deposit rates raise the savings rate, and increased real rates raise investment. However, the offsetting income and substitution effects of increased interest rates suggest that the net impact on savings must be ambiguous. Evidence from the United States and other industrialized countries supports skepticism in that virtually no study has demonstrated a discernible net effect. In the case of developing countries, the lack of data and their poor quality make it much harder to establish the facts (Dornbusch and Reynoso 1989). Again, there is insufficient evidence to show the existence of a causal relation between increased real rates and investment. In addition, with inflationary pressures prevailing in the developing nation, any attraction such options offer will soon disappear after the first or second round.

In place of the above, we propose a government-backed scheme of making prices of future purchases of consumer goods (in real terms) more attractive than present prices even after discounting interest gains. One way would be to introduce a kind of prepayment installment system for specific goods selected by the consumer to be delivered in the future, on price terms that are more competitive than present prices after discounting interest gains. Rather than incurring a debt and mortgaging future income, the consumer will receive a premium for postponing certain kinds of enjoyment to the future. Of course, the government needs to command sufficient credibility for the scheme to be successful, and it needs to honor its contracts by delivering the goods on time. The scheme should spread over a fairly long period, during which consumers will be enticed to work harder in order to keep up with the agreed installments. The government, of course, will have to provide a subsidy since it promises to supply future goods at less than their present values, but in the long run such a subsidy could be partly offset, or even more than offset, by the increased earning power of its consumers and, thereby, by their tax contributions.

The proposed strategies in the above discussion should help clarify the kind of role appropriate to a government in a developing country and how government actions might help eliminate potential hazards that lurk in the path of development. With these design principles and proposals in the background, we will turn in the next chapter to a most controversial issue in developing economics, namely, agriculture, and show how China, being essentially an agricultural economy, could make the best out of its situation.

NOTES

1. The term "structuralism" first entered the vocabulary of development in the 1950s debates about the causes of inflation in Latin America (Little 1982).

2. F. A. Hayek is a notable exception in so far as he recognizes the contribution of knowledge to economic activities. (See, for example, Hayek 1948).

3. As espoused by the subjective theories of value.

4. This does not, however, prevent the capitalist economy from developing into a divisible system.

5. To be fair, some animals, such as chimpanzees, do use and manipulate symbols in their "thinking," but symbol manipulation, although essential to the development of imagination, is not equivalent to the use of imagination itself.

6. In the case of China, the visions of its people are, however, built around the future of their offspring. This accounts for the disproportionate amount of income that parents spend on their child (most families in the urban areas are single-child families).

7. Opposed to the findings in Mundell's work, Henry Wallich's (1969) study of 43 countries, however, found a negative relationship between inflation and growth. Thirlwall and Barton (1971), U Tun Wai (1959), and Dorrance (1966) also found that among developing countries growth declines when annual inflation exceeds 10 percent.

4

The Case for Agriculture and an Appraisal of Agricultural Development in China since 1949

THE CASE FOR AND AGAINST THE PRIMACY OF AGRICULTURE AS A VEHICLE OF DEVELOPMENT

There is little need to restate the importance of agriculture to the Chinese economy. In spite of its emphasis on industrial development, China remains fundamentally an agriculture-based economy. Presently, agriculture accounts for half its gross national output and engages 70 percent of its total labor force. With over a billion people, or about one-quarter of the world's population, to feed, and with only 13 percent of its land being arable, the importance of agricultural development in China can hardly be overemphasized. Given the importance of agriculture, it is clear that China should continue, at least in the short to medium term, to develop a solid agricultural sector, regardless of whether in the long run agriculture will only be a stepping stone to its efforts towards modernization, in the sense of China becoming a full-fledged, industrialized nation. In this regard, it is imperative that we look at the place of agriculture in development and the kind of strategies for agricultural development that are appropriate to the conditions of China. In this chapter, we will first review the changes in the perceived role of agriculture in developing economics. We will then discuss the advantages and disadvantages of agriculture as a vehicle to development, and whether it is justified to give priority to investments in agriculture. We will critically review the development of agriculture in China since 1949 and evaluate its performance and present state.

Changes in the Perceived Role of Agriculture in Development

Since the founding of development economics, the perceived roles of agriculture in development have undergone big changes. In the founding period of development economics, namely, in the "economic growth-and-modernization" era of the 1950s and 1960s, when development was defined largely in terms of growth of average per capita output, most development economists viewed the role of agriculture as "instrumental" and transitory. Indeed, development was believed to consist of and result in the decline of agriculture's relative share of gross national product. Arthur Lewis's seminal paper "Economic Development with Unlimited Supplies of Labor" (1954) pioneered the view that the rural sector is characterized by the existence of abundant surplus labor and that development represents the transfer of this surplus labor from the subsistence sector (where the marginal productivity of a laborer approaches zero as a limiting case) to the capitalist sector. From this view, many development economists drew the conclusion that the rapid transfer of surplus labor from agriculture to industry, entailing that agriculture's relative importance in a developing economy will decline in due course, was an appropriate short-run development strategy.

This view was congenial to some prevalent and influential views against the possible existence of long-run potentials of agriculture for development. In 1949 R. Prebisch and H. W. Singer each argued separately that since the terms of trade tend to turn against countries that export primary products and import manufactured goods, the scope for expanding output through agriculture is highly restricted.[1] A. O. Hirschman, in his *Strategy of Economic Development* (1958), asserted that whereas "agriculture certainly stands convicted on the count of its lack of direct stimulus to the setting up of new activities through linkage effects—the superiority of manufacturing in this respect is crushing" (pp. 109–10), investment in industry would lead to more rapid and more broadly based economic growth. Besides, it was generally believed that the income elasticity of the demand for unprocessed food is less than unity and declines with higher incomes. As a result, the demand for raw agricultural products will grow more slowly than consumption in general. In addition, it was also widely held that the overall increase in the productivity of agriculture is unlikely to surpass that of industry unless it is extensively aided by mechanization and chemical fertilizers. The employment of these inputs means that the demand for labor in agriculture will be drastically reduced, dwarfing its relative importance in the economy over time.

The above view, however, rapidly underwent drastic changes. Agriculture was soon seen to make important, positive contributions to the process of development. The need to avoid food shortages, which may choke off growth in the nonfarm sector, was stressed by G. Rains and J. Fei (1961, 1963, 1964), as well as by S. Enke (1962), who recommended rapid investments in agriculture in order to accelerate the growth of its agricultural surplus. B. F. Johnston and J. W. Mellor (1961) argued that agriculture contributes to the structural transformation of the developing economies by providing labor, capital, foreign exchange and food to a growing industrial sector and by providing a market for domestically produced industrial goods. The case for the interdependence of agricultural and industrial growth was also stated by W. H. Nicholls, whose influential work "The Place of Agriculture in Economic Development" (1964) stimulated economists to view agriculture as a positive factor. In these writings, the longer-term potentials of agriculture to development were clearly recognized.

The potential contribution of agriculture to development was also seen from a novel angle by T. W. Schultz who, in his classic *Transforming Traditional Agriculture* (1964), advanced the view that farmers and herders in the developing countries are, contrary to generally held conceptions, rational and calculating economic actors. The cause of rural poverty does not lie in the inherent

irrationalities of these economic actors, nor in their cultural idio-
syncracies. Their actions are merely bounded by inefficient and
nonprofitable technical packages and by their inadequate ability to
rapidly exploit changing agricultural technologies. In his view, the
key to overcoming such inadequacies consists in the improvement
of agricultural productivity. This is achievable through the adoption
of agricultural technologies, to be supported by the right kind of
agricultural research and rural education.

The 1970s witnessed the onset of the "growth-with-equity" era
in development economies. During this period, the harmful effects
of uneven development were recognized and the conventional
goals of development were called into question. Increasing attention was given to the questions of employment, distribution and
"basic needs." This new orientation had significant ramifications
for the perceived role of agriculture in development. For example,
agriculture came to be seen to have a more powerful employment
effect than was previously believed. It became apparent that urban
industries in most countries could not expand quickly enough to
provide employment for the expanding rural labor force (Eicher,
Zalla, Kocher, and Winch 1970). The emphasis on more equitable
income distribution also enhanced the perceived role of agriculture. Evidence became available to show that the economies of
scale expected for tropical agriculture are more limited than previously believed and that the improvement of small farms often
results in greater output and employment per hectare than large-
scale farming. Also, it became more apparent that certain types of
rural industries are more efficiently run than their urban counterparts. The orientation toward the provision for the "basic needs"
of the population also underscored the importance of agriculture
in a developing economy, an orientation underlined by a growing
awareness of the increasing landlessness in many parts of the Third
World, particularly in South Asia and Latin America, and of the
increasing need to create productive employment in rural areas (see
Streeten 1981).

As a result of these orientations, studies on the microaspects of
the rural economies and on different models of agricultural growth

proliferated during this era. It also witnessed expansion in theoretical and empirical researches on the interdependence between agricultural and nonagricultural growth (see Johnston and Kilby 1975, Mellor 1976), generating an increase in knowledge about farmer behavior, about the linkages between agricultural research and extension institutions, and about the complexity and location-specific nature of the agricultural development process. As a result of these studies, development economists gradually came to view agricultural growth not only as a desirable instrument to foster industrial development, but probably also as a desirable end in itself. The subsequent ascendency of the "substainable development" paradigm further reinforced this view. With agriculture becoming the focal point of a new development strategy, we seem to have come to a big "U-turn" in development economics.

Controversies over the Principles and Strategies of Agricultural Development

While the relative importance of agriculture is increasingly being recognized, a clear-cut consensus within development economics as to what constitutes sound and tenable strategies for agricultural development is still lacking. In fact, within the camp of proponents for agricultural development, controversies abound, ranging from questions of fundamental principles to matters of policies and programs. At the level of basic development philosophy, one can discern debates over the place of agriculture in development, and in particular over the question of whether agriculture should be development's means or end. At the level of agricultural science, one can discern two conceptual polarities, namely a nature-centered agriculture (minimal human effort and intervention so that the "laws of nature" are allowed to work fruitfully) versus a technology-based agriculture (maximal human input in order to generate the highest possible level of present yield). At the level of reform strategy, controversies loom over the benefits of the technocratic or modernization strategy (agriculture development without simultaneous and profound changes in social structure; see Barraclough 1973) and those of the radical strategy (agriculture development through radical changes in social and political structures; see Gurley 1973) as well as proponents of the reformist strategy (an eclectic position; see, for example, Heck 1979). Within the sphere of the modernization strategy, there are conflicting approaches, such as the "crash" modernization strategy versus the "progressive" modernization strategy. The former emphasizes the fruitfulness of investing in the leading sectors—for example, in the most promising regions and the most progressive farmers—while the latter calls for mobilizing resources to improve the most backward regions or the performance of subsistence farmers (see Johnston and Kilby 1973). Concerning the agency for directing agricultural development, differences in opinion also exist over what respective roles the government and the market should play. For those who favor substantial government action, controversies exist over what types of support government should give to agriculture. On the specific issue of income support, one also witnesses differences in opinion over the cost-effectiveness of different income support programs, such as input subsidy versus product subsidy and deficiency payments versus import levies (Ritson 1977). Other relevant debates include whether small holdings are superior to large holdings, whether monoculture is preferable to multiple culture, and similar topics.

The above examples aim neither to catalogue nor to exhaust the debates in the sphere of agricultural economics. They are merely meant to show some of the complexities involved. Many issues in agriculture are complex because they involve questions concerning both matters of fact and matters of value, and that cut across an exceedingly large number of domains and disciplines. Where value judgments are involved, insurmountable difficulties often exist either because the articulation of such values is difficult to achieve or because they require intertemporal utility comparisons about which we have only scant information. For example, to what extent should we allow ecological considerations (which entail the moral question of how responsible we should be to future generations) to override the aspirations of the present generation to better its material conditions? As another example, should we aim at more egalitarian results in farmer performance or should we aim at producing the largest "global pie" for the agricultural sector regardless of the problem of income distribution? Clearly, difficulties of this sort arise because they involve intertemporal comparisons of welfare that do not lend themselves to easy articulation and because the propositions themselves are barely subject to testing or refutation.

With these difficulties, does it mean that we can never hope to objectively evaluate agricultural strategies for development or that we are in no position at all to appraise the role of agriculture without committing ourselves beforehand to a certain ideology? Without a doubt, some of these issues cannot be easily disentangled or resolved, especially those that involve ecological considerations. Fortunately, however, there is no lack of fundamental principles in development—for example, those of the kind that we discussed in the previous chapter—that we can use in appraising issues in agriculture, in particular in appraising the central question of whether agriculture should be taken as a means or as an end in itself. For example, we can ask to what extent an agricultural strategy is hazard-free or how far it satisfies our criterion of human capital formation. Before we turn to these issues, let us first address a basic issue, namely, is the case for according a primary role to agriculture in development justified?

The Case against the Primacy of Agriculture

While many development economists would now gladly concede that agriculture does have an important role to play in development, especially in the many types of support it gives to other sectors during the development process, it is doubtful whether they all agree to accept the thesis of the primacy of agriculture in development. It is still less likely that they would accept agricultural development as an end of development. In this section I will contend that whereas it is difficult to resolve the issue of taking agriculture as an end of development, it is plausible to argue for an agriculture-first strategy for many developing nations, of which China is a paradigmatic case. I will also contend that in spite of the many apparent weaknesses of agriculture as a vehicle to development, there are compelling reasons why this pathway is, everything considered, a superior one.

Arguments against the primacy of agriculture can be classified into two broad categories. The first category is founded on the grounds that agriculture is an ineffective means of development, especially in comparison with industry. The second category is based on the grounds that this particular pathway of development is beset with a number of formidable potential hazards. We can call the first category "arguments from ineffectiveness" and the second category "arguments from hazards," and we will consider them in turn.

Agriculture is seen to be an ineffective vehicle to development for a number of reasons. We have already mentioned the relatively weak linkage effects between agriculture and development. Another formidable argument, since David Ricardo, is that, land being a fixed input, agricultural activities are subject to the principle of diminishing returns. In addition, agriculture, necessitating the cooperation of nature, is a fairly rigid production activity that cannot be artificially speeded up. Indeed, both Adam Smith and David Ricardo saw manufacturing and commerce as progressive, as compared with agriculture, which was the sinecure of an unprogressive landed aristocracy (See Schultz 1987). The view that there is slim chance of upgrading the productivity of agricultural land over time entails too that there is a limit to the increase in productivity or agricultural activities. Moreover, even if one were to grant that an increase in productivity in agriculture is possible, one could contend that the rate of productivity increase of agriculture is still lower than that of industry. Giving top priority to agriculture for a developing economy would mean that it would be compelled to forgo the chance of catching up with the industrialized West and might thereby suffer persistently from adverse terms of trade in its transactions with the industrialized countries.

Another formidable argument against the effectiveness of agriculture as a vehicle of development is the conservatism of the average farmer. There are a number of factors leading to this trait. First, farmers invariably operate under uncertain regimes. Occasional natural hazards can wipe out years of gain, and many of these hazards are unpredictable. Second, land quality, location, and so on are rather specific factors, and it requires considerable time before the farmer can develop sufficiently specific knowledge about their characteristics to exploit them profitably. This means that the farmer tends to stick to his indigenous practice and is hesitant to try new techniques. Third, unlike an industrial system where input-output relations are well defined by a particular set of technologies and where performance is monitored by a hierarchical organization, production in agriculture, which is subjected to ecological factors, is a relatively open system whose variables are difficult to track, where abnormal results take time to reveal and where anomalies can be explained by a variety of reasons. Besides, the farmer usually does not have to account for his performance to other parties. Considering, too, that he is generally lacking in extra resources and can hardly afford even a single major failure, it is nothing but obvious that risk-aversion will dominate his considerations and prevent him from adopting an entrepreneurial attitude. Considering too that it takes considerable time for a human actor to accept a new idea, it will be a Herculean task to alter such a risk-aversion mentality.

Arguments based on the hazards are no less formidable. Agriculture is alleged to suffer from hazards of different types, including, inter alia, natural hazards, ecological hazards, economic hazards and social hazards. With respect to natural and ecological hazards, we will postpone discussion to a later section. It suffices to mention here that disruptions to the environment are caused as much by subsistence farming which relentlessly exploits marginal land, thereby causing irreversible soil erosion, as by mechanical and chemical farming which wipe out delicate ecological balances by monoculture and by breaking up natural food chains in the pest world. With respect to economic hazards, since most developing nations lack a full-fledged food-processing industry with a steady demand for agricultural output, and since the demand for agriculture products is relatively inelastic, increases in output by the average farmer do not always result in higher revenues and income. More often than not, bumper harvests lead to substantial price drops, and unless storage and refrigeration facilities are amply available or preservation techniques are well developed, may result in an unacceptably low level of income for many producers. Increases in agricultural productivity leading to higher levels of output, therefore, do not entail a corresponding increase in the income of the farmer or in savings for investment activities. Additionally, out of the intention to keep up a minimum standard of living for their agricultural populations, governments usually take measures to protect their domestic markets, rendering access by foreign producers a difficult proposition. On the one hand, overinsurance provided by government support programs has the effect of diminishing the self-reliance of farmers, but on the other hand, underinsurance has the effect of increasing the misery of certain hard-stricken sectors and thereby the ability of the farmers in question to invest for better farming conditions. These dilemmas suggest that sustaining farmer incentive is no easy task.

Since the bureaucratic machinery of government is often an impediment to efficiency and since the government has an indispensable role to play in agriculture, holders of the view that agriculture should be a primary vehicle to development are open to the challenge that emphasis on agricultural development means subjecting the development process to extensive bureaucratic intervention, corruption and abuse. We have said that expansion in agriculture may not necessarily yield higher income for the farmer unless his output can be sold in time, can be absorbed by a sufficiently large market without substantially depressing farm product prices, or can be absorbed by the government, which must commit to procure such output at favorable prices. The former requires substantial infrastructural investments in storage and transportation as well as a well-developed network of supporting services, investments that are not always properly handled by government. Income support programs, such as government procurement of farm products at fixed prices, on the other hand, once initiated, often unwittingly commit the government to indefinite long-term subsidies. In many instances, income support programs have differential benefits on farms of different sizes and different endowments, and may be biased against the smaller and less resourceful farmers.

The Case for Agriculture

It is to the arguments from ineffectiveness that T. W. Schultz has persistently launched his counterattack. In his view, the supply of agricultural land is not a fixed factor. It is augmentable by investments of various types. Advances in microbiology could alter the genetic structures of different plants making possible, for instance, shorter maturation periods or rendering certain species more pest-resistant. Agricultural research on the whole, along with complementary inputs, has proven to be highly successful in developing substitutes for cropland, or, differently put, in land augmentation. Actual increases in yield per hectare have held, and may well continue to hold, the key to increases in crop production. According to Schultz, the U.S. yield of maize in 1931 was 1,500 kilograms per hectare (kg/ha), but by 1978 the yield had risen to 6,300 kg/ha. In 1929, the yield of sorghum grain was 870 kg/ha. By 1978, it had risen to 2,800 kg/ha (Schultz 1984). The upshot of his argument is that, confined to the short view, one becomes beholden to a highly inelastic supply of agricultural products and food. However, if one takes the long view, the supply of agricultural products is clearly elastic over time. Knowledge from research is an effective substitute for agricultural land. Advances in that knowledge mean that the supply of land is no longer fixed in quantity, in quality or by location, and that the productivity of land is becoming increasingly a man-made phenomenon (Schultz 1987).

In Schultz's view, gains in agricultural productivity are manifestations of the principle of increasing returns, a principle ignored by conventional economics in the latter's obsession with the logic of equilibrium. Increasing returns are possible in agriculture by virtue of increases in the specialized human capital embodied in the farmer and the agricultural scientist. Such capital can be sustained by an expanding market that induces further specialization. Agricultural research and the education of farmers are thus the key to increasing returns on agricultural activities. On this basis, Schultz rejects the forebodings, whether past or present, that are based predominantly on assessments of the declining physical capacity of the earth. On the contrary, increases in our acquired abilities and advances in knowledge will continue to hold the key to future economic productivity.

Schultz's account of increasing returns presupposes that new research knowledge is readily transmittable to farmers from agricultural research centers. In this regard, he is insightful in realizing that research entrepreneurship, an important factor in producing useful knowledge, is scarce in supply and has to be nurtured by the right types of research institutions (1984). On the other hand, however, he seems to assume that entrepreneurship among farmers is not a serious problem. He believes that given sufficient education and government persuasion, farmers will unproblematically take on the entrepreneurial task of adopting returns-increasing and state-of-the-art knowledge from agricultural research.

However, as we have shown in the preceding section, we cannot take it for granted that the problem of farmer entrepreneurship has been solved. Another objection to Schultz's account is that he does not deal in any systematic way with the different potential hazards that beset agriculture. Until the problems of entrepreneurship and potential hazards are satisfactorily addressed, we cannot consider that the thesis of primacy of agriculture in development has been established.

To justify the primacy of agriculture, we have to adopt a different route. Admittedly, as previous arguments have shown, agriculture as it has generally been practiced is far from being qualified to serve as the primary vehicle for development. However, this does not disqualify "agriculture in theory" from such a role. In other words, we would contend that whereas existing modes of conducting agriculture are not sufficiently effective, in theory there may exist certain modes that are capable of unleashing higher states of productivity among the farmers while keeping potential hazards to a minimum. It is possible that once certain thresholds have been crossed or certain constraints removed, existing modes of agriculture will undergo changes that will unleash the theoretical advantages that agriculture as a production system enjoys. Alternatively put, existing modes of agriculture are ineffective and hazardous because they are either overconstrained by existing socioeconomic institutions or because they lack the right kind of preconditions for transformation into effective agriculture.

Apparently there can be more than one set of formulae that leads to effective agriculture. In the next chapter, we will offer some specific recommendations that we believe in principle will permit effective agriculture. At present, we will spell out the advantages that a regime of effective agriculture would enjoy, and explain why we consider such a regime worthy of pursuit. We will, in other words, argue the case that a regime of effective agriculture satisfies our canons of feasible development.

For the moment, let us assume that there is no need to deal with ecological issues and that the goal of development is the accepted goal of material enhancement. Let us also assume that some kind of effective regime of agriculture is in force, which entails in particular that a sizable number of farmers are now motivated to take on new approaches to increase their output. The theoretical advantages of this regime are manifold. In the first place, agriculture seems to have more advantages to confer to a budding entrepreneur. Entry is relatively easy. Starting requirements in terms of skill and knowledge are less demanding than their counterparts in industry. Nature, which plays an important part in agricultural production, makes up for much of the ignorance of the entrepreneur-farmer in the early phases of his career. Admittedly, the dominance of nature's role also means that the farmer-entrepreneurship is subject to the element of luck and is easily harmed by nature's hazards. This is a real and important problem to which we will turn. For the time being, let us assume that this problem is surmountable through institutional arrangements and that farmer entrepreneurship is sustainable in spite of potential hazards.

With easy entry, and on the assumption that farmer entrepreneurship is sustainable, the long-term effect of such development would be the creation of a strong base of human capital. With nature playing a dominant role, it will take considerable time before the farmer-entrepreneur will accumulate sufficient knowledge and skill, and the process will be slow. However, the importance of eventually having a strong base of farmer-entrepreneurs who are continually willing to expend efforts or invest for more output tomorrow, in spite of the negative impacts of natural hazards, is far-reaching. It goes beyond the possibility that the agricultural system will finally be able to rid itself of the need for government subsidies, that it will be able to contribute its surplus to support a growing commercial and industrial sector, that it will be able to upgrade its productivity to the extent that it can release surplus labor to the urban sector or even that it will build up a foreign exchange earning capability. The buildup of such a base is important in that it implies the transformation of the mentality and quality of most of the population of the economy in question. This transformation consists in the realization by its economic actors that knowledge is a key input to production, that active and systematic adaptation to production are important, and that it is indispensable to take calculated risks. The result of such a transformation will be that the rural sector will become the force behind the generation of a large pool of quality entrepreneurs who have the will to accumulate surplus for making new investments, possess an expanding vision of the future and remain undaunted in the face of uncertainty and hardship. Part of such human capital will be ploughed back into the agricultural sector, while the rest will spill over to other sectors. The process might not be rapid but it will surely engender solid results over time.

As a matter of fact, the relatively slow pace at which farmer-entrepreneurship develops is not necessarily a disadvantage. It could, on the contrary, turn out to be a blessing in disguise. One major hazard to development, as we have explained, is the rapid polarization of income among different sectors or different classes of economic actors within the same sector. Given that the initial pattern of factor endowment in agriculture is relatively even (as in the case of China), a slower rate of progress in farmer-entrepreneurship and in the rise of farm income may mean more solid progress at the collective level in the long run. Slower but more solid progress also might mean that the commercial hazard of occasional oversupply or abundance could be reduced because a steady and across-the-board rise in purchasing power in the rural sector would leave it on the whole better equipped to absorb such extra supply. A steadily growing market also would mean that specialization was further encouraged, providing new opportunities for the entrepreneurally inclined. Slower but across-the-board increases in prosperity in conjunction with a more diversified range of agricultural output would mean that the system would become more resilient to contingencies and unforeseen factors. Provided a proper collective insurance system was also in force, the individual farmer would be much better placed to overcome such impacts.

In comparison, rapid expansion of industrial capacity as a vehicle to development faces hazards of a no less formidable magnitude, though of a different kind. Rapid industrial expansion entails the concentration of both capital and labor. As we have shown, concentration of capital in a developing economy tends to create rent-seeking opportunities for the elites and to create white elephant projects that become burdens to the economy in the second round. It is seldom the case that the centralized capital would be wisely and efficiently used, and even if it were the case, it would benefit only a relatively small percentage of the entire population.

Concentration of labor proves to be even more hazardous. On the one hand, it leads to rapid urban sprawl, resulting in a drastic deterioration of living conditions. More potentially dangerous is the fact that the concentration of labor in the cities means concentrations of unemployed people. In this regard, it is useful to note the difference between unemployment in the city and unemployment in the countryside. Unemployment in the countryside is never absolute: There are peak periods when surplus labor can always be absorbed. Unless unemployment is entirely voluntary, the unemployed can always take up some kind of productive work even in off-peak seasons or help out in others' work, by virtue of the fact that jobs in agriculture are never rigidly defined. However, unemployment in the urban areas is a clear-cut phenomenon, and a person is always either employed or unemployed. The political ramifications of large-scale unemployment in the city are familiar and require little elaboration. A politicized unemployed labor force, which poses a big threat to any government, has to be appeased by provisions that are essentially unproductive, if not counterproductive, to development, such as costly welfare programs and minimum wage legislation. In contrast, an economy with more people relying on their land for subsistence is far more stable politically and less dependent on such provisions.

Concentration of labor produces not only an army of urban unemployed but also a pool of people easily infected by consumption expectations. This does not mean that farmers are not susceptible to demonstration effects, but with lags in information, the effects will generally be less formidable and easier to contain. With less expectations, less political demands, less need to provide for the urban infrastructure and more ability to sustain a subsistence level of living, the amount of subsidy that a government expends in real terms on a person in the rural sector will probably be much less than what it has to pay for a person in the urban sector. Compared on these terms, subsidy to agricultural development is likely to be a lesser evil, even if we take into account the fact that the foreign exchange earning power of industrial output is generally higher than that of agricultural output.

Sustainable Development, Climatic Hazards and the Future of Agriculture

In the above discussions, we have not taken ecological considerations into account. While it is clear that rural activities and urban industrialization are both causes of pollution, emphasis on agriculture at least has the advantage that we will be more concerned with and sensitive to the role of nature and how farming systems could eventually be harmonized with the environment. With increased interest and sensitivity, we will naturally be led toward the direction of evolving farming systems that are sustainable. In this regard, it is useful to briefly look at the concept of sustainable development and the "sustainable development paradigm" which has recently been on the ascendency in development economics.

The relevance to agriculture is that in this paradigm, agriculture becomes the focal point, partly because attempts to operationalize sustainability in the ecological sense inevitably involve agricultural processes and activities, and partly because sustainable agricultural development, if it turns out to be a feasible proposition, will offer an alternative mode and a new hope of development for the Third World. Exactly what constitutes "sustainable agriculture" or "SD in agriculture," unfortunately, remains highly imprecise and controversial. Part of the controversy arises from the fact that the terms "sustainable agriculture," "low-input agriculture" and "organic farming," which differ in meaning and connotation, are used interchangeably (Buttel and Gillespie 1988). Also contributing to the confusion is the fact that many international organizations are still confusing sustainable agriculture in terms of minimal damage to the quality of the environment with the mere maintenance of the growth of agricultural production.

It is clear that the single-minded pursuit to maintain the growth of agricultural output, for both developing and the developed countries alike, is incompatible with ecological sustainability, which must constitute the core meaning of sustainable development in order that the latter be a meaningful concept. Within the realm of thought on sustainability, different opinions exist as to what constitutes the proper trade-off between maintaining agricultural growth using man-made inputs and protecting the environment from rapid degradation. There are, too, a variety of positions representing the different extents to which one should copy the wisdom of nature and the extent to which we should inject human knowledge and technology, to either make up for nature's deficiencies or speed up nature's work. We have, for example, the purist position held by Masanobu Fukuoka, who recommended a complete trust in nature's wisdom and thereby minimal human toil (1978, 1985). At the opposite extreme, we have agronomists from, for example, the New Alchemy Institute in Falmouth, Massachusetts, who enlist the help of computers, advanced polymers and geodesic domes in the quest for ever more elegant legerdemain, trying to match old wisdom to new science and creating such things as argon-insulated bioshelters; small-scale aquaculture tanks; and vacuum-bagged constant-camber, wood-epoxy fishing boats, all of which were designed to be made cheaply and simply anywhere in the world (Eisenberg 1989, p. 84). There are others who advocate somewhat similar ideas but under different labels. We have, for instance, the idea of "permaculture" coined by Bill Mollison, who saw it as the conscious design and maintenance of agriculturally productive ecosystems which have the diversity, stability and resilience of natural ecosystems (1989). Right now, at virtually all fronts, we are witnessing the flowering of different approaches to natural and organic farming, such as the double-digging system advocated by John Jeavons or the do-nothing gardening of Ruth Stout.

These developments are, of course, at once encouraging and confusing. There are many misconceptions that will have to be weeded out, and there are inappropriate approaches that will eventually be eliminated as the idea of sustainability becomes better articulated and as the trade-off relations between upgrading agricultural productivity and protecting the long-term well-being of the environment become more manifest and precise. Out of these diverse approaches, we could reasonably expect that some kind of grand synthesis will form, respecting the wisdom of nature on the one hand, yet injecting human knowledge that is compatible with or mimics that wisdom on the other. Such a grand synthesis will not have been possible without first reorienting our focus and interest on the nature of agriculture, with its power and its limitations. Hence, we have an additional case for taking agriculture seriously.

It may be feared that by the time we have unlocked the wisdom of nature to the point where we believe we are well placed to complement or enhance it, nature may have already undergone important changes that outdate our acquired knowledge. The vigorous ways that we, in our ignorance, build up our modern, technology based civilization seem to have effected an irreversible impact on key factors that govern our environment and the atmosphere. The gradual warming of the planet owing to the greenhouse effect and the depletion of the ozone layer through the buildup of chlorofluorocarbons, with their far-reaching consequences on human life, seem in their broad outline to have become well-established and commonly accepted theses among the scientific community. The rates at which these phenomena progress and the specific consequences they will trigger are still highly controversial and subject to wild speculation, but the possibility of adverse consequences can no longer be ignored, even as steps are now being taken across the international community to take remedial action and enforce agreements reached, such as the agreement to control the use of chlorofluorocarbons. Whereas this is a matter of life-and-death importance to humanity and deserves immediate and great attention, the purpose of this book will permit only some speculations of the broad impact on agriculture and how agriculture might be organized in principle in order to survive them. It is hoped that the overall impact will be relatively mild or containable by some self-regulating mechanisms not yet known to us, and that no major disruptions will eventually ensue. Wishful thinking apart, however, it is wise of agricultural systems to build in some features in order that the disruptive effects, if any, can be kept within manageable bounds.

Let us assume that more instability in the weather, including more heat and more drought, lie ahead. These changes will affect factors like moisture, temperature and the growing season. A longer growing season will be favorable to agriculture, but a lack of moisture will obviously hurt it. If temperatures stay warm, plants will grow nicely, but if temperatures get really hot, plants will wither while pests and diseases may proliferate. Climatic models, with too many variables to properly take into account, are generally too crude to project with any precision what will happen in a given area. How far the various climatic factors will interact, enhance or cancel each other out is difficult to estimate. In an agricultural area, as large and diverse as China, gains in some regions will surely be offset by losses in others, with the net result being anyone's guess. Should the erosion of the ozone layer further intensify, the number of hours of our possible exposure to the sun will be limited and much outdoor activity, on which agriculture largely depends, will have to be restricted. Should this become the case, agriculture will become a major casualty. Clearly, the list of miscellaneous effects that will result from changes in the atmosphere is literally infinite, especially when we take into account the fact that these effects will interact with one another ad infinitum. In the present study, we will have to assume that the effects will be relatively mild and that the uncertainties that will increase still lie within our ability to adapt.

To reduce the impact of the uncertainties ahead, an insurance-intensive mode of agriculture seems to be essential. Ideally, such a scheme should cover both the micro and the macro aspects of agriculture from, say, the choice of plants to the network of distribution. The basic idea is to spread risk across the entire spectrum of agricultural activities. In the realm of production, the insurance scheme should consist in diversifying the range of crops and in developing certain crops that are resistant to more extreme conditions—for example, crops with drought-resistant and pest-resistant properties—even if these trends may entail trade-offs in productivity. An insurance-conscious agricultural system naturally means that large-scale monoculture should be reduced. It entails more reliance on small holdings, within which diversities of output are to be further encouraged. Moreover, in ancitipation of large-scale crop failures due to climatic forces, investment in storage facilities and efficient transportation will become essential. To forestall the possibilities of prolonged famine, national stocks of grains to buffer adverse periods should be significantly enhanced. In addition, efficient transportation will be necessary to minimize waste from bumper harvests that some regions would unexpectedly experience aas a result of prolonged growing seasons.

On the assumption that uncertainties in climatic changes are not disruptive beyond our ability to adapt, an insurance-intensive agricultural system with small holdings, diverse crops, substantial collective investments to forestall natural hazards, and so on, would be better placed to meet the challenges of tomorrow.[2] China, with its relatively egalitarian holdings, relatively diverse patterns of crops and a historically well-developed collective system to mobilize people and materials seems to possess the essential elements for adopting an insurance-intensive agricultural system, although certain features would have to be strengthened or modified. With a vast population to feed, agriculture will remain the mainstay of China's economy for many years to come, and given that agriculture can be highly productive of human capital in the proper environment and that an insurance-intensive agricultural system is better placed to meet climatic hazards, the paramount importance of promoting agriculture in China should be clear to everyone.

The future of agriculture is also closely tied to advances in biotechnology and genetic engineering. Advances in this realm are important in that they will systematically improve the productivity of many existing types of plants, enhance their resistance to climatic hazards and enlarge the stock of possible crops that we could rely on. In some sense, the future of humanity will be intimately pegged to how far we can develop weather-resistant seeds and plants, which depends critically on the progress made in biotechnology. Without much speculation, biotechnology is the industry of the future. This, in turn, makes agriculture more dependent on human knowledge than on land, and also makes it more essential than other industries. Agriculture is no longer a stepping stone on the path to industrialization. With these advances, future agriculture might well become a knowledge-rich, biotechnology-based industry, a primary sector that insures humankind against the hazards of food shortages caused by the numerous changes in the environment. Moreover, it is likely to become the ultimate instrument for human survival.

A CRITICAL APPRAISAL OF CHINA'S AGRICULTURAL DEVELOPMENT SINCE 1949

Factors Governing Agricultural Development in China

Agricultural development in China was guided by two strands of philosophy, and specific policies that were pursued clearly reflected such underlying beliefs. It goes without saying that China's agriculture, being part of the socialist system, partakes of standard socialist features and takes on the socialist instruments of economic development, namely the egalitarian, collectivist approach and the reliance on planning and command. In addition, as a corollary to the Stalinist model of communist development, modernization of agriculture means its mechanization.

In spite of their professed acknowledgment of the importance of agriculture, Chinese leaders in general, like most politicians in the developing nations, have seen agriculture only as a stepping stone to industrialization. Agriculture was looked on as a sector that would eventually decline in importance as China became modernized. This "instrumentalist" strand of thought formed the backbone to China's basic philosophy toward agriculture and persisted regardless of apparent differences in the specific approaches or organizational strategies adopted during different periods of the Communist regime. These philosophies apart, a persistent feature that has characterized China's agriculture has been frequent reversals of policy caused by drastic political changes and ideological swings. Within Mao's regime alone, one could witness several swings in policies and approaches in this area. The agricultural policy under Deng's regime has been more consistent, but one is not entirely certain whether the recent swing toward political conservatism will eventually cause changes in policies in the countryside.

Collectivization of Agriculture under Mao

With the aid of the above framework, the specific policies and approaches that were adopted in China's agriculture for the past

40 years can be easily comprehended. In 1950, the stage was set for a system of socialist agriculture with the advent of land reform. The land reform was essentially a political movement aimed at destroying the traditional order in the countryside and preparing it to be replaced by a new collectivist machinery. As such, it was a halfway measure toward a full-blown socialist, collectivist agriculture which coincided with the unfolding of the First Five-Year Plan (1953–1957). Characteristic of the Leninist-Stalinist approach, the plan gave top investment priority to industry, which received 52.4 percent of total national investment, 89 percent of which was for heavy industry. Only 7.8 percent of the budget was given to agriculture. In spite of the relatively low funding, agriculture received much organizational attention. Impetus was given to the collectivization of agriculture under the leadership of Mao, who believed that collectivization was a precondition for agricultural modernization. Thus, the period of the First Five-Year Plan witnessed the rapid transformation of individual farms into collective farms, from the creation of mutual aid teams consisting of six neighboring households to the creation of elementary agricultural producers' cooperatives consisting of 20 to 40 households, and finally to the creation of advanced agricultural producers' cooperatives consisting of 100 to 300 households formed by merging elementary cooperatives. Within a span of five years, China's rural population had been organized from individual peasants into members of some 752,000 advanced cooperatives (Hsu 1982).

Collectivization in agriculture, as one might expect, was a two-edged sword. On the positive side, collectivization laid the foundation for an egalitarian system, the implementation of which helped China avoid the serious problems of polarization faced by many other developing economies. Thanks to this move, the Gini coefficient which measures the degree of income inequality was kept low by international standards in rural China. Unwittingly, it also made possible the unleashing of productive energies and impressive outputs under the earlier phase of Deng's regime of de-collectivization. By way of contrast, K. N. Raj pointed out that agriculture in India, which was plagued by inequality of holdings, fragmentation, and irrational land use, impeded the improvement of yields under a family farming regime (1983).

In addition, the command structure of collective agriculture enabled it to pool resources for projects needed to protect farms from major natural hazards—for example, flood control, pest control, and water conservation projects—as well as projects that directly enhance the productivity of farming—such as the building of small hydroelectric stations and irrigation projects. In this regard, the collective system was particularly effective in mobilizing farmers during off-peak months. Also of importance was the fact that the system enabled some degree of research and development as well as the transmission of important discoveries in farming techniques. Substantial economies of scale were also reaped in the mechanical aspects of farming, such as the use of tractors and the sharing of plough animals. Last but not least, the collective system at times served as a stabilizing factor, buffering the countryside from extreme sufferings under adverse conditions, like famines.

The following impressive results achieved under the collective regime are worth mentioning. As a result of collectivization, great improvements in irrigation and drainage were made, expanding the irrigated area at an average rate of slightly over one million hectares per year. By 1980, the total irrigated area was 47.3 million hectares, about 48 percent of total cultivated land. The expansion in irrigated areas made it possible to extend multiple-cropping and to achieve high, stable yields in many areas. In the realm of plant breeding, the collective system facilitated the speeding up of systematic breeding and the distribution of new varieties for large-scale adoption. For example, in 1964 the Chinese government began to distribute the high-yielding dwarf indica varieties of rice. By 1965, 3.3 million hectares in the south had been sown using these varieties and by 1977, these varieties were being grown on 80 percent of total rice land in China. A similar rate of diffusion also characterized the new hybrid rice first developed in 1971, which accounted for 34 percent of national rice acreage in China by 1987. As a matter of fact, China is the first country in the world where hybrid rice technology was successfully developed and used in large-scale cultivation (Barker and Herdt 1985, Lin 1989). In a similar vein, the rapid multiplication of improved seeds can be attributed to the existence of the collective system.

In certain aspects in the realm of technology and mechanization, the collective system also proved to be effective. For example, short-term training programs at the local level flourished under the collective system and helped to promote the dissemination of knowledge in operating farm machinery, handling farm chemicals and carrying out maintenance. The system also enabled the rapid diffusion of proven technologies, such as the generation of biogas. In the sphere of plant protection, the power of the collective system was obvious. Available evidence shows that China's plant protection programs could be considered outstanding, with the sucess due, to no small extent, to the organization of pest control encompassing different levels of agricultural units across the country. The communes, for example, had their own insect and disease forecasting stations, and the brigades and teams had plant protection workers in the field. Together with the country plant protection workers, they formed a countrywide network for crop protection.

Having said this much for collectivization, one should not, however, underestimate its negative aspects. Waste and inefficiency are universal to the collective system. The distribution and application of chemical fertilizers is a case in point. Estimates are that as much as 20 percent of the fertilizers were spoiled or wasted in the process of transportation, storage and distribution, amounting in 1980 to an annual loss of as much as 1.2 million tons. Objectionable, too, was the fact that collectivist concerns tended to override regional variations and locational differences, even in areas where those factors had a lot to contribute. Indeed, for a long stretch of time, most farming communiites did not have an accurate idea of the soil conditions of their land and did not apply the appropriate mix of nutrients.

As can be expected, a collective system gave much administrative power to party cadres who had little knowledge about farming and often made wrong judgments. By extension, the command system made it possible for a few top party leaders to impose their will on the system. Indeed, virtually all important aspects of agriculture were vulnerable to the whims and convictions of a few—including, among other elements, crop priorities, research emphases, investment priorities, procurement prices, agricultural taxes and loans. By corollary, changes in the leadership had a profound and unsettling effect on agriculture.

One of the most far-reaching negative impacts of collectivization was that it destroyed the traditional pattern of China's agriculture. Contrary to what the Chinese communists preached, precommunist Chinese agriculture was far from a backward system. By all accounts, it was fairly complex and sophisticated from the viewpoint of the evolution of cropping and marketing patterns (Lardy 1984). There was a great deal of regional specialization supported by extensive interregional trade. Innovative Chinese farmers generally adopted crops in regions where they enjoyed comparative advantages. One could perhaps say that beginning in the ninth century, the subsistence nature of China's rural economy was gradually transformed into a sophisticated program based on specialization and trade. Specifically, the development of interregional markets in rice and other staple commodities began as early as the Tang dynasty in the seventh century and accelerated during the twelfth and thirteenth centuries as the increased cultivation of sugar cane and other cash crops on the southeast coast was facilitated by shipments of rice and other staples from surplus regions in the Yangtse delta, the Canton delta, and the central Kan river valley. It appears, too, that even before the Ming dynasty, population densities on the southeast coast were clearly supported by the cultivation of cash crops traded for rice from surplus grain regions.

In line with its tacit philosophy of treating agriculture as a subsidiary to industry, in the autumn of 1953, China imposed the producer levy system, a system of compulsory deliveries at fixed prices, and subsequently introduced a system of coupon rationing to distribute state-procured cereals and vegetable oils to the urban populations. Expectedly, the effects on agriculture were negative. The farmers in effect began to subsidize the urban population, for government procurement policies invariably tended to lower the prices they received. Worse still, the rural markets and, by extension, interregional trade, suffered, as private traders now came under the administrative jurisdiction of the Ministry of Food and its local agencies. As a result, the volume of transactions in rural markets fell considerably. In the case of cotton, cotton growers were, as a matter of fact, prohibited from privately selling raw cotton, yarn or homemade cloth. The curtailment of local marketing reduced not only the prices peasants received and their opportunities to earn income from the sale of commodities not subject to state producer levies, but also reduced their opportunity to specialize in their production. The rural markets and interregional trade received a further blow during the Great Leap Forward (1958–1960). With the onset of the Cultural Revolution, trade declined further still. By 1978, the interprovincial trade of domestically produced cereals had shrunk to a few hundred thousand tons, or less than 1 percent of domestic production.

To briefly summarize, while in general the collective system in agriculture helps to alleviate extreme cases of suffering for a small part of its rural population for a particular period and helps to maintain a certain level of collective capital which is required for individual farming, the shortcomings and inertia of the system clearly override its advantages. The strategy of urging farmers to contribute under the collectivist ideology may well work during the first phase, when a large part of the farming population is operating below the subsistence level, but the momentum can hardly last long, for there is a limit to the persuasive power of the collective system and that limit usually comes quickly. Subsequent increased affluence and adversity alike would not make the individual farmers more motivated to give extra support to the collective system. In better times, a collective system enables most individuals to stay somehow above the level of subsistence, while in worse times, most individuals share the same fate and suffer together. On the average, production tends to stabilize or fluctuate around the line of subsistence, but there is hardly any possibility of escape.

The Great Leap Forward (1958–1960)

Treating agriculture as subsidiary to industry means, too, that the farm sector was forced into the unfortunate position of absorbing the shocks caused by mistakes made in the industry. Agriculture in China thus faced a double difficulty in adverse periods. The Great Leap Forward (1958–1960), which followed the First Five-Year Plan, illustrates this point clearly. The ill-conceived plan, which put its bet on heavy industry, led to excess industrial capacities, a high rate of unemployment, a shortage of raw materials for industry, inflationary pressures and lowered rural demand for industrial output. The Great Leap Forward was launched by Mao to correct such an adverse situation and to restore some balanced proportions among agriculture, light industry and heavy industry. It was also meant to absorb and exploit the surplus resources that appeared to exist in the countryside in order to maximize economic growth.

The Great Leap Forward (1958–1960) was thus an ambitious movement to mobilize all possible rural resources to attain the highest possible rates of growth. In a sense, the movement could be said to reflect Mao's "engineering" conceptions of development, namely, that the parameters governing development lay well within the control and persuasive ability of the government and that it was imperative for China to catch up with the West within the shortest possible time. It was therefore both necessary and possible to make up for the time China had lost during the First Five-Year Plan. To mobilize all the resources available would necessitate a formidable command system. To this end, People's Communes were set up starting in April 1958, with the whole of the nation becoming organized into some 26,400 communes through amalgamating the advanced agricultural producers' cooperatives, each of which consisted of 4,000 to 5,000 households. These communes, organizing large rural enterprises and capital projects and providing commune-wide services, began to dominate the entire life of the individual farmers.

The strategies adopted by the Great Leap Forward were to launch vigorous programs to build small, labor-intensive industrial plants in the countryside and big infrastructural projects for agriculture. Indigenous, labor-intensive plants employing local resources and raw materials were set up, such as iron and steel foundries, coal and iron ore mines, food processing plants, fertilizer factories, cement factories, and so on. It was believed that by making use of surplus resources existing in the country-side, these projects were capable of fostering a high rate of growth.

As might be expected, the Great Leap Forward turned out to be a failure and a disaster. The plants that mushroomed simply lacked the right kind of expertise and management to carry the new policies through. On the other hand, the increased political inter-ference and the imperative of the local units to match their perform-ances with the rhetoric and propaganda of the party meant that many of the projects were ill-conceived and of low quality. Instead of making use of surplus resources that allegedly existed in the rural sector, the Great Leap Forward ended up distorting the existing pattern of resources, damaging the environment with its poorly built projects and putting the farmers into an enslaved state. The result was a crisis of unprecedented magnitude. Again agricul-ture fell victim to the false image of modernization and the com-mand instrument that had made the mobilization of resources possible on such a scale.

Recovery and Cultural Revolution (1961–1976)

The period that followed was one of recovery and adjustment (1961–1965). It was directed by Liu Shaoqui, the country's chair-man and vice-chairman of the party, who set out to correct the excesses of the Great Leap Forward and to restore stability to the countryside. He emphasized the role of material incentives as opposed to the ideological purism of Mao. Under Liu, some private plots and rural markets were restored. Substantial progress was made in introducing and desseminating various types of agricul-tural technology. Water cónservation projects were improved and rural electrification was also stepped up. The recovery, however, was short-lived, and was brought to a halt as Mao launched his counterattack on what he perceived as the advent of "revisionism" in Liu's policies.

The subsequent period, the Cultural Revolution (1966–1976), reversed much of what had been gained in the period of recovery. The extreme leftist ideology downgraded the role of techniques and knowledge, as many schools and universities were closed for from one to four years. Under the banner of egalitarianism, political interference with peasant incentives and farming activities was deliberately increased. Allowing political matters to override economic considerations, the authority emphasized self-sufficiency of grain production regardless of locational characteristics. Once again agriculture fell victim to political struggles and ideological swings.[3] No matter how vigorously the collectivist ideology was pursued, there was a limit to the positive effects it could generate, and the rate at which they were generated was clearly subject to the law of diminishing returns. In spite of the emphasis given to grain production, grain output stagnated in 1968–1969, 1971–1972, and 1975–1977.

The death of Mao in 1976 and the arrest of the Gang of Four opened up a new era in China's development. Consistent with the traditional communist view, the new chairman of the party, Hua Guofeng, called for renewed development efforts in the newly drafted Ten-Year Development Plan (1976–1985), with emphasis to be put on heavy industry. Within agriculture, farm mechanization was given top priority. Under the plan it was envisaged that by 1985 at least 85 percent of all farm work would be mechanized, and that grain output would be increased to 400 million metric tons from the level of 285 tons in 1977. By 1979, however, it had been recognized that this essentially Soviet model was not suitable to China's situation and that some new breakthrough toward the direction of decentralization and the unleashing of the individual incentive was needed. That new breakthrough became the foundation of the 10-year reform undertaken under the direction of Deng.

Deng's Rural Reform and the Present State of Agriculture (1979–)

In 1979, a consensus developed among policymakers who began to recognize the serious imbalances existing in the economy as well as the stifling effects of the command system on productivity. By the time Deng assumed control, with Zhao Ziyang leading the way in his "experiments" in Sichuan Province, the stage was set for a radical reform in the organization of agriculture. The Third Plenum of the Eleventh Central Committee in December 1978 was looked on as the turning point in the change. Briefly, the decisions of the Third Plenum, as far as agriculture was concerned, consisted in raising farm prices (with grain quota procurement prices going up 20 percent from the summer harvest of 1979 onward), forbidding the higher authorities to intervene with the rights and decisions of commune subunits, especially the production teams, and permitting contracting output to small groups within the production team. Subsequent policy changes of importance included raising the limit on the size of private plots and relaxing the policy of enforced self-sufficiency in grain. The most dramatic change, however, came along with Document 75 issued by the Central Committee in late September 1980, which almost unconditionally permitted contracting output and indeed, everything else, to the household. This in effect ended the commune as a composite unit combining political and economic authority. In a matter of three years, the household was almost completely restored as the basic unit of production in agriculture.

The whole process of de-collectivization (baogan daohu) could be seen to consist of three stages. Under the first phase, the means of production, such as draft animals, tools, and equipment, were divided among households, while the team was to retain the power to set sales quotas and tax obligations. After meeting its sales and tax obligations, the household was free to dispose of its surplus. It could sell to the state at above-quota prices and beyond that at still higher "negotiated prices," or it could sell in the free market. Thus, an increase in productivity would result in a disproportionately higher increase in income for the household. The second phase of decollectivization, rendered effective with Document Number 1 in 1983, witnessed more important steps forward. The household was then free to hire labor, to buy its own motor vehicles and farm machinery, and to market its surplus product (namely, what was above state quotas) across administrative boundaries. These advances were further consolidated with the issue of Document Number 1 of 1984, which essentially permitted a free enterprise system in agriculture. Lease-like arrangements between households, permitting concentration of land in the hands of the more efficient ones, were legislated, as were household investments in different kinds of private and cooperative enterprises. To consolidate the farmer's incentive and to discourage the predatory use of land, contracts between households and government were lengthened to periods of more than 15 years. As households became free to lease their land, farmers were, by corollary, free to pursue their occupation and to go after what they perceived as better opportunities. A class of farmers-turned-entrepreneurs thus sprang up, engaging itself vigorously in a multiplicity of rural enterprises or becoming employed in different types of nonfarm work such as industry, construction, transport, commerce and services. At the end of 1984, about one-quarter of the rural labor force was said to be engaged in nonfarm activities. Thus, within a matter of six years, a kind of "peasant capitalism" entirely replaced collectivism as the dominant mode of rural organization and production, reaching proportions no less than those of a revolution.

The results of these changes were impressive. Agricultural output increased at an annual rate of 7.5 percent between 1980–1982 and 13 percent between 1982–1986. Most components of farm output grew faster than the rates registered in the prereform period. Except for grain, all components registered phenomenal growth, nongrain crops growing by 13.2 and 9.4 percent in the periods 1980–1982 and 1982–1986 respectively. Animal husbandry grew by 10.1 percent throughout 1980–1982. Most dramatic of all was the growth of subsidiary output and rural industries, registering 40 and 43.1 percent annual growth respectively in 1982 and

1986. Indeed, nearly 60 percent of the increase in output in the years 1983–1986 was accounted for by rural industries (Perkins 1988). Although grain output grew at a slow rate of 3.9 percent and 2.5 percent during the periods 1980–1982 and 1982–1986 respectively, these increases were achieved in spite of a 10 percent drop in the acreage sown. These results speak of an indisputable success and indeed, it was this phenomenal success that gave Chinese leaders both the will power and the political capital to subsequently launch a large-scale reform of the urban industries. Within the realm of agriculture, further reforms continued. At the beginning of 1985, Zhao Ziyang announced the phasing out of mandatory quotas. Prices of all agricultural products, with the exception of grain and cotton, were to be set by market forces. In the latter case, the state would contract to buy smaller quantities than before, leaving the farmers more freedom to sell in the market. The latter measure was, of course, also intended to reduce the heavy grain subsidy the state had been incurring, which amounted to about 10 percent of total government expenditures in 1981.

While the de-collectivization drive was undoubtedly a success, it too was marred by the myopic, instrumentalist philosophy that Chinese policymakers adopted towards agriculture, which led them to ignore the hazards of progressing too rapidly. They did not seem to realize that the phenomenal success in farm performance was due in part to the legacy handed down by the collectivist past, which included the clearing away of institutional obstacles against a more rational distribution of land and means of production, a more equitable access to material inputs such as seeds and fertilizers, and more equal selling rights to the official collection/distribution agency. The collective mode of rural organization, too, enabled indispensable public infrastructures to be erected, as well as permitting easier dissemination of technological information. Had the Chinese policymakers been more sensitive to the importance of the foundation to their success, they would have taken measures to replenish at least a significant part of such collective capital, the rapid depletion of which became unavoidable under an individualist regime. Bread, as always, was perceived to be the

intermediate good used for producing steel. In 1978, total government investment in agriculture accounted for about 10.6 percent
of overall government expenditures. In 1986, when agriculture was
contributing importantly to the growth of the national output, it
received only about 3.3 percent of government expenditures. As a
result, rural infrastructural capital was depleted at a much faster
rate than it was replenished. In many areas, irrigation works and
their maintenance received inadequate attention. Instead, much of
the increase in household income went into consumption, including traditional activities such as weddings, ceremonies and religious celebrations, and into housing. Indeed, the amount of irrigated
area fell between 1978 and 1983. According to an estimate made
by R. Du, the development of the rural economy would call for an
investment level of 1,000–1,500 billion yuan between 1985 and
the year 2000 if it were to sustain its then-prevailing rate of
development (1985). However, the amount to be contributed by
the state in the current plan was only about one-fifth of this
estimate. Any provision beyond that would have to be taken care
of by other agencies, such as the farmers themselves, private or
collective enterprises or the banking system.

It would be a gross mistake to infer that there was lack of funds
in the agricultural sector. A lot of funds were available, but they
were in the hands of private households or in the banking system,
and intended largely for investment in the nonfarming sector,
namely the rural industries and commerce. Such a development
was intentional. It was in line with the thinking of the Chinese
policymakers, who considered that nonfarm activities represented
the hope and the future of China's rural population. As we have
previously mentioned, some officials even predicted that by the
year 2000, the proportion of the rural labor force engaged in
agriculture would decline from 80–85 percent in 1987 to about 30
percent, with the difference to be absorbed by rural industry and
commerce, mining, forestry, services, and so on (Delfs 1984). The
Chinese policymakers also expressed hope that by then China's
farms would be well consolidated and mechanized. Presently, the
average farm size is one-third of a hectare. The Chinese policy-

makers believed that for effective mechanization, the average farm size should be 2 hectares instead. The ideal situation would be that the farms could be continually enlarged and mechanized, yielding higher levels of output as well as surplus labor that would again be absorbed into the nonfarm sector.

Such an ideal is false. It assumes that the consolidation of farms would be able to proceed smoothly. This, however, is unlikely to be the case. Many farmers, out of their traditional land-bound attitude, still keep their lands and work on them half-heartedly while striving to make extra gains in nonfarm activities. Besides, the authority seems to underestimate the impetus given to rural population growth by the household responsibility system. The increased rate of population growth clearly renders the desired rate of farm consolidation a lot more difficult to attain. Furthermore, the success of raising productivity in agriculture is contingent on a multiplicity of factors, of which mechanization and scale, while important, are not necessarily the most crucial.

Given their instrumentalist frame of mind, Chinese policy-makers were expectedly insensitive to the destablizing effects of the disproportional growth of the nonfarm sector. These destablizing effects were multidimensional. First, nonfarm projects, especially industries producing consumption goods, fulfilled latent demands that had previously been suppressed under the collective regime, and hence stood to profit easily. Protected by the local province or county, they quickly took over the traditional market shares previously controlled by the state enterprises. As a result of their profitability, they easily acquired more funding from the local banking system. The result was that long-term investments in agriculture proper were ignored. Second, as it was liable to generate quick and large profits, the nonfarm sector unwittingly bred an unbridled aspiration for consumption. The demonstration effects that were created, in turn sucked more resources and funds out of agriculture. As might be expected, the farmers who moved off their land were no longer inclined to go back except in extreme cases. As the nonfarm sector grew into a significant size, it tied its fate to the business cycle of the urban industrial system and shared its ups and downs. Hence arose another dimension of instability. Needless to say, unemployment in the nonfarm sector was always more of a problem than the same level of unemployment in the farm sector because the capacity to create employment in the latter was more flexible.

Apart from the disproportionate growth of the nonfarm sector, there were other problems that resulted from the rapid de-collectivization. These included, among others, the destruction of collective property; an enhanced sense of insecurity among some of the farmers; the increased tension between local cadres and the households, with the former being losers in the exchange; an increased rural birth rate spurred by the demand for household labor; increasing polarization in income among different households and regions; and conflicts between the production of the farmers and the planners' preferences (Riskin 1987). Some of these problems were not insurmountable but they did merit serious attention. Many of the natural disasters that have occurred recently should not be attributed to climatic factors alone: The rapid de-collectivization clearly had to bear part of the responsibility. Erosion of soil caused by the reckless felling of trees and the clearing of forests for fuel or building materials used in the construction of houses and by the rural industries must have contributed, to no small extent, to the environmental degradation of the countryside. Some of these problems, such as the polarization of income, caused little harm during the brighter days but could well be amplified when compounded with other problems.

Thus, in spite of a promising start, subsequent developments did not sustain the initial success of the rural reform. By 1986, it was obvious that the success had run its course, with output having reached a plateau for major items. Since 1986, grain production has stagnated, with the total output in 1988 remaining at the same level as that of 1986 (394 million tons). Cotton production, in fact, registered declines. In 1986, total output reached 4.14 million tons, but in 1988 it dropped to 4.06 million tons. The stagnation was temporarily compensated for by growths being registered in other farm items and the nonfarm sector, until the weaknesses of the rural reform were thrown open and compounded by the setbacks in the urban industrial reform. A crisis, indeed, seemed to have been gradually in the making in the countryside since 1988.

Troubles began as inflation began to climb in the city starting in 1987, caused by a sustained expansion drive across the nation that was backed up by a strong credit expansion. The escalating inflation reduced, on the one hand, the real income of urban workers and their effective demand, and on the other hand, led to shortages and hoarding of materials in the industries, raising the cost of essential inputs to agriculture, notably chemical fertilizers. Matters then worsened as the government started to impose austerity measures in order to curb the overheated demand. One result was that some provinces found themselves short of finances with which to procure grain from the farmers, and were compelled to issue them IOUs. Another result was that the nonfarm sector, which depended on credit available from local banks that was no longer forthcoming, had to throw thousands of people in the countryside out of jobs. The negative impacts of these developments on agriculture began to unfold starting in 1987. Agricultural output stagnated. Both acreage sown and total output in 1988 fell below the 1987 level. In 1988, imports of grains grew to 15.33 million tons, doubling the 7.73 million tons imported in 1986. The 14.7 million tons of fertilizers imported in 1988 almost tripled the level of 5.1 million tons registered in 1986.

In response to cost increases, reduced demand and the uncertainty caused by the issue of IOUs, farming behaviors in China are undergoing changes. Let us assume that the government, out of political considerations, stops issuing IOUs for forthcoming harvests and thereby avoids a crisis of nondelivery from the farmers. This does not mean, however, that it will be able to honor its commitment to supply fertilizers at stipulated prices and to make preproduction deposits to the farmers in time. The medium-term consequence will be that the rational farmer, in response to the lack of inputs and finance and to the uncertainty of payment, will cut back production especially as oil prices and prices of chemical fertilizers are on the increase. Cutbacks in farm production will mean that consumers shopping in the free market may experience a further increase in prices. Increases in prices may, in turn, reduce the overall effective demand, justifying further cutbacks of production on the part of the farmer.

The possibility that government will not issue IOUs directly does not mean that it will have the full ability to pay for its procurement. To do so, it may have to resort to printing money. To a cash-hungry government, the temptation to do so is irresistible. Unfortunately, the consequence of printing money is that more inflation will lie ahead. Farmers who come to realize that they receive deflated values for the crops they submit will resist fulfilling the full quota that is imposed on them. The result is either that government will have to raise the procurement price, which will send its budget further into the red, or it will have to apply some kind of coercion. The former may help for a while, but the latter will likely generate resistance, for the average farmer is no longer the same as under the regime of Mao. The taste of prosperity and freedom has made him too individualistic to accept blind coercion. The result of the above developments is that the overall level of procurement may be on the decline. To combat this situation, the government may consider recentralizing the rural organization, but clearly it is no longer practical to do so. Such a move would not only reverse the cardinal achievement of Deng, it would also mean an immediate sharp drop in output, the political consequences of which could hardly be ignored by the policymakers. At any rate, inadequate procurement and the subsequent shortage for distribution to the cities, coupled with rising prices in the free market, may make the already discontented urban workers panic unless the government steps up its imports in time. Beyond a point, rationing may have to be reinstituted in some cities. Were such a tense atmosphere to develop nationwide, the news of riot in a particular place could trigger large-scale disturbances. Some kind of time bomb seems to have been set, and it may require only certain conditions or contingencies for the explosion to take place unless something drastic is done.[4]

NOTES

1. For a summary of this thesis, see Prebisch (1959).

2. Care must, however, be taken to ensure that the insurance system will not dampen farmer incentives and entrepreneurship.

3. These general trends, of course, concealed small and gradual improvements in different areas, although on the whole this was a period of setback if not stagnation.

4. Since 1989 there have been occasional unconfirmed reports of farmers rioting against the authorities in some countries.

5

An Agenda for Effective Reform

WHAT LESSONS HAVE WE LEARNED?

China is clearly in a state of predicament, and there is an unmistakable need for continuing the reforms. However, exactly what types of reforms are still being tolerated, what types can be vigorously pursued and what types will be effective within the political constraints and ideological regime of the day are controversial issues. The present chapter will sketch an agenda for reform, drawing lessons from what we have discussed so far. Based on fundamental principles, the agenda recommended here will have to ignore the question of ideology, although caution will be exercised to make sure that the recommendations do not directly contradict or challenge the existing political framework. From Chapter 1 we have learned that partial reform of the type conducted by Deng and Zhao is not tenable because the system under reform is irrational and highly indivisible. Being indivisible in character, it is capable of transmitting its irrational elements throughout the system and sustaining these irrationalities. Without a thoroughgoing price reform compelling the system to become completely divisible, there will be no penalty system sufficiently powerful to offset or check the excesses caused by the incentive schemes that are needed to unleash reform energies. In addition, the irrational price system set free by the reform tends to create runaway inflationary pressures that are politically unpalatable. The reform undertaken was, as we pointed out, not completely lacking in chances for success. The years 1984–1985 were a golden opportunity for a complete decontrol of prices. However, to grasp such an opportunity would require the policymakers in question to possess at once the understanding, the will, the political capital and the ideology needed to justify a change of such a nature and magnitude. Needless to say, such a combination of favorable conditions cannot be expected to recur often enough to be readily exploited.

From our analysis of socialism in Chapter 2, and in particular from our moral critique of socialism, two points should be transparent. First, any "end-result–based" economic system aiming to promote egalitarianism for every individual, regardless of his or her level of effort, has the countereffect of demolishing the basis of self-responsibility wherein lies the moral strength of any robust economy. Second, any centrally planned economy designed to attain specific results will encourage hypocrisy and create a class of privileged moral guardians who can impose moralistic interpretations on others at will. In short, the entire command system is highly indivisible. As a result, the straightforward reward-effort relations so essential to its effective operation and, indeed, to the effective operation of any economy, are rendered highly invisible. However, the theoretical demise of an egalitarian system does not imply the demise of the second-best ideal of continually maximizing opportunities for the maximal number of economic players based on a preset system of ground rules of reward and penalty. To avoid the mistakes of socialism, this system must not be end-result–based. It must, on the contrary, operate impartially on a set of initial principles known in advance to all economic players, plus a set of self-regulative corrective devices, the rules of which are also to be made known to the players ahead of time. Whether such a system embodying a maximal number of historical principles of justice is called a kind of modified socialism or a modified capitalism is not important.

From our analysis of the drawbacks of existing development theories, we have learned that a tenable development strategy needs to be two-tiered, aiming on the one hand to promote the formation of capital in the generalized sense (which consists importantly of human capital), and on the other hand, to avoid the emergence of anticapital, thus forcing the economy toward the hazardous path of hyperdeficit and inflation. We have also examined the respective roles of the market and the government in development and the potential hazards of relying overly on either of the two agencies before the market reaches a mature state. Based on this analysis we have recommended some plausible strategies that are compatible with the general principle of generating continually maximal opportunities for the maximal number of players without leading the economy toward either a state of explosive disequilibrium or the trap of a low-level equilibrium. These strategies and principles are of relelvance to China's situation, and will form a part of the basis of our recommended agenda for reform.

From our analysis of the place of agriculture in development and the nature of hazards facing it, we should be able to appreciate the plausible role of agriculture as a vehicle to development, as well as the preconditions that make such a role fruitful. We should appreciate the enormous potential contributions that agriculture can make to human capital formation once the system has overcome the obstacles to farmer-entrepreneurship, which is hard to come by in agriculture. We have also examined current controversies over what mode of farming is compatible with the concept of environmental substainability and have seen, in light of the increasing vagaries of the earth's climate, the need for an insurance-intensive farming system. It remains to be seen in what way entrepreneurship could be spurred in an agricultural system like that of China, which is a country populated by conservative, resource-poor farmers, and in what way the market could be gradually nurtured to play a more important role in order that government subsidies could finally be phased out. Our analysis of China's agricultural development in the Communist regime also shows how ideological swings and the instrumentalist mentality held by policymakers in China toward agriculture have led to the different disasters and difficulties that plagued Chinese agriculture.

The above-mentioned frameworks, which we have elaborated in the preceding chapters, are pertinent to the situation of China, for China is at once a socialist country, a developing economy, and a predominantly agricultural system. They will form the basis of our proposed agenda for reform. As can be expected, our prescriptions will have to concentrate on broad directions and strategies rather than on specific policies, for the crisis that China is now facing goes deeper than either its financial predicament, the low level of productivity that plagues its industrial system, or the interlocking debts haunting its different enterprises. The most important part of the crisis is the lack of self-knowledge of its policymakers and the lack of a sense of direction toward which reform efforts can be fruitfully applied and resources can be properly allocated. In short, it is a crisis of ignorance, a crisis that has plagued the Communist regime since its inception. The policy prescriptions we make are, of course, tailored to the characteristics of China, but their usefulness should not be restricted to China's situation. Some of the prescriptions are sufficiently general for wider application, as many of the principles embodied are fundamental.

Before we go ahead, a foretaste of my prescriptions may be in order here. In its long-term interest, China should adopt a lasting agriculture-first policy. This policy should remain as a permanent feature of China's economy. Agriculture should be looked on as the regular source of entrepreneurship and a major stabilizing factor to the economy. The countryside rather than the urban city should be made the ideal place for future human settlement. From the instrumental stance, we will contend that agriculture is the least hazardous point of departure for reform. China's urban industrial system is plagued by the existence of interlocking vicious circles to the extent that it is next to "nonreformable" without a sweeping and comprehensive package of reform policies supported by strong political will and power. However, the present political situation in China no longer permits partial reforms of the type pursued during Zhao's rule, let alone a comprehensive reform consisting of a complete price decontrol. The agricultural system remains the only area free of the contagious irrationalities of the urban industrial system, and is also the only area on which favorable conditions for a comprehensive reform could gradually be reinstated.

In spite of its present setbacks, China's agricultural system on the whole, and especially the farm sector, is still in a relatively healthy state. For all its current stagnation, China's agriculture is still blessed by many positive aspects, such as its largely rational and egalitarian holdings, a collective machinery that is experienced in infrastructural building, a nationwide network for efficient dissemination of information and techniques, and a potentially large internal market with much room for regional specialization. There are, of course, many drawbacks to the system, but comparatively speaking, it is in the best possible position to serve as the spearhead for future reform.

In a nutshell, our first agenda for reform is to create a powerful agricultural base for China, on which self-contained rural industries can be rebuilt. Before such a strong base emerges, steps must be taken to insulate the agricultural system from being affected by the irrationalities of the urban industrial system. In the meantime, steps should be taken to render the urban industrial system less indivisible and less invisible. With more divisibility and visibility, it is hoped that more of its irrational components could be identified and avoided by its economic actors, while at the same time its rational elements could be enhanced and further strengthened. Eventually we can expect that with the integration between the rural and the urban systems, a free market for all would emerge.

ADOPTING THE AGRICULTURE-FIRST POLICY

Building the Missing Link of Entrepreneurship

The crucial missing link in agricultural development is the lack of entrepreneurship. Operations on the farm, unlike those in an industrial plant, are not well structured. Much room therefore exists for managerial improvement and for the upgrading of productivity, but these improvements clearly lie beyond the resources of the typical farmer who responds largely to the flow of events or is confident only in using conventional techniques. The farm, however small in size, is a self-contained commercial unit consisting of a multiplicity of jobs, ranging from financing, accounting, production and distribution to marketing. Even granted that the farmer is a technically competent, hard-working and efficient individual, it is inconceivable that he would be fully competent in these different aspects. In fact, it is the fundamental complexity of agricultural work that calls for specialization and thereby justifies larger-scale farming. For reasons already stated, however, large-scale farms are not tenable modes of farming. Large-scale farms of the collective type suffer from incentive problems, and large-scale private, commercial, plantation-type farms are liable to create the serious problem of income polarization in the process of development. Their profit positions are subject to the vagaries of the international commodity markets and, more often than not, they fall victim to international protectionism. It seems, therefore, that some middle course has to be steered. Farms should stay relatively small, but at the same time, specialization of farm jobs should be encouraged to increase productivity.

The way to do this would be to nurture a class of "agromanagers" who would play the role of management and technical consultants as well as researchers, coordinators and business agents to the farmer. Let us construct the following scheme: Suppose there are groups of agro-managers who are organized into teams, with a team being headed by a senior agro-manager who is assisted by a few junior ones. Each team is assigned to serve, say, 10 farms in the neighborhood. As a management and technical consultant, the team is to help to raise the efficiency of the farmer and his household by way of, say, developing or keeping some effective accounting system for the farm, initiating work and motion studies appropriate to the farm's nature and scale, and developing viable inventory, storage systems, and so on. As a research center, the team is to disseminate research information to the farms it serves and to test out some of the new techniques available. In this connection, the team will have to keep in close touch with the regional experimental stations or experimental farms. As a coordinator, the team is to closely monitor the interests of the farm it serves in conjunction with the interests of farms in other areas, for example, pest control, water conservation and rural public works. As a business agent, the team is to assist or to represent its farms in marketing their output, negotiating credits with banks, procuring farm inputs and farm machines, planning their cash flows, monitoring their changes in profitability, dealing with government officials over procurement matters and similar things.

These agro-managers can in the first phase be government employees or even party cadres. While they are to receive state remuneration, some kind of bonus system could be designed to peg their bonus to the medium-term increases in output or profit of those farms that they are assigned to serve. The bonus can be fully borne by the government until the farms are willing to do so. The important point to note is not how much government will subsidize, because government subsidy is a must in the first stage. However, after a period of, say, five years, by which time a considerable number of the farms they serve might come to accept the value of their services, the teams could choose to become independent, deriving their income solely from farms or, if the conditions are not yet completely favorable for financial independence, they could opt for some kind of intermediate status, drawing income on the government on the one hand while operating part of their services on a commercial basis. Whatever the case, the idea is that commercially based agro-management services should gradually evolve as farmers come to appreciate the value of these services and are able to pay for them. Of course, not all agro-managers will choose to establish commercial services, and some may be content to remain as government employees. Some agro-managers may even choose to become farmers themselves. Again, the important point is that under such a scheme, agro-managers who are entrepreneurally minded will have the opportunity to commercialize their services and in due course to expand their operation and range of services.

Some of these agro-managers need, of course, some background training in agriculture sciences, including, say, agrochemistry, agrobiology, agrology, agrostology and agrotechnology. One would expect some of them to be graduates from agricultural schools or to have completed courses in agriculture in the universities. Assistants or junior members in the team can have lesser qualifications, and it is important that lack of qualification does not handicap any of them in their future career. Indeed, some of these assistants should preferably be young people, say, graduates from rural schools and should have some practical knowledge in farming. One cannot expect, of course, that any particular team would be able to effectively discharge all the functions we have outlined in the above discussion, and much of the expertise of the team might well be acquired on the job. Since these teams would be part of a larger network, they would be able to call on help and resources from their regional headquarters, experimental stations or national agricultural research institutes. Indeed, these teams in the field would be accountable to officers vested with regional responsibilities whose duties are to coordinate the activities of these different teams in the region. To provide back-up services to these teams in the field, there should also be "specialist" teams that operate from some regional headquarters. Although the various teams in the field have to be made accountable to their respective headquarters, they should in principle be autonomous units. Disputes that might arise between these teams and their farms or among the teams themselves should, of course, be resolved at the level of the regional headquarters.

The nurture of a nationwide class of agro-managers is by no means an easy task. Available statistics, according to the World Bank (1983), show that there is an acute shortage of agricultural technicians working on farms and in extension services. The low aggregate national enrollment in agriculture education is equally disappointing. The World Bank statistics for China show that in 1979 there were only 110,000 students in technical agricultural schools and 226,000 in senior secondary schools with agricultural programs (or about .6 percent of the relevant age group) in a society where agriculture occupies 75 percent of the labor force. Consider the following example: According to the same World Bank report, a prefecture in Hubei, with a population of 2.6 million, of which well over 90 percent are rural inhabitants and depend on agriculture for their living, has 2,400 primary schools with 450,000 students, 553 general secondary and primary teacher training schools with 164,000 students, yet only 1 agricultural school with 335 students and 1 farm machinery school with 200 students.[1] Of the 40,000 senior secondary and post-secondary–level students in the prefecture, only 1 percent study agriculture and farming. Even more disappointing, only 25 percent of the 335 students in the Hubei agricultural school had agriculture as their first choice for further training, despite the shortage of agronomists and abundant employment opportunities for trained agriculturists in the prefecture (World Bank 1983, p. 157). Due to the prevailing social ethos against a career in agriculture, even graduates from agricultural schools who came from rural backgrounds did not prefer working in agriculture, and few returned to direct farming activities. On the nonformal front, efficient on-the-job training for agricultural workers and technicians for agriculture is generally difficult to develop. The situation may have somehow improved after 1979 with more emphasis being put on agriculture. No current statistics are available, but the World Bank surmises that there have been no radical changes since then (World Bank 1985, p. 27). Short of a drastic institutional change, the prospect remains a dismal one.

Against this background, it is imperative that a handsome initial salary be paid to the agro-managers in order to attract promising students into agricultural schools and colleges. At any rate, it has been claimed in Cuba that a change in the salary structure so that agronomists are paid higher salaries than academicians and technicians has successfully solved this problem (World Bank 1983). In our case, it is obvious that the same strategy is necessary, though not sufficient, for the purpose. It is hoped that the new package for the agro-managers, namely a higher salary, a profit-sharing scheme and the possibility of ownership in a commercial enterprise, might attract students to pursue a career in agriculture. To strengthen this strategy, an additional approach would be to grant higher subsidies to students who enter the agriculture stream and to penalize them if they subsequently abandon this career. Granted even partial success, the above scheme would call for an extensive expansion of slots in agriculture courses in schools or colleges, the establishment of new schools or training institutions and a vigorous program of nonformal education in agriculture.

The above scheme has a strong motivating component. Since agro-managers know that after a stipulated period they will run their services as commercial enterprises and hence will face competition for business from other teams, it is in their interest to serve their first assigned clients as well as they can and to win a reputation before commercialization occurs. Even those agro-managers who decide to remain in government service can hardly afford to ignore the competition they will encounter when the commercialization phase begins. Competition for client patronage means that the agro-managers will naturally be forced to develop better techniques and to strive for more useful information. Farms in different regions will therefore stand to benefit, both in information and techniques, from the cross-fertilization of knowledge among the agro-managers. With rapid dissemination of knowledge and techniques, fewer farms will be able to outperform the rest by wide margins for a long period and, accordingly, a pattern of even performance will likely prevail.

Modes of Farming and Land Policies

We have pointed out that the early success of Deng's rural reform was very much dependent on the collectivist legacy of Mao. We have also mentioned that different regimes in the history of the People's Republic of China, regardless of differences in their ideological bent, invariably have favored large-scale, mechanized farming. We have also mentioned that Chinese policymakers under Deng's regime, in recognition of the predatory use of land by household farms, wisely extended the duration of contract to 15 years and beyond. All these are complexly and intricately related to two key issues in Chinese agriculture, namely what particular mode of farming China should promote and what land policy it should adopt. Clearly, decisions pertaining to these issues have far-reaching ramifications for rural employment, the farm size, the rate of income polarization, the rate of rural population growth, the willingness of farmers to plough surpluses back into their farms, their visions of the future and indeed, almost every important aspect of agriculture.

Traditional Chinese agriculture is characterized by labor-intensive farming, employing organic fertilizers such as human and animal manure to maintain soil fertility. Two directions of technical progress were favored during the Communist regime, namely, the promotion of the use of chemical fertilizers and the promotion of mechanization. The former is not incompatible with the traditional system, whereas the latter has required changes in land policy. Whereas during Mao's regime farms were centralized by political organization, it is the intention of the reformers in the Deng era that existing farms should evolve into larger sizes so that mechanization would become possible. Regardless of the difference in the approaches adopted, the policymakers concerned all have failed to grasp the potential hazards inherent in this particular mode of farming in both the short and the long run. Briefly, being capital-intensive and land-intensive, this mode of farming works against the factor endowments of China's rural system. Successful mechanization, apart from the sizable level of capital initially required, presupposes a steady supply of inputs such as electric power, gasoline and an efficient backup system of machine repair and maintenance, as well as the ready availability of spare parts and other technical services, most of which are underdeveloped in China's countryside. It also presupposes a certain level of organizational ability as well as the ability to absorb risk on the part of the farmer. Without such backup, it is doubtful whether mechanization could easily attain the increasing returns to scale that are hoped for. Even if we grant that the mechanization process is successful, it will quickly aggravate the problem of rural unemployment and will bring about a rapid polarization of income among farms of different sizes. All these will have destabilizing effects on the rural sector. Besides, when one considers that mechanization invariably promotes monoculture, and that monoculture is potentially hazardous in an era of uncertain climatic conditions, the case for large-scale mechanization as a universal strategy for agricultural development can hardly be established, although, as we will explain later, there is still a case for maintaining a certain proportion of large farms. Reformers under Deng's regime implicitly assume that rural unemployment can be more than offset by a growing nonfarm sector, but clearly they have not fully taken into account the detrimental effects of relying on the nonfarm sector.

Giving up the large-scale, highly mechanized mode of farming leaves us the alternative of small-scale, labor-intensive farming. Small-scale farming, however, need not entail a limit in the scope of productivity. In the short run, small-scale farming is invariably labor intensive. However, labor-intensive farming is not incompatible with our development criteria for maximal entrepreneurship, maximal employment opportunities and minimal rate of income polarization. Labor-intensive farming is, moreover, not necessarily backward and does not mean low productivity. A comparison of Asian countries in labor inputs per hectare shows striking intercountry differences, with the most advanced Japanese system having labor inputs four or five times as high as those in West Bengal (Reynolds 1975). This suggests strongly that there is great potential for labor absorption and labor productivity increases within many existing agricultural systems.

In the long run, the kind of small-scale farming we have in mind is "knowledge farming." With a new class of agro-managers promoting farm entrepreneurship and land substitutes, farming should gradually move from being manual-labor intensive to being knowledge-labor intensive, or simply to being knowledge intensive. Knowledge farming can be both labor intensive and non–labor intensive. Knowledge farming is labor intensive in the sense that since agricultural output is highly sensitive to rainfall, temperature, soil condition, altitude, length of day during the growing season, and other factors, all of which are highly locational and specific, we have to diligently adapt research findings and techniques to local conditions. This also explains the important role of the agro-managers, part of whose work is to test out the applicability of different technologies to the local conditions governing their clients' farms. Ecological considerations and the need for an insurance-intensive system of farming is also congenial to knowledge-intensive farming and small-scale farming. The advent of knowledge farming means that the farmer will be in a better position to adapt himself to the vicissitudes of climatic factors. It helps him, for example, to more rapidly and more confidently select new plants with weather-resistant characteristics and similar qualities. The prevalence of small-scale farming also means that there will be an increased diversity of agricultural outputs within any particular region, thus reducing the negative impacts of climatic hazards.

Knowledge farming of the labor-intensive type is, however, not the only mode of knowledge farming available. We have mentioned briefly the kind of farming Fukuoka promoted, namely natural farming (1978, 1985). Natural farming is essentially knowledge farming of a higher order, and is non–labor intensive. In part, Fukuoka's idea, along with similar ones held by other innovators in the field, is a response to the predicaments faced by the present mode of agriculture, which include, among others, the rising cost of chemical fertilizers and labor, and threats to the environment. These predicaments challenge the basis of traditional labor-intensive farming as well as chemical-intensive agriculture. As a matter of fact, wheat has already become a financial loss crop in many places, and rice is quickly becoming another. The idea behind natural farming is to dispense with cultivation, weeding, the use of chemical fertilizers and chemical pest control. This mode of farming, if it were capable of being universally applied, would entail not only that the environment could be revitalized and preserved, but also that the severe overpopulation problem which causes great distress to the farmer and the developing country could be alleviated. Part of the pressure to produce large families is due to the need for more labor. However, as Fukuoka pointed out, this process is self-defeating, as land would have to be subdivided due to an increasing population. Indeed, both environmental degradation and uncontrolled population growth became serious problems facing the countryside during the later days of Deng's rural reform.

Fukuoka's methods, if his claims could be ultimately substantiated, would eliminate as much as 90 percent of the labor conventionally required, as the land is never cultivated. The goal of his methods is to revitalize the land by providing it with basic nutrients through nonchemical means such as cover cropping, use of green manure, sheet compositing and pond culture. According to Fukuoka, the three modes of farming—traditional, chemical and natural—yield comparable levels of harvest in the short term, but differ markedly in their effects on the soil in the longer term. Using the traditional method, the condition of the soil tends to remain about the same over the years. The farmer receives a yield in direct proportion to the amount of compost and manure he puts in. The soil in the fields of the chemical farmers, however, becomes lifeless and depleted of its native fertility in a relatively short span. With natural farming, however, the soil improves with every season.

The most important implication of Fukuoka's proposal is that rice can be grown without flooding the field throughout the growing season. In his view, natural farming can completely eliminate the need for irrigation in many places. If his thesis is true, rice and other high-yielding crops could be grown in areas not previously thought suitable. Steep and marginal land could be brought into production without danger of erosion. In addition, soils already damaged by careless agricultural practices or by chemicals could be effectively rehabilitated. Growing crops in such a healthy environment also protects them from diseases and insects, and the crops are seldom devastated.

Natural farming in different versions is still in the stage of experimentation, and there is insufficient evidence to show that its application can be universal and can provide widespread substitutes for the kind of traditional or chemical farming practiced in most of the arable lands of China. Even if it turns out to be technically feasible, its ramifications for labor employment in the short term would be staggering as far as China is concerned. Furthermore, it is questionable in theory if one should subscribe completely to the laws of nature, for there is no a priori reason why human knowledge could not improve on such laws. Clearly natural farming could always be supplemented by new techniques gained from biotechnology. In addition, we would have to assume that manmade impacts on nature are reversible. Clearly this is no longer a valid assumption, as much of the environment has already been changed by human ignorance or design. Fukuoka, for instance, did not deal with the possible effects of a warming earth on his mode of farming. In spite of such limitations, natural farming may be instrumental in opening up vast marginal lands in China as well as those lands that were once considered to lie beyond effective agriculture.

The above inconclusive discussion means that we cannot rely on any particular mode of farming in a lopsided way. Knowledge farming takes time to develop, while the merits of natural farming remain to be confirmed. In such a background of ignorance, and partly for insurance and pragmatic considerations, we propose to adopt an eclectic approach and to develop a balanced portfolio consisting of the traditional (organic), the chemical (now being promoted), and the mechanical, as well as knowledge and natural farming. The way to do so is to set up some broad ratios for each type of farming as well as to stipulate their respective farm sizes, with these stipulations subject to review from time to time. Such broad ratios and their changes will reflect the overall direction of emphasis to be given, which in turn should reflect changes in our knowledge of the respective merits and suitability of these different modes in the particular context of China's development.

Setting up arbitrary scales of farms for different modes of farming might appear restrictive. However, the restrictiveness is only apparent. Under the regime of fixed scale, both the farmer and the agro-managers will concentrate their attention on raising productivity via intensive use of land or through developing land substitutes. Such development fits well with the labor-intensive characteristic of China's agriculture in the first stage. In turn, the increasing adoption of land-saving techniques will stimulate the complementary development of labor-saving techniques especially those of the manual kind. These changes will eventually alleviate the joint pressures on arable land and labor supply, both of which underlie the traditional rural misery and poverty. The rate of productivity increase of this scheme for the agricultural system as a whole may be lower than that of a system with unrestricted modes and scales of operation, but the hazards of the latter, such as income polarization and monoculture, may well be avoided in the present scheme.

As far as land policy goes, within our proposed framework one should expect several stages of development, each requiring a different set of strategies. With more people presently thrown out of jobs in the nonfarm sector, in particular in the rural industries which are now in trouble, we would expect an increasing demand for farmland as an increasing number of people return to their homelands to seek a living. Even if we discount this contingency, we expect the demand for land to increase as our proposed scheme starts to be implemented. Increased government spending in agriculture and the emergence of agro-managers will attract more people to work on the land, reversing the movement of labor from the cities to the countryside. To meet the increasing demand for farmland, several sources of supply are available. One source would be the production of new farmlands with the aid of infrastructural projects, such as irrigation. However, we have reservations about producing land extensively in this manner, for not only is the cost of land production going to be formidable, its negative impacts on the environment could also be serious. Although in the course of land production, a considerable number of unemployed laborers could be absorbed, it clearly is not advisable to employ this method extensively. Instead, if initial experiments turn out to be favorable, we would recommend the opening up to natural farming of marginal lands hitherto not considered profitable for agriculture. Another source of supply would be from the return of farms from disinterested farmers, from confiscation of land from non–tax-paying farmers, and from land presently subleased by nonproducing farmers. All in all, the guiding principle during this first period should be that only the farmer who is committed to working on the land should be granted a lease, and that he should concentate on upgrading the productivity of his land rather than increasing his output by expanding the scale of his farm.

In the medium term, the overall demand for farmland should stabilize, although the rates of demand among different types and sizes of farmland will differ. Demand will increase as the profitability of farming improves, but at the same time it will ease as labor-saving techniques become more dominant. Demand will also ease as more farmers decide to have fewer children to provide manual labor for the farm. Since the cost of rearing a child to the point of turning him into a knowledge farmer will far exceed that of rearing a child in order to make use of his manual labor, the cost of education will gradually impose a constraint on the rate of population growth and hence the demand for farmland. In the long term, as the profitability of farming becomes more steady and predictable, the government might start to relax its control over land transfer and might consider introducing an auction system, or indeed, any system that will foster competition and maintain the momentum of knowledge acquisition and development. Such a system should further stimulate the drive toward productivity increases while generating more revenue for the government.

Low-Hazard Schemes for Sustaining Peasant Incentives

One major problem of development in agriculture is to sustain peasant incentives, particularly in the earlier phases of development. The problem is a complex one. We have mentioned that on the supply side, the peasants are too conservative to plough back their surplus into their farmland for fear of potential natural hazards and are too ignorant to know what types of investments will bear fruitful results. The demand side is no less hazardous. Increases in output, if not matched by effective demand and steady prices, may incur losses on the part of the farmer. Increases in output, too, might backfire if the terms of trade between agricultural output and consumer/capital goods become highly unfavorable. Exporting, on the other hand, is a remote possibility for the small farms, and those that have the capability to do so invariably experience disturbing price fluctuations in the international commodity markets. All these factors are liable to dampen the incentives of the farmer and tend to inculcate a fatalistic mentality, inducing him to spend more on present consumption than he saves for investing into the future.

To sustain peasant incentives requires a steady demand for their output. There is presently an additional need to sustain the level of demand for farm output in China: Increasing rural unemployment and the declining real income of urban workers are jointly depressing the present level of demand. It is imperative in the short run that the Chinese authority make a serious effort to take care of this problem. In this connection, collective investments in infrastructure, as well as our proposal to develop teams of agro-managers and give them attractive pay, will help to offset part of the slackening demand.

In the medium to long term, the most important route to step up effective demand in a country with a vast terriority and many interregional differences is via the expansion of interregional trade. The economic history of China has testified to the viability of this route, and we have already dealt with this point. To promote interregional trade requires an extensive buildup of infrastructural facilities which include, among others, communication, storage and transportation facilities as well as a dense network of market centers. It is neither necessary nor possible for government to plan such provisions down to every detail or to finance every project, but nonetheless government clearly has a role in taking the lead. Given the vast size of China, the room for regional specialization and interregional trade is enormous and would, in the long term, provide the impetus needed in sustaining demand for farm output. Once the first hurdles and thresholds have been crossed, the system will become self-generating. Before this point is reached, government may, as a buffer, continue to help the existing farms via an income support scheme, although this could be designed on a diminishing basis. In the meantime, to encourage the plough-back of farm surpluses, a system of input subsidies relating the level of subsidy to output performance might be considered.

Readers may notice that thus far we have not mentioned the export of agricultural output as a vehicle to sustain production. Given the vagaries of the international commodity markets and the existence of different types of international agreements and cartels on agricultural products, the capability to export successfully would require conditions such as physical facilities and commercial and financial skills, which are far beyond what the individual farmer or his local marketing organization possesses. It is also doubtful whether state trading organizations that operate rigidly in a communist regime are able to cope with the vagaries concerned. Since China is blessed by the size of its domestic markets, it could well bypass such a hazardous path in the earlier phases of its agricultural development.

The same, however, should not be said of processed food, which is a mainstay of demand for farm products. No effort should be spared to promote this industry, both at the rural and urban level, as it has strong forward linkage effects and could eventually make steady inroads into the international markets. The development of this industry, however, must be viewed as a long-term process, and it should be built from the local level with indigenous resources. As interregional trade develops, the industry would grow as specialization gradually takes place. The potentials of this industry are vast, as can be witnessed in the developments of the same industry in Japan. Indeed, given the vast size of China's domestic markets, the food industry could well become a major industry, and China might, given sufficient time and effort, become a leader in the world market in this field.

Eventually, when the farmer has raised himself well above the level of subsistence, the point will be reached when he will start asking why he should continue to expend his energies on increasing his output and productivity. He will ask why he should continue to invest for the future instead of directing his surplus to immediate consumption activities. He will query the meaning of continuing investment if he cannot insure for his future by accumulating marketable properties, or if he cannot consume at will the goods so highly valued by consumers in the urban centers or in foreign countries. Sooner or later, he must give new meaning to his vigorous activities and find justification for making extra efforts. We have already noted how farmers in China are strongly addicted both to traditional, ceremonial and ritualistic types of consumption and to modern consumption. In a country like China where private property rights are extremely restricted and where the transfer of these rights is not legitimized or legally protected, it is small wonder that farmers turn to immediate consumption as soon as they lift themselves above the poverty line. As affluence grows in the rural area, it is important that the Chinese authority consider unconditionally permitting some kind of marketable property rights in order that farmers can make lasting investments. As we know too well, incentives are the key to material progress and, within some limits, private property ownership offers the strongest bond linking work and rewards.

The Financial Aspects of Agricultural Development

The schemes recommended in the preceding sections will, upon implementation, require substantial public financing. To reiterate, finances will be needed for land production, temporary unemployment relief (for the rural unemployed), executing the nationwide agro-manager program (including formal and nonformal training facilities and activities), infrastructural projects necessary to maintain the arability of existing farmland and infrastructural building to promote interregional trade. This list could be further expanded. The critical question is how these activities are to be financed. By corollary, one would also ask whether the revenue from these investments would ever pay off, whether such spending and subsidies would go on indefinitely, and if not, what kind of payback period one should assume. Unless these questions are satisfactorily answered, policymakers will be hesitant to undertake expenditures of such a scale, particularly as China is presently facing a deteriorating financial deficit. We do not have backup figures to quantify the range of expenditures these projects will incur. We will, however, attempt to show that over time such expenditures should stabilize at a certain level, as the revenue from these investments will gradually be on the increase. Hopefully, at some point the gap may be closed.

In the first period, during which a colossal amount of funding is necessary, the funds, apart from the normal budget earmarked for agriculture, could conceivably come from cutbacks of expenditure in other sectors and increases in savings deposits via more attractive interest rates, as well as from regional loans. Transfer from other sectors would be politically sensitive, and resistance could be expected from industries dominated by powerful vested interests such as the heavy industries. Given the considerable amount of capital accumulated in the rural sector over the past 10 years, government may consider acquiring such capital that still remains idle and stays clear of the banking system by offering higher rates of interest or by offering participation in government projects with a guaranteed rate of return. Getting more funds from international agencies such as the World Bank should not be an insurmountable task.[2] This is because these international agencies have now been converted to the view that the most meaningful path for development is sustainable development, and that the buildup of a sustainable agriculture is one major pillar of a sustainable development program. More important, as we will show below, the payback capacity of our proposed program is likely to be significant. Furthermore, international security considerations would prompt some Western countries to shortly resume making loans to China.

The reason why our proposed program is financially viable is that the overall expenditure involved will, at some point, level off. Infrastructural projects to facilitate trade are largely one-shot investments, as are training facilities for farmers and agro-managers.

Infrastructural projects to maintain existing arable land also tend to stabilize at a certain level. Similarly, marginal land production is also likely to stabilize at some point, as the promotion of natural farming could be undertaken at a low cost. The only burden will be the heavy recurrent expenditure on personnel enumeration for agro-managers and trainers, but since we expect that some of these people will become private practitioners, the wage bill to be borne by the government will decline over time. In addition, since our proposed program to increase rural productivity should attract a sizable population from the city, the amount of food subsidies in real terms might be lowered over time. All these factors considered, the rate of investment necessary to sustain the momentum of development should peak at some point and then decline. The overall level of investment, though massive, is not entirely without some upper limit.

Predictably, the yield from this investment program will grow over time. With more farmlands being opened up and more inter-regional trade developing, one would expect that government would draw increasing revenues from its levies. Increased productivity from the farms should yield higher returns, making it possible for government to derive more revenue at one point or another, or at least to reduce the level of its income support. Commercialization of agro-management services will also in due course yield extra revenue for the government. It is, of course, difficult to determine the particular point at which the deficit can be eliminated. However, with increasing revenue accompanied by a gradual reduction of government commitments (such as insurance, financial services, technical consultancy, and pest control, which will be partially commercialized in the long run), it is not unreasonable to hope that the gap will some day be reduced if not altogether closed. To get an idea of the magnitude of the finances needed and the rate at which the gap may be closed, we suggest that further research be conducted so that different plausible scenarios can be constructed. Needless to say, care should be exercised to balance the need to raise revenues and the need to maintain peasant incentives so that changes in tax structures will have little dampening effects on incentive. At any rate, the overall direction will be a positive one.

All the above discussions presume that agricultural policies and measures are rather uniform across different provinces and that their administration is more or less standardized. In reality, local authorities have much elbow room in executing such policies and in modifying them to suit local conditions. To ensure that such local power will not distort the strategies recommended in the preceding sections, it is important that the central government make explicit the rules concerned and enforce their uniform application across the board.

A New Vision of the Countryside

Let us presume that knowledge farming becomes a reality at some time in the future, generating steady advances in productivity. Let us also presume that the increases in production will be absorbed by growing interregional demand, spurring further specialization in farming. Finally, let us presume that this virtuous circle is firmly erected, raising the profitability of farming without putting pressure on the demand for manual labor and thereby on land. At this point, conventional wisdom might lead us to think that we should, using such agricultural surplus, start to promote vigorous investments in industries and in the buildup of urban cities. This, however, is where we part company from conventional wisdom. We believe, in the long-term interests of China, that it should continue to build on the strength it has developed in agriculture and should use a substantial part of its surplus to build an attractive countryside. In other words, creating a most habitable countryside in conjunction with sustaining a prosperous agriculture, rather than propelling the entire economy toward maximal industrial growth, is, in our opinion, a more desirable goal of development. The countryside, it must be reemphasized, is where China's future lies.

In the short to medium term, developing an attractive countryside will go a long way toward relieving the problems of China's industrial sector, which is currently oppressed by an irrational price regime. It will help to avert the type of exodus of rural workers into the cities that we recently witnessed with its destabilizing effects. A more prosperous countryside, being able to take up more employment, will reduce the colossal amount of subsidy now needed to keep the urban population afloat. In addition, a prosperous countryside also has much to offer in alleviating the shortage of agricultural products and raw materials as well as the inflationary pressures in urban China.

With hindsight and increased knowledge, the issue of whether the mode of development that the industrial West has pursued is in the best interests of humanity in the long run has become a questionable proposition.[3] The opportunity cost of the quest for incessant growth, as we now have come to learn, is colossal. The prosperity thus brought about was purchased at the expense of ecological imbalances and the degeneration of the environment. It was attained at the expense of the rapid depletion of nonrenewable resources or, alternatively put, at the expense of the interests of our future generations. Environmental degeneration or the depletion of nonrenewable resources is not, of course, restricted to the industrial nations. Population pressures in a typical developing country invariably lead its members to unthinkingly exploit their land (although their impacts are dwarfed by those made by the industrial West). China is no exception. Already, experts in China are extremely worried over the rate of depletion of the country's natural resources and the degradation of the environment. A statement recently made by a group of scientists showed great concern over the imbalance of the ecological system; the rate of deforestation; the rate of desert formation; the overgrazing of the grassland; the depletion of water; the accumulation of wastes, especially around the urban areas; acid rain; and so on—phenomena that are already manifest in many parts of China. Apart from the contributions made by the urban population and industries, both agriculture and the flourishing rural industry in China clearly must be held responsible for this unfavorable development.[4] To build a prosperous yet ecologically sustainable countryside must therefore be a major item on our reform agenda.

As ecological considerations will impede the development of productivity and, therefore, negatively affect the profitability of investments, it is difficult to take these factors completely into account at the initial stage of rural development. However, as prosperity in the rural sector begins to appear, farmers should be persuaded to compromise their short-term profitability in favor of the long-term sustainability of their environment. On the other hand, new knowledge and available expertise might help to lower the trade-off cost. In this regard, our proposed strategy to restrict the proportion of large-scale farming is relevant in that it helps to limit the extent to which China has to depend on inorganic farming, a mode that has proven to be highly detrimental to the environment. Another strategy we suggest is to switch gradually toward ecological and natural farming, if it can be shown that their adverse effects on output are tolerable. It is hoped that our knowledge might reach a stage where a kind of high-yield ecological farming (based on knowledge) becomes possible. Before this stage, however, once they have reached a certain level of affluence, farmers should be persuaded to pay more attention to the idea of sustainability.

To create a healthy countryside to the extent that the natural environment could be well preserved and its natural resources conserved, it is important for farmers to plough back from agriculture a considerable portion of their surpluses. To discourage people from migrating to the cities in the long run, one prerequisite would be to provide in the countryside adequate public amenities that people will find in the cities. In this regard, a proper step would be to erect extensive cultural amenities, with a view to promoting more awareness and interest in the nonmaterial, non–zero-sum aspects of social life. Surpluses that accumulate in the countryside should therefore be used to provide for such amenities so that rural life and work can become both lively and comfortable.

All these measures can jointly generate a virtuous circle. Increasing employment opportunities will attract an inflow of people into the countryside, which helps to increase production and maintain the effective demand for farm products. The increase in effective demand makes it possible to sustain the development of high-yield knowledge farming. The raise in productivity through knowledge farming enables more funds to be made available in improving the quality of the countryside, which in turn makes it more tempting for city dwellers to consider moving there. Such developments may not excite or even interest those who are attuned to the Western model of industrialization and mode of living, but to the Third World, this might represent the "optimal" path of development and might even constitute the ideal.

INTEGRATING THE RURAL AND URBAN SECTORS

Rural Insulation: Building a Self-Contained Economic Base in the Countryside

By the time a relatively prosperous countryside has appeared, measures could be taken to reintegrate the booming countryside and the urban industrial system. There is no need to rush toward this integration, particularly if the agriculture-first policy were to be jeopardized or compromised. The key to the integration consists in the development of a powerful base of rural industries, which already has a strong foundation in the Chinese countryside. Readers may point out that since we have criticized the vigorous expansion of rural industries in Deng's rural reform, we are contradicting ourselves by assigning this important role to rural industries. We therefore need to reconcile our positions. Admittedly, rural industries have much to contribute to development. They are the breeding ground for many a rural entrepreneur, and they make important use of farm outputs. The income they earn provides the effective demand for farm products, and thus they contribute to the creation of employment opportunities. They also help to diversify the source of income for the countryside and, in this sense, they serve as a kind of insurance system.

There are, however, many negative aspects to the unfettered development of rural industries, especially if they are vigorously pursued before the farm sector has attained a high level of productivity. Farming and industry, it should be pointed out, operate and mature in two very different time frames, knowledge farming in particular. Since knowledge farming requires a longer incubation period before leaps of productivity can be realized, rural industries appear to have an edge both in return and in productivity in the short run. However, given the primacy of farming (for reasons we have already elaborated), it would surely be a mistake to allow the proliferation of rural industries at the expense of the resources that should first be channeled to the building of a solid farm system.

Another problem with the rapid development of rural industries in China, as we have also pointed out, was that as these industries grew in an unfettered manner, they became infected by the irrationalities of the urban industrial system. Less hampered by bureaucratic reins, these industries attracted vast funding from local and provincial banks and thus became increasingly dependent on the credit system of the urban industrial complex, not unexpectedly causing a capacity expansion that was out of line with effective demand. As they grew, they increasingly made use of the inputs from the urban industrial system, and thus their price structures began to partake of the irrationalities of those of the urban industrial system. It is not surprising, therefore, that when the recentralization policy was enacted, the rural industries immediately felt the pinch and became the major casualty. The present predicament of China, in fact, is contributed to, to no small extent, by the difficulties faced by these industries. Had these industries evolved more slowly and depended more on their own resources, they would have built a stronger base over time, although they would still experience their own cycles of boom and bust. Another objection to the existing rural industries is that they are a major factor contributing to the environmental degradation of China's countryside, a point that needs no further elaboration.

In view of the above, Chinese policymakers would be well advised not to indiscriminately rescue all the rural enterprises that are now in trouble (apart from the obvious fact that the government does not have the resources to do so), in spite of the unemployment effects they will create. Where the government decides to embark on a rescue program, it should concentrate selectively on those rural industries least linked to the urban industrial system, namely industries that depend minimally on the supply of inputs from the urban industrial system as well as those whose outputs hardly depend on the demand of the city dwellers. In other words, the rural industries that are to be rescued or further developed in the future should be insulated as far as possible from the urban industrial system, and should remain so until a strong, self-contained industrial base gradually reemerges in the countryside, or until the urban industrial system itself becomes a significantly divisible and rational system.

From the above, some measures to guide the sound development of rural industries can be deduced. In order that rural industries will not outgrow the resources needed for the development of the farms, some kind of discriminatory taxes might be considered. In a similar vein, a discriminatory tax system could be applied to discourage the development of those rural industries that are closely linked to the urban industrial system. The idea is, of course, to allow rural industries to grow from their own resources and to evolve linkage effects among themselves. To protect the environment, a system of surcharges might be developed to discourage the proliferation of those industries that have negative impacts on the environment, together with certain laws that limit the kind of rural industries to be permitted. These are restrictive measures that will impede the rapid development of the rural industries and the rate at which it is going to absorb rural labor. Considering, however, the potential hazards of the rapid development of these industries, a slower rate of development may well turn out to be a blessing in disguise.

Dissolving the Seamless Web of Irrational Prices

We have said in various parts of this book that partial reform under an irrational price system is an impossible proposition. The crux of the problem is that apart from effecting a complete price decontrol, no part of the system could become a starter for reform because irrationalities pervade different parts of the system. This is not unexpected. Since all decisions of the economic actors are somehow expressed in prices, the irrationality of some prices in one part of the system will be transmitted to and infect the rest of the system. It follows, therefore, that any move to improve the system by changing any particular parameter inside it stands little chance of success because it cannot alter the system's basic irrationality. Another fatal limitation on reform under an irrational price system is that without rational prices to penalize inefficient acts or wrong decisions, incentive schemes alone will lead the system toward a state of explosive disequilibrium, as was the case in China.

Economists disagree substantially in their prescriptions for China's reform. Some economists, notably Milton Friedman, prescribe a monetarist-cum-free-market approach (Friedman 1990). They believe that the runaway situation experienced in the later days of Zhao was due to the joint effects of a liberal credit expansion and the irrational price regime. Naturally, their solution consists in a restriction of the money supply together with a comprehensive lifting of price controls. While such a heavy dose will doubtlessly work given sufficient time, the solution is politically not palatable. Indeed, one could hardly expect a socialist government, keen on preserving its power, to be willing to bear the political consequences of the inflationary pressures that are to be unleashed by a wholesale price decontrol, and merely restricting money supply without decontrolling prices would leave the irrational system intact and would therefore be no starter at all. Indeed, under a restrictive money supply regime, the least politically sheltered parts would bear the brunt of the impact, aggravating the irrationality of the system rather than alleviating it.

Micro-policy measures to contain inflation, such as taxing the price-raising party (say on net inflated turnover or on increased gross profit due entirely to price increases, for example) are, in principle, sound measures (see Wallich and Weintraub 1971, Weintraub 1970, Woo 1984). They are sound measures in principle because they aim at rooting out the benefits of inflation that the price-raisers set out to reap, thereby refocusing the attention of the producers on productivity increases or product innovation rather than on price manipulation. However, these measures are not easily applicable in a developing nation, where accounting systems are underdeveloped and accounting procedures are not standardized. Enforcement is, needless to say, also an almost insurmountable problem because of corruption, red tape or both.

To overcome such difficulties, a two-tiered strategy is recommended. First, measures are taken to render the irrational industrial system relatively less important to the extent that it will become over time the "second" economy, with its position taken over by the agricultural system, which is expected to rise in importance. Second, measures are to be taken to de-scale enterprises in the industrial system to the point that the irrationalities haunting the system become more transparent to the economic actors and more containable by the policymakers. By corollary, measures should be taken to insulate the agriculture system as far as possible from the urban industrial system, a point with which we have already dealt.

Methods to de-scale the industrial sector consist of reducing the level of resources to be channeled into this sector, in allowing bankruptcies of state enterprises, encouraging state enterprises to break up and allowing the free movement of labor. The first measure needs little elaboration. With respect to the institution of bankruptcy laws, it should be noted that although Zhao had been pushing such legislations ahead with great vigor, he was only able to get them passed in the final days of his reform. As a result, the bankruptcy laws have never been seriously enforced in the state enterprise sector. State enterprises in trouble are, as a rule, being bailed out. While the tightening of credit under the austerity program is triggering a chain of collapses among both the private enterprises and the collective enterprises, making bankruptcy a reality by default in the nonstate sector, the state enterprises remain unscathed. As a matter of fact, to avoid the chain effects spreading far and wide, state enterprises have been given ample subsidies regardless of their performances.

It would be a great mistake if the Chinese policymakers were to continue to insulate the state enterprises from the effects of these widespread bankruptcies, although it might be partly justified on employment grounds. Our proposal to step up spending in agriculture should in time absorb a large number of the urban unemployed. Thus, increases in unemployment in the industrial sector caused by bankruptcies of the state enterprises should not be feared. Too many workers in the state enterprises have been in a state of "disguised employment," drawing income very much out of line with their work and productivity. The adversity that is now facing the economy should give the government a good excuse to accept bankruptcy as a normal rule of the game, and, by corollary, to adopt the policy of free mobility of labor.

Enforcing bankruptcy laws and instituting a free labor market will have far-reaching benefits. They will compel more rational allocations of resources within a highly irrational regime. Although by themselves these measures are still insufficient to reduce the overall irrationality of the industrial system, they are essential steps for further reform. Of great importance, they go a long way in de-scaling the industrial system. Recent steps taken by many collective enterprises to absorb their spin-offs or joint ventures into the parent system amount to a rescaling of the industrial system, and will have highly detrimental effects on productivity.

The importance behind de-scaling, to repeat, is twofold. First, it renders the irrational elements in an irrational price system more visible and avoidable. Second, it makes more straightforward and transparent the relations between rewards received and efforts contributed by the economic participants. Different ways of de-scaling industrial organizations are possible. Sophisticated contractual arrangements can be set up for de-scaling to take place without physically dislocating or actually disintegrating existing enterprises. It is possible, for example, to devise rules to facilitate the breaking up or the spinning off of certain parts of an organization that would be better run as independent operations. The management of different parts of an existing enterprise should be encouraged to negotiate with the parent management for more autonomy in decision making, or to become independent specialized units or to become separate enterprises. Lease and buy-back agreements could be instituted for the spin-offs to take over and buy back the assets of the original enterprises on an installment basis. Franchise-like agreements can also be used to retain parent–spin-off relations. The above steps may well be the starting point of a rudimentary system of private property rights, although there is no need to rush into this institution. Under a still-irrational regime, what can be hoped for in the short to medium run is the gradual dilution of the most obvious irrational elements. As long as an important number of prices within the system are still arbitrary, the prices of private properties (should the latter be allowed) will remain less than rational, for people who opt for such properties will still have to operate under far-from-perfect information and make less-than-optimal decisions.

To add impetus to the process of de-scaling, policymakers may consider the rule that it will be the responsibility of the parent management to justify why it does not grant a spin-off contract to the applicants rather than the other way around. Courts should be set up to arbitrate these negotiations. With the above schemes, a new class of "intrapreneurs" seeking autonomous management responsibilities will spring up. Some loss of economies of scale may be possible, but we believe that as a whole, the industrial units in China are far oversized and that too many of the existing state enterprises have already been operating under diseconomies of scale. The real question therefore is not whether de-scaling is desirable, but rather what method of de-scaling would be more appropriate.

The result of de-scaling will be that managerial decision making will become highly decentralized. Such a state of affairs is often viewed by the Chinese authority, especially by the conservatives, as a state of chaos. This view, however, is not justified. Decentralized decision making under a regime of irrational prices breeding speculation and manipulation may be chaotic. However, if employees can now be fired, if a large range of prices are now rationalized under lease arrangements and franchise contracts, and if bankruptcies are now allowed, the system will become increasingly self-regulative and the manifest chaos will become more apparent than real. Critics may also contend that decentralized decision making may provide more chances for corruption and bureaucratic manipulation. Corruption may well remain, but with more enterprises becoming de-scaled and decentralized, the chances of syndicated corruption should also be reduced. Conversely, chances for the enforcement of the rule of law should be enhanced as vested interests are slowly dissolved under the de-scaling process. The emergence of competition will further trim the margin now available for large-scale corruption. Bit by bit, the irrationality of the system will melt.

These measures are, of course, not inconsistent with the open-door policy still said to be fully pursued. Foreign firms and joint ventures can still coexist with de-scaled state or collective enterprises, and foreign firms will no doubt benefit from a free labor market. Critics may argue that the austerity imposed on the urban industrial system, coupled with de-scaling, may further weaken the export performance of China's industries. The result would be a further curtailing of China's power to earn the foreign exchange needed to sustain the import of raw materials and technologies. However, if one considers that many of China's imports are of doubtful value and that sophisticated technologies purchased from abroad barely match the human capital structure of the enterprises concerned, one would wonder who actually benefits from these costly imports. As far as exports go, it is believed that a considerable part of what was exported was sold under cost by foreign exchange–hungry enterprises, a phenomenon very much facilitated by the dual price structure of the yenminbi. If such were the case, one could say that a considerable part of China's merchandise exports amount, in effect, to the export of its capital assets. Were the above interpretation correct, it would pay China to both export and import less in the short to medium term. Hence, a shrinking industrial system with less capability to import and export would not necessarily mean disadvantages for China.

In line with this argument, we would suggest that the two-tiered exchange rate system of the yenminbi be abolished as soon as the irrationality of the urban industrial system becomes less apparent. With this abolition, the black market will go. In the short run, this measure will throw a number of enterprises into jeopardy and will affect the existing pattern of imports and exports. However, if the government can allow bankruptcy among its enterprises caused by this change, it would be advisable that the two-tiered system be abolished as soon as possible. With the elimination of the two-tiered exchange rate, a significant aspect of the irrationalities in China's industrial system will be removed, preparing it for the final stage of complete price decontrol.

It may be useful to repeat the overarching economic principle behind our proposal. An irrational-cum-indivisible price system is a self-sustaining system. Because the system is characterized by chunks of indivisibilities, irrational prices in a part of the system tend to produce irrational prices in another part, and irrational prices existing in the first round will produce irrational prices in the second round. Hence, partial reform is bound to fail. To combat such a self-generating machinery, one needs to make the system increasingly more divisible. All the measures we propose for the urban industrial system, including allowing bankruptcies and labor mobility and promoting de-scaling of enterprises, are based on the principle of creating a fundamentally more divisible economy. In this way, the irrationalities that exist will become diluted until a point is finally reached when their negative effects become small enough to be easily contained. In other words, all these measures set the stage for the eventual uplifting of all price control and thereby the abolition of arbitrary prices.

One Free Market for All: Complete Price Decontrol under the Least Hazardous Conditions

In mid-1988, in a desperate attempt to once and for all wipe out the irrational price system that had clearly hampered effective reform, Deng strongly expressed his will to back the price decontrol program. Shortly after his strong statement, he quietly ate his words. The political risks of the escalating inflation that accompanied price decontrol were too formidable even for a political figure as powerful as he. The lesson is a resounding one. To effect price decontrol without incurring economic and political hazards in an irrational industrial system requires a set of favorable conditions that need to be carefully cultured. A rash move will only backfire.

By the time the measures we propose have taken root, we believe the conditions for a plausible comprehensive price decontrol will be gradually emerging. With the expansion of the economic power of the countryside, prices of farm products will be able to be kept at a steady level. With increasing income earned in the countryside, the demand for output from the urban industrial system will be on the increase, providing new opportunities for the more competitive enterprises there. The rural industries, through the operation of both vertical and horizontal linkages, will by this time have developed a more solid base. Outputs from these rural industries, either for final consumption or as intermediate inputs to other industries, will gradually make their way into the urban industrial system. Although in the early stage the types of outputs of the rural industries will overlap little with those produced in the urban industrial system, a point we have already elaborated, the linkage effects that both systems generate will gradually bring about an integration between them. Competition among the rural industries will lead to the lowering of the prices of their outputs, and, more important, will provide the urban industrial system with alternative sources of supply. As can be expected, the converse also holds. In this connection, the price system of the rural industries, which is essentially a rational one, will probably take the lead to reduce the irrationality of the urban system, particularly as the former grows in importance. As an integration between the two systems takes place, competition will further move their respective price structures toward a common, rational level.

These external stimuli, together with internal changes in the urban industrial system brought about by the measures we have discussed—namely, allowing bankruptcies and labor mobility and promoting de-scaling and decentralization—will gradually create the right conditions for an entire lifting of control over all kinds of prices. In the first phase of complete decontrol that is to take place, policymakers may consider applying a temporary income support program to be phased out according to some preset time table. Also in the initial stage of a complete price decontrol, some prices will go up, but they will effectively stimulate supply-side factors because the price now signals scarcities more accurately. In due course, some kind of dynamic equilibrium between the two sectors will be attained. The market, with its supreme signaling power of relative scarcities and opportunities, will become the chief guiding principle of resource allocation. Subscribing to the market function to stimulate growth does not, of course, mean that one should phase out the initial built-in self-correcting devices to ensure the continuing existence of maximal opportunities for most economic players, a point we will not repeat here.

Our vision of a future China is very different from that held by China's policymakers or the so called "architects" of the Four Modernizations for China. In our vision, a future China is to be populated by a mass of knowledge workers engaged permanently in farming. It is to be characterized by an attractive countryside promoting knowledge, education, art and culture. It will probably house the world's leading food industry and food-related industries. A future China will be characterized by a life-style that is different from what one finds in the industrial West. Industry will still be promoted but continuing growth will not be mandatory, especially if the environmental quality would be compromised. Sustainability is the chief consideration in long-range economic investments. The markets are basically free, but large-scale operations will be discouraged in ways and for reasons already given. Intrapreneurs will flourish and rewards will somehow be directed toward the operating persons rather than the inactive shareholders. All these ideas we have already argued for at length, and they will not be repeated.

China does not need modernization in the sense it is commonly conceived. Modernization in the material sense is a misleading concept and, at best, bad rhetoric. China needs to bypass the phase of material modernization. It should leap straight into the phase of "postmodern" society, in the way we have characterized above. Modernization via the route of vigorous industrialization as a developmental pathway is a misconceived strategy, costly to attain and not sustainable. Being a latecomer, China should be able to benefit from the experiences of other nations. Whether it is actually capable of doing so, of course, will depend on how open-minded its policymakers can be.

NOTES

1. There are, in addition, schools in forestry, trade and nursing, which together have 1,560 students (World Bank 1983).

2. The World Bank has recently approved two loans to fund agricultural projects in China (*Hong Kong Economic Journal*, 16 June 1990).

3. Although we confine our discussion to economic benefits, we are aware of the sociological and psychological cost of modern urban living.

4. *Ming Pao*, 27 June 1989.

Bibliography

Abramovitz, M. "Resources and Output Trends in the United States since 1870," *American Economic Review* 44 (May 1956): 5–23.

Amihud, Y. and B. Lev. "Risk Reduction as A Managerial Motive for Conglomerate Mergers." *Bell Journal of Economics* 12 (1981): 605–17.

Antal, L., L. Bokros, I. Csillag, L. Lengyel, and G. Matolcsy. "Fordulat es Reform" (Turnaround and Reform). In *Kozgazdasagi Szemle*, 34 (June 1987): 642–663.

Arndt, H. W. *Economic Development—The History of an Idea*. Chicago: University of Chicago Press, 1987.

Arnon, I. *Modernization of Agriculture in Developing Countries*. New York: John Wiley, 1987.

Arrow, K., and F. Hahn. *General Competitive Analysis*. San Francisco: Holden-Day, 1971.

Arthur, W. B. "Self-Reinforcing Mechanisms in Economics." In P. W. Anderson, K. J. Arrow, and D. Pines, eds., *The Economy as an Evolving Complex System*. Reading, MA: Addison-Wesley, 1988.

Barker, R., and R. W. Herdt. *The Rice Economy of Asia*. Washington, D.C.: Resources for the Future, 1985.

Barone, E. "The Ministry of Production in the Collectivist State." In F. A. Hayek, ed. *Collectivist Economic Planning*. London: Routledge and Kegan Paul, 1935.

Barraclough, S. L. "Rural Development and Agrarian Reform." In C. Gotsch, ed., *Rural Development and Employment*. Ford Foundation Seminar. Nigeria: Ibadan, 1973.

Bauer, T. *Tervgazdasag, Beruhazas, Ciklusok*. (Planned Economy, Investments, Cycles). Budapest: Közgazdasagi es Jogi Kiado, 1981.

Bergson, A. *Productivity and the Social System—the U.S.S.R. and the West*. Cambridge, MA: Harvard University Press, 1978.

Brabant, J. M. van. "Socialist Economics: The Disequilibrium School and the Shortage Economy." *Journal of Economic Perspectives* 4, no. 2 (1990): 157–175.

Brody, A. "Gazdasagi Növekedesunk Uteme 1924–töl 1965–ig" (Rates of Our Economic Growth, 1924–1965). In *Közgazdasagi Szemle*, no. 4, 1967.

Bronowski, J., *The Ascent of Man*. London: British Broadcasting Corp., 1973.

Buttel, F. H., and G. W. Gillespie, Jr. "Agricultural Research and Development and the Appropriation of Progressive Symbols: Some Observations on the Politics of Ecological Agriculture." Bulletin No. 151. Ithaca: Cornell University, Department of Rural Sociology, 1988.

Chai, J.C.H., and C. K. Leung, eds. *China's Economic Reforms*. Hong Kong: University of Hong Kong, Centre of Asian Studies, 1987.

Chao, K. *Agricultural Production in Communist China 1949–1965*. Madison: University of Wisconsin Press, 1970.

Coats, A. W. "Autopoiesis, Dissipative Structures, and Historical Process in Economics." Draft, introduction to session at the Richmond History of Economics Society meetings, Toronto, 1988.

Colander, D. C., ed. *Neoclassical Political Economy: The Analysis of Rent-Seeking and DUP Activities*. Cambridge, MA: Ballinger Publishing Company, 1984.

Davis, C. and W. Charemza. "Introduction to Models of Disequilibrium and Shortage in Centrally Planned Economics." In C. Davis and W. Charemza, eds. *Models of Disequilibrium and Shortage in Centrally Planned Economics*. London-New York: Chapman and Hall, (1989): 3–25.

Dawisha, K. *Eastern Europe, Gorbachev and Reform: The Great Challenge*. Cambridge: Cambridge University Press, 1988.

Delfs, R. "Reverse for Full Ahead." *Far Eastern Economic Review*, 11 October 1984.

———. "Agricultural Yields Rise, but the Boom Cannot Last." *Far Eastern Economic Review*, 13 December 1984.

Denison, E. *The Sources of Economic Growth in the United States and the Alternatives Before Us*. New York: Committee for Economic Development, 1962.

———. *Why Growth Rates Differ: Postwar Experience in Nine Western Countries*. Washington, D.C.: Brookings Institution, 1967.

Domar, E. "The Problem of Capital Accumulation." *American Economic Review* 37 (March 1947): 34–55.

Dornbusch, R., and A. Reynoso. "Financial Factors in Economic Development." *The American Economic Review* 79, no. 2 (1989): 204–209.

Dorrance, G. S. "Inflation and Growth: The Statistical Evidence." *International Monetary Fund Staff Papers* 13 (March 1966): 82–102.

Du, R. "Second-Stage Rural Structural Reform." *Beijing Review* 25, 24 June 1985.

Eicher, C. K. and J. M. Staatz, eds. *Agricultural Development in the Third World.* Baltimore: Johns Hopkins University Press, 1984.

―――, T. Zalla, J. Kocher, and F. Winch. *Employment Generation in African Agriculture.* East Lansing: Michigan State University, Institute of International Agriculture, 1970.

Eisenberg, E. "Back to Eden." *The Atlantic Monthly.* November 1989, pp. 57–89.

Enke, S. "Industrialization through Greater Productivity in Agriculture." *Review of Economics and Statistics* 44 (February 1962): 88–91.

―――. "Economic Development with Limited and Unlimited Supplies of Labor." *Oxford Economic Paper* 14 (June 1962): 158–172.

Feuchtwang, S., A. Hussain, and T. Pairault, eds. *Transforming China's Economy in the Eighties. Volume 1: The Rural Sector, Welfare and Employment. Volume 2: Management, Industry and the Urban Economy.* Boulder, CO: Westview Press, 1985.

Frank, A. G. *Capitalism and Underdevelopment in Latin America.* Harmondsworth: Penguin Books, 1971.

Friedman, M. *Friedman in China.* Hong Kong: The Chinese University Press, 1990.

Fukuoka, M. *The Natural Way of Farming, the Theory of Practice of Green Philosophy.* Trans. F. P. Metreaud. Tokyo: Japan Publications, 1985.

―――. *The One-Straw Revolution—An Introduction to Natural Farming.* Trans. edition C. Pearce, T. Kurosawa, and L. Korn. Emmaus, PA: Rodale Press, 1978.

Fung, K. K. "Surplus Seeking and Rent Seeking through Back-Door Deals in Mainland China." *American Journal of Economics and Sociology* 46 no. 3 (1983): pp. 299–317.

Galbraith, J. K., and S. Menshikov. *Capitalism, Communism and Coexistence.* London: Hamish Hamilton, 1988.

Greenshields, B. L., and M. A. Bellamy, eds. *Rural Development—Growth and Equity.* Aldershot, Hampshire: Gower Publishing, 1986.

Greenwald, B., and J. E. Stiglitz. "Externalities in Economics with Imperfect Information and Incomplete Markets." *Quarterly Journal of Economics* 101 (May 1986): 229–264.

―――. *Financial Market Imperfections and Productivity Growth.* Paper given at Stockholm conference, June 1988.

Griffin, K. *Institutional Reform and Economic Development in the Chinese Countryside.* London: MacMillan Press, 1984.

Gurley, J. G. "Rural Development in China, 1949–1972, and the Lessons to be Learnt from It." In C. Gotsch, ed., *Rural Development and Employment.* Ford Foundation Seminar. Ibadan, Nigeria: 1973.

Harrod, Roy F. "An Essay in Dynamic Theory." *Economic Journal* 49 (March 1939): 14–33.

Hayek, F. A. *Collectivist Economic Planning.* London: Routledge and Kegan Paul, 1935.

————. *The Road to Serfdom*. London: Routledge and Kegan Paul, 1944.

————. *Individualism and Economic Order*. London: Routledge and Kegan Paul, 1948.

————. *Knowledge, Evolution, and Society*. London: ASI (Research) Limited, 1983.

————. *The Fatal Conceit*. Chicago: University of Chicago Press, 1988.

Heck, B. van. *Participation of the Pool in Rural Organizations*. Food and Agriculture Organization of the United Nations, 1979.

Hirschman, A. O. *The Strategy of Economic Development*. New Haven: Yale University Press, 1958.

Hoppe, H. H. *A Theory of Socialism and Capitalism*. Deventer, the Netherlands: Kluwer Academic Publishers, 1989.

Hou, C. M., and T. S. Yu, eds. *Agricultural Development in China, Japan and Korea*. Taipei, Taiwan: Academia Sinica, 1982.

Hsu, R. C. *Food for One Billion: China's Agriculture since 1949*. Boulder, CO.: Westview Press, 1982.

Jantsch, E. *The Self-Organizing Universe: Scientific and Human Implications of the Emerging Paradigm of Evolution*. Oxford: Pergamon Press, 1979.

Johnston, B. F., and W. C. Clark. *Redesigning Rural Development*. Baltimore: Johns Hopkins University Press, 1982.

Johnston, B. F. and P. Kilby. *Agricultural Strategies, Rural-Urban Interactions and the Expansion of Income Opportunities*. Paris: OECD Development Centre, 1973.

————. *Agriculture and Structural Transformation: Economic Strategies in Late-Developing Countries*. New York: Oxford University Press, 1975.

Johnston, B. F. and J. W. Mellor. "The Role of Agriculture in Economic Development." *American Economic Review* 51, no. 4 (1961): 566–593.

Kaleczki, M. "Introduction to the Theory of Growth in a Socialist Economy." In M. Kaleczki, ed. *Selected Essays on the Economic Growth of a Socialist and Mixed Economy* (pp. 1–118). Cambridge: Cambridge University Press, 1972.

Katz, M., and C. Shapiro "Technology Adoption in the Presence of Network Externalities." *Journal of Political Economy* 94 (1986): 822–841.

Kis, J., F. Koszeg, and O. Solt. "Tarsadalmi Szerzödes. A Politikai Kibontakozas Feltetelei." (Social Contract. Preconditions of the Political Rejuvenation). In *Beszelo*, no. 12 (1987): 1–60.

Kornai, J. *Overcentralization in Economic Administration*. Oxford: Oxford University Press, 1959.

————. *Rush versus Harmonic Growth*. Amsterdam: North Holland, 1972.

————. *The Economics of Shortage*. Amsterdam: North Holland, 1980.

————. Shortage as a Fundamental Problem of Centrally Planned Economies and the Hungarian Reform." *Economics of Planning* 18, no. 3 (1982): 103–113.

————. "The Dual Dependence of the State-Owned Firm in Hungary." In G. Tidrich and J. Chen, eds., *China's Industrial Reform*. New York: Oxford University Press, 1987.

Lam, W.W.L. *Towards a Chinese-Style Socialism, an Assessment of Deng Xiaoping's Reforms*. Hong Kong: Oceanic Cultural Service, 1987.

Lange, O. *On the Economic Theory of Socialism*. ed. B. E. Lippincott, University of Minnesota 1938, New York: McGraw-Hill, Reprint 1964.

Lardy, N. R. "Prices, Markets and the Chinese Peasant." In C. K. Eicher, and J. M. Staatz, eds., *Agricultural Development in the Third World*. Baltimore: John Hopkins University Press, 1984.

Lavoie, D. *National Economic Planning: What Is Left?* Cambridge: Ballinger Publishing Company, 1985.

Lee, P.N.S. *Industrial Management and Economic Reform in China, 1949–1984*. New York: Oxford University Press, 1987.

Lewis, W. A. "Economic Development with Unlimited Supplies of Labor." *Manchester School of Economic and Social Studies* 22, no. 2 (1954): 139–191.

Lin, J. Y. *Market Size and Hybrid Rice Innovation in China*. Paper presented at the Third Workshop on Differential Effects of Modern Rice Technology on Favorable and Unfavorable Production Environments. Dhaka, Bangladesh, March 31–April 2, 1989.

Lippit, V. D. *The Economic Development of China*. New York: M. E. Sharpe, 1987.

Little, I. *Economic Development: Theory, Policy and International Relations*. New York: Basic Books, 1982.

Little, I., T. Scitovsky, and M. Scott. *Industry and Trade in Some Developing Countries: A Comparative Study*. London: Oxford University Press, 1970.

Marcus, A. J. "Risk Sharing and the Theory of the Firm." *Bell Journal of Economics* 13 (1982): 369–378.

Marshall, A. *Principles of Economics*. London: MacMillan 1890, 9th ed., 1961.

McKinnon, R. *Money and Capital in Economic Development*. Washington, D.C.: Brookings Institution, 1973.

Mellor, J. W. *The New Economics of Growth: A Strategy for India and the Developing World*. Ithaca: Cornell University Press, 1976.

Mollison, B. *Permaculture: A Designer's Manual*. Tagari Publications, 1989.

Mueller, D. C. *Public Choice*. Cambridge: Cambridge University Press, 1979.

Mundell, Robert A. "Growth, Stability and Inflationary Finance." *Journal of Political Economy* 73 (April 1965): 97–109.

Myrdal, G. *Development and Underdevelopment*. Cairo: National Bank of Egypt, 1956.

Naughton, B. "Financial Reform in China's Industrial System." In E. J. Perry and C. Wong, eds., *The Political Economy of Reform in Post-Mao China*. Cambridge: Harvard University Press, Council on East Asian Studies, 1985.

Nicholls, W. H. "The Place of Agriculture in Economic Development." In C. K. Eicher and L. W. Witt, eds., *Agriculture in Economic Development* (pp. 11–44) New York: McGraw-Hill, 1964.

Nove, A. *Socialism, Economics and Development.* London: Allen and Unwin, 1986.

Nozick, R. *Anarchy, State and Utopia.* Oxford: Basil Blackwell, 1974.

Ohlin, B. *Interregional and International Trade.* Cambridge: Harvard University Press, 1933.

Olson, M. "Beyond the Measuring Rod of Money." Manuscript, 1988.

Perkins, D. H. "Reforming China's Economic System." *Journal of Economic Literature* 26 (1988): 601–645.

Perroux, F. *A New Concept of Development.* Paris: United Nations Educational, Scientific and Cultural Organization and Croom Helm, 1983.

Perry, E. J., and C. Wong, eds. *The Political Economy of Reform in Post-Mao China.* Cambridge, MA: Harvard University Press, 1985.

Polanyi, M. *Personal Knowledge: Towards a Post-Critical Philosophy.* Chicago: University of Chicago Press, 1958.

Popper, K. R. *The Poverty of Historicism.* London: Routledge and Kegan Paul, 1957.

Portes, R. "Macroeconomic Equilibrium and Disequilibrium in Centrally Planned Economies." *Economic Inquiry* 19, no. 4 (1981): 559–578.

———. "The Theory of Measurement of Macroeconomic Disequilibrium in Centrally Planned Economics." In C. Davis and C. Wojciech, eds., *Models of Disequilibrium and Shortage in Centrally Planned Economies* (pp. 27–47). New York: Chapman and Hall, 1989.

Prebisch, R. "Growth, Disequilibrium, and Disparities: Interpretation of the Process of Economic Development." In *Economic Survey of Latin America*, United Nations Economic Commission for Latin America. New York, 1949.

———. "Commercial Policy in the Underdeveloped Countries." *American Economic Review* 64, no. 2, (1959): 251–273.

Prigogine, I. *Order out of Chaos.* New York: Bantam Books, 1984.

Rains, G., and J.C.H. Fei. "A Theory of Economic Development." *American Economic Review* 51, no. 4 (1961): 533–565.

———. "Innovation, Capital Accumulation, and Economic Development." *American Economic Review* 53, no. 3 (1963): 283–313.

———. *Development of the Labor Surplus Economy: Theory and Policy.* Homewood, IL: Richard D. Irwin, 1964.

Raj, K. N. "Agricultural Growth in China and India: Role of Price and Non-Price Factors." *Economic and Political Weekly* 18, no. 3, 1983.

Reynolds, L. G., ed. *Agriculture in Development Theory.* New Haven: Yale University Press, 1975.

Riskin, C. *China's Political Economy, the Quest for Development since 1949.* New York: Oxford University Press, 1987.

Ritson, G. *Agricultural Economics—Principle and Policy.* London: Granada Publishing, 1977.

Robert, A. M. "Growth, Stability and Inflationary Finance." *Journal of Political Economy* 73 (April 1965): 97–109.

Robinson, J. *Aspects of Development and Underdevelopment.* Cambridge: Cambridge University Press, 1979.

Rosenstein-Rodan, P. N. "Problems of Industrialization of Eastern and Southeastern Europe." *Economic Journal* 53 (June–September 1943): 202–211.

———. "Notes on the Theory of the Big Push," in Howard S. Ellis, ed., *Economic Development for Latin America.* London: Macmillan, 1951.

Schultz, T. W. *Transforming Traditional Agriculture.* New Haven: Yale University Press, 1964.

———. "The Economics of Agricultural Research." In C. K. Eicher and J. M. Staatz, eds. *Agricultural Development in the Third World.* Baltimore: Johns Hopkins University Press, 1984.

———. *The Long View in Economic Policy: The Case of Agriculture and Food.* Panama City, Panama: International Center for Economic Growth, 1987.

Sen, A. *On Ethics and Economics.* Oxford: Basil Blackwell, 1987.

Shand, R. T., ed. *Agricultural Development in Asia.* Canberra: Australian National University Press, 1969.

Shirk, S. L. "The Politics of Industrial Reform." In E. J. Jerry, and C. Wong, eds., *The Political Economy of Reform in Post-Mao China.* Cambridge, MA: Harvard University Council on East Asian Studies, 1985.

Singer, H. W. "The Distribution of Gains between Investing and Borrowing Countries." *American Economic Review* 40, no. 2 (May 1950): 473–485.

———. "Education and Economic Development" (1961), reprinted in *International Development: Growth and Change.* New York: McGraw-Hill (1964): 66.

Solow, R. "Technical Change and the Aggregate Production Function." *Review of Economics and Statistics* 39 (August 1957): 312–320.

Stavis, B. *China's Green Revolution.* Ithaca: Cornell University, 1974.

Stiglitz, J. E. "Markets, Market Failures, and Development." *American Economic Review* 79, no. 2 (1989): 197–213.

———, and A. Weiss. "Credit Rationing in Markets with Imperfect Information." *American Economic Review* 71, no. 3 (1981): 393–410.

Streeten, P., S. Burke, M. Haq, N. Hicks, and F. Stewart. *First Things First: Meeting Basic Needs in Developing Countries.* Oxford: Oxford University Press, 1981.

Sunkel, O. "National Development and External Dependence in Latin America." *Journal of Development Studies,* (October 1969): 32.

Szelenyi, I. "Eastern Europe in the Crisis of Transition—the Polish and Hungarian Cases." In B. Misztal, ed. *Poland after Solidarity.* New Brunswick: Transaction Books (1985): 97–102.

Tang, A. M., and C. J. Huang. "Changes in Input-Output Relations in the Agriculture of the Chinese Mainland 1952–1979." In C. M. Hou and T. S. Yu, eds. *Agricultural Development in China, Japan and Korea.* Taipei, Taiwan: Academia Sinica (1982): 319–348.

Taylor, D. *Mind.* London: Century Publishing, 1983.

Taylor, F. M. "The Guidance of Production in a Socialist State." In B. E. Lippincott, ed. *On the Economic Theory of Socialism.* University of Minnesota, 1938. New York: McGraw-Hill, Reprint 1964.

Thirlwall, A. P., and C. A. Barton. "Inflation and Growth: The International Evidence." *Banca Nazionale del Lavoro Quarterly Review* no. 99 (September 1971): 263–275.

Tidrick, G., and J. Chen, eds. *China's Industrial Reform.* New York: Oxford University Press, 1987.

U, T. W. "The Relation Between Inflation and Economic Development: A Statistical Inductive Study." *International Monetary Fund Staff Papers* 7 (October 1959): 302–17.

von Mises, L. *Socialism: An Economic and Sociological Analysis.* 1922. Trans. J. Kahane. Indianapolis: Liberty Press, 1981.

———. *Human Action: A Treatise on Economics.* 1949. 3d ed. Chicago: Henry Regnery, 1966.

Wallich, H. C. "Money and Growth: A Country Cross-Section Analysis." *Journal of Money, Credit, and Banking* 1 (May 1969): 281–302.

———, and S. Weintraub. "A Tax Based Incomes Policy." *Journal of Economic Issues* vol V, no. 2 (June 1971): 1–19.

Weber, M. *The Protestant Ethic and the Spirit of Capitalism.* Trans. T. Parsons. Charles Scribner's Sons, [1904–5] 1976.

Weintraub, S. "An Incomes Policy to Stop Inflation." *Lloyds Bank Review.* January, 1970.

Wicksteed, P. H. *The Common Sense of Political Economy and Selected Papers and Reviews on Economic Theory.* London: Routledge and Kegan Paul, 1933.

Winiecki, J. *The Distorted World of Soviet-Type Economies.* Pittsburgh: University of Pittsburgh Press, 1988.

Wong, C. "Material Allocation and Decentralization." *In The Political Economy of Reform in Post-Mao China.* Cambridge, MA: Harvard University Council on East Asian Studies, 1985.

Woo, H.K.H. *The Unseen Dimensions of Wealth.* San Francisco: Victoria Press, 1984.

———. *Cognition, Value and Price: A General Theory of Value.* Forthcoming.

World Bank. *China: Socialist Economic Development, the Social Sector, Population, Health, Nutrition and Education.* Washington, D.C.: World Bank, 1983.

————. *China, Issues and Prospects in Education.* Washington, D.C.: World Bank, 1985.

Wu, J. "Choosing a Strategy for China's Economic Reform." *Social Sciences in China* 9, no. 4 (1988): 27–41.

Zeleny, M., ed. *Autopoiesis, Dissipative Structures and Spontaneous Social Orders.* Boulder, CO: Westview Press, 1980.

Index

Abramovitz, Moses, 121

agriculture: arguments against primacy of, 170–73; biotechnology and, 183; collective system of, 189; complexities of, 168–69; conservativism in, 170–71; controversies over, 167–68; development and, 164, 165–66, 167, 169; ecological considerations and, 168, 169, 171, 179, 215; economic hazards of, 171–72; effectiveness of existing modes of, 175; employment effect of, 166, 177–78; entrepreneurship in, 174, 175–76, 205; Fukuoka and, 179–80, 215, 216–17; genetic engineering and, 183; Gorbachev's reform and, 82; government role in, 168, 171–73, 178; human capital and, 173–74, 176, 183, 205; in India, 185–86; in Japan, 214; in West Bengal, 214; insurance-intensive, 182–83; labor demand for, 165; labor surplus and, 176; land as fixed asset and, 173; large-scale, 208; market role in, 168; modernization strategy for, 168; natural (organic), 167, 179, 180, 213, 215, 216–17, 227; nature's role in, 175, 176, 180–82; product demand and, 171–72; progress rate of, 176–77; research on, 173, 174; Schultz cited on, 173–74; Stalin and, 72–73; sustainable, 179, 223; technology for, 166, 167, 179–80; vs. industry, 44, 164–65, 170–71, 196, 225; yield increase and, 173. *See also* agriculture in China

agriculture-first policy, 206–7; agro-managers and, 208–12, 214, 215, 217–18, 220, 224; countryside attractiveness and,

ABOUT THE AUTHOR

HENRY K. H. WOO is the Chairman of the Hong Kong Institute of Economic Science (1983–   ) and Chairman of the China Foundation, Hong Kong (1988–   ). He was an economics graduate from the University of Hong Kong (1969), and has been an economist at the Hong Kong Trade Development Council, an economic columnist of the *Hong Kong Standard* and a contributing editor of *Hong Kong Business Today*.

He is a Founding Council Member and Hong Kong Representative of the Society for the Advancement of Socio-Economics, Washington, D.C.; a Founding Member and Hong Kong Representative of the International Society for Intercommunication of New Ideas, Boston, Mass.; a Founder and Executive Director of the International Network for Economic Method, Hong Kong, and a Trustee of the Hong Kong Centre for Economic Research at the Chinese University of Hong Kong.

His publications include *A Reconstruction of Education* (1977), *Understanding Economic Affairs of Hong Kong* (1979), *The Unseen Dimensions of Wealth—Towards a Generalized Economic Theory* (1984), and *What's Wrong with Formalization in Economics?—An Epistemological Critique* (1986).